lonely

Miami and the Keys

The Everglades &
Biscayne National Park
p107

Miami
p44

Florida Koyo &
Key West
p134

Jesse Scott, Terry Ward

Art deco building, Miami Beach (p50)

CONTENTS

South Beach, Miami (p51)

Airboat tour, Everglades
National Park (p112)

FELIX MIZIOZNIKOV/GETTY IMAGES

Wynwood (p73)

MIAMI & THE KEYS
THE JOURNEY BEGINS HERE

Growing up in Fredericksburg, Virginia, South Florida was an annual Christmas destination for my family. Dad and mom would drive to my grandpa's house in Fort Lauderdale. There was no better place on Earth for this red-headed only child – the warmth of my beloved family all under one roof, the warm weather and Sunshine State adventures aplenty. I have no doubt that my grandpa has rubbed off on me – he and the family memories I hold so dear are inevitable reasons why my wife and I have ended up here and called South Florida home for nearly a decade. I've scoured Miami and the Keys as a correspondent for some of our region's biggest news outlets – *Miami New Times, Forbes Travel Guide, Time Out, Eater* and *Aventura Magazine* among them. Consider my findings a love letter to this culturally diverse, geographically dazzling foodie haven like few others. It's a letter that continues to be written.

Jesse Scott

@jesserobertscott

Jesse is a South Florida–based writer who has written about food, entertainment, culture and travel for 20-plus years. Jesse wrote The Everglades & Biscayne National Park and Florida Keys & Key West chapters.

ADORNED PHOTOGRAPHY

My favourite experience involves meandering around Miami's **Wynwood Arts District** (p73). Be it Wynwood Walls' ever-changing graffiti exhibits or fresh splashes of art donning buildings' facades, there's always something new and funky to gawk at.

WHO GOES WHERE

Our writers and experts chooses the place that, for then, define Miami and the Keys.

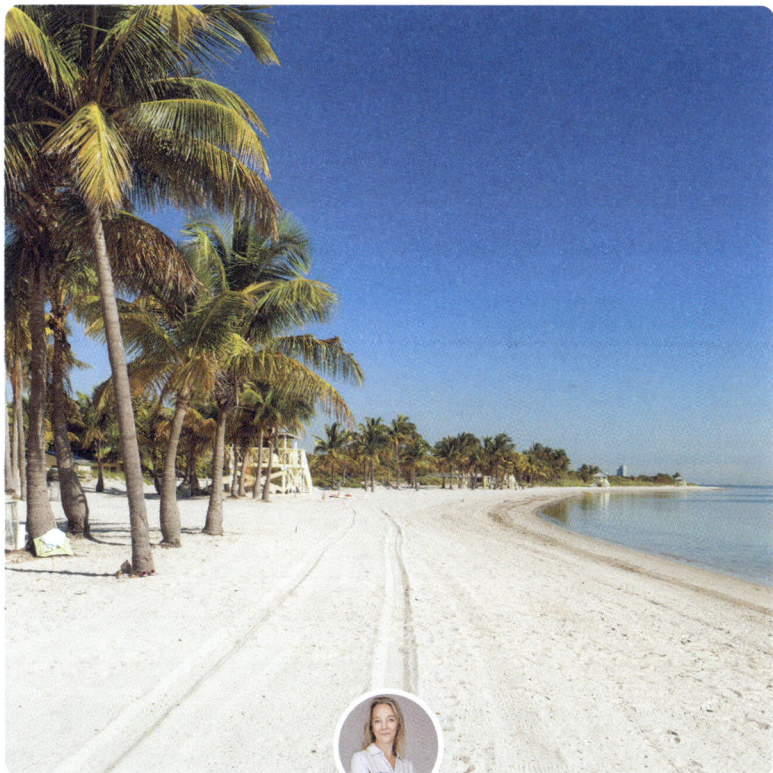

When Miami has me feeling overstimulated, I make for the barrier island of **Key Biscayne** (p101) to recharge. It feels like an escape in the middle of the city. On weekdays, it's particularly easy to find a quiet stretch of sand at Bill Baggs Cape Florida State Park for relaxing within steps of the ocean. When the day's shadows start growing long, I head to No Name Harbor and The Cleat for a cold beer and ceviche at what I'm convinced is Miami's best waterfront bar for sunset.

Terry Ward

@terrywardwriter

Terry is a writer about travel and culture and a keen scuba diver. She wrote the Miami chapter.

Everglades City

Nosh on stone crabs from the source (p122)

Everglades National Park

Alligator spotting and airboat rides (p112)

Key West

Drink where Hemingway once did (p161)

Bahia Honda State Park

Kayaking, camping and pristine beaches (p154)

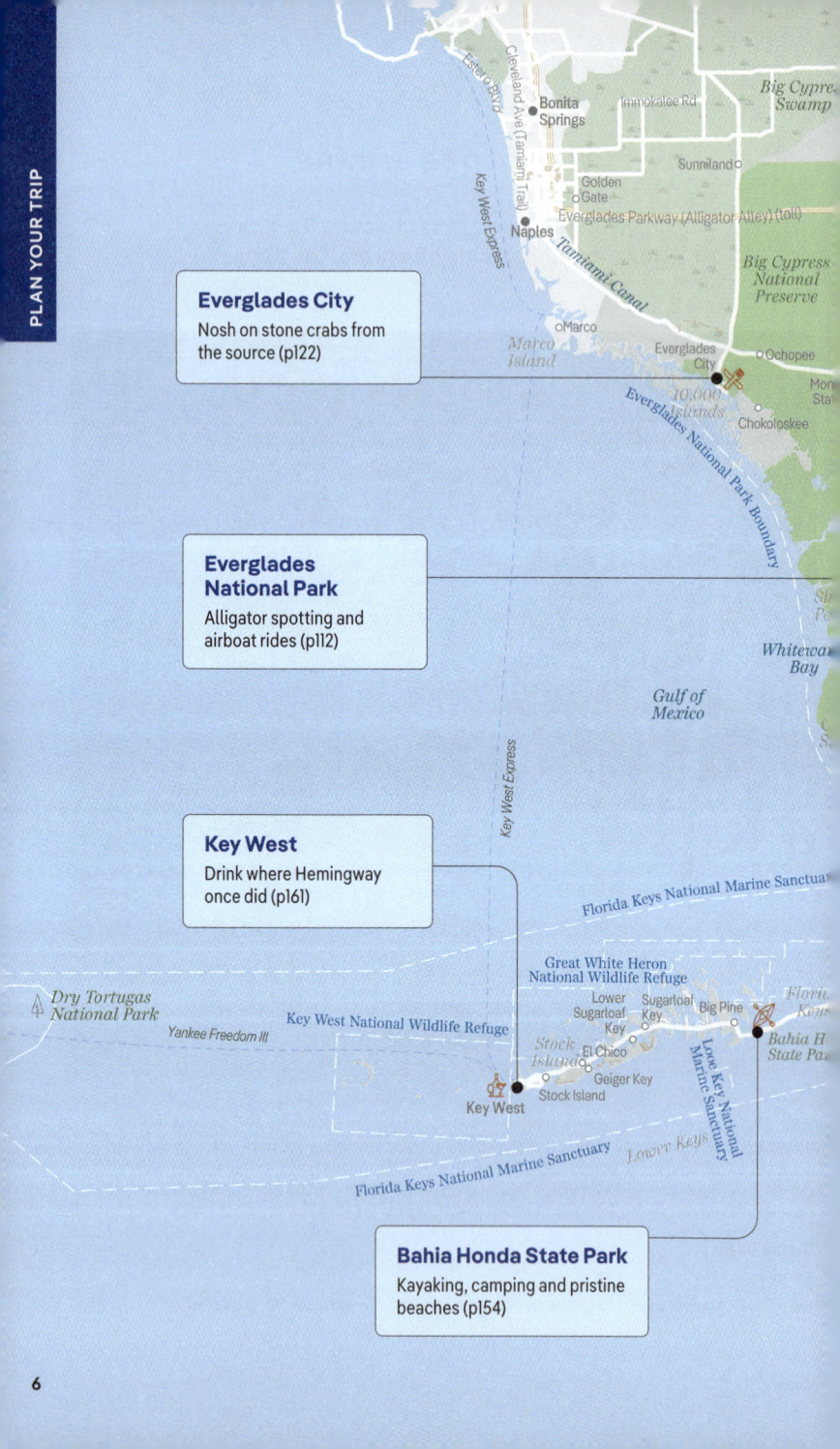

Big Cypress Swamp

Immokalee Rd

Bonita Springs

Cleveland Ave (Tamiami Trail)

Lester Blvd

Sunniland

Golden Gate

Everglades Parkway (Alligator Alley) (toll)

Key West Express

Naples

Tamiami Canal

Big Cypress National Preserve

Marco

Marco Island

Everglades City

Ochopee

Mon Sta

10,000 Islands

Chokoloskee

Everglades National Park Boundary

Gulf of Mexico

Whitewater Bay

Sl Po

S

Florida Keys National Marine Sanctua

Key West Express

Great White Heron National Wildlife Refuge

Dry Tortugas National Park

Key West National Wildlife Refuge

Lower Sugarloaf Key

Sugarloaf Key

Big Pine

Flori Key

Yankee Freedom III

Stock Island

El Chico

Geiger Key

Looe Key National Marine Sanctuary

Bahia H State Pa

Key West

Stock Island

Florida Keys National Marine Sanctuary

Lower Keys

Wynwood

Graffiti art, modern galleries, edgy boutiques (p73)

Miami Beach

Towering resorts and umbrella-draped sands (p50)

South Beach

See titans of art deco design (p51)

Key Biscayne

Island adventures adjacent to Downtown Miami (p101)

Calle Ocho

Little Havana's pulsing Latin heart (p81)

John Pennekamp Coral Reef State Park

Snorkel paradise and an underwater statue (p140)

New River Canal

Loxahatchee National Wildlife Refuge

Boca Raton

Miami Canal

Coral Springs

Florida's Turnpike (toll)

Everglades Parkway (Alligator Alley) (toll)

Sunrise

Lauderdale-by-the-Sea

Fort Lauderdale

The Everglades

Weston

NORTH MIAMI BEACH

Dania Beach

Hollywood

Big Cypress National Preserve

North Miami Beach

Surfside

Miami Beach

Hialeah

Wynwood

South Beach

op Rd

Tamiami Trail

Miccosukee Village

Calle Ocho

MIAMI

Shark Valley

Kendal

Key Biscayne

Everglades tional Park

Peters

Goulds

Biscayne Bay

Long Pine Key Trail

Homestead

Florida City

Biscayne National Park

hitewater y

Barnes Sound

John Pennekamp Coral Reef State Park

Key Largo

Flamingo

Key Largo National Marine Sanctuary

Key Largo

Florida Bay

Islamorada

Key

Overseas Hwy

Hawk Channel

Upper Keys

on

iddle Keys

Straits of Florida

ATLANTIC OCEAN

NW 17th Ave (Krome Ave)

| 0 | | 50 km |
| 0 | | 25 miles |

WHITE SANDS & MORE WHITE SANDS

The beach isn't going anywhere around these parts. Sure, the water may be cooler come wintertime, the sand may sizzle to a point of needing flip-flops on it during summer, but it's always beautifully right there. The beach is the heartbeat of Miami and the Florida Keys – architectural marvels are built with vistas of sandy expanses front and center, and even the staunchest of 'I'm staying indoors' folks inevitably find themselves dipping a toe in the water.

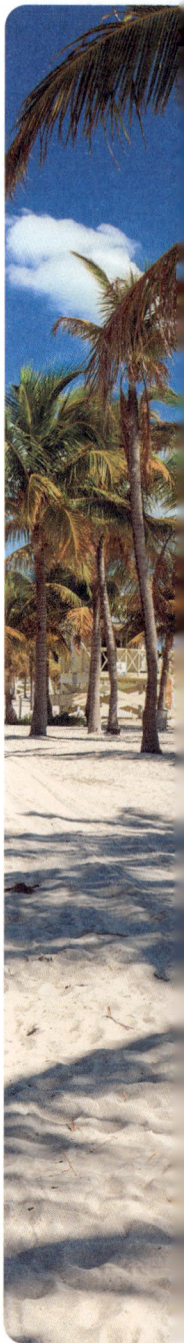

Arrive Beach-Ready

Pack sunscreen, shades and water shoes for South Florida's beaches. Depending on the beach, coral reefs, soft sands, ocean breezes – or perhaps a little of each – await.

Man-Made Miami Beach

Perhaps the region's most famous stretch of golden goodness is man-made. Miami Beach was transformed from a swampy island landscape into a beach with imported sand in the early 1900s.

Sunrises & Sunsets

Set the alarm clock and plop on Miami's sands for an often orange-y sunrise. You can catch the sunset over Florida Bay in the Keys from a variety of sandy nooks.

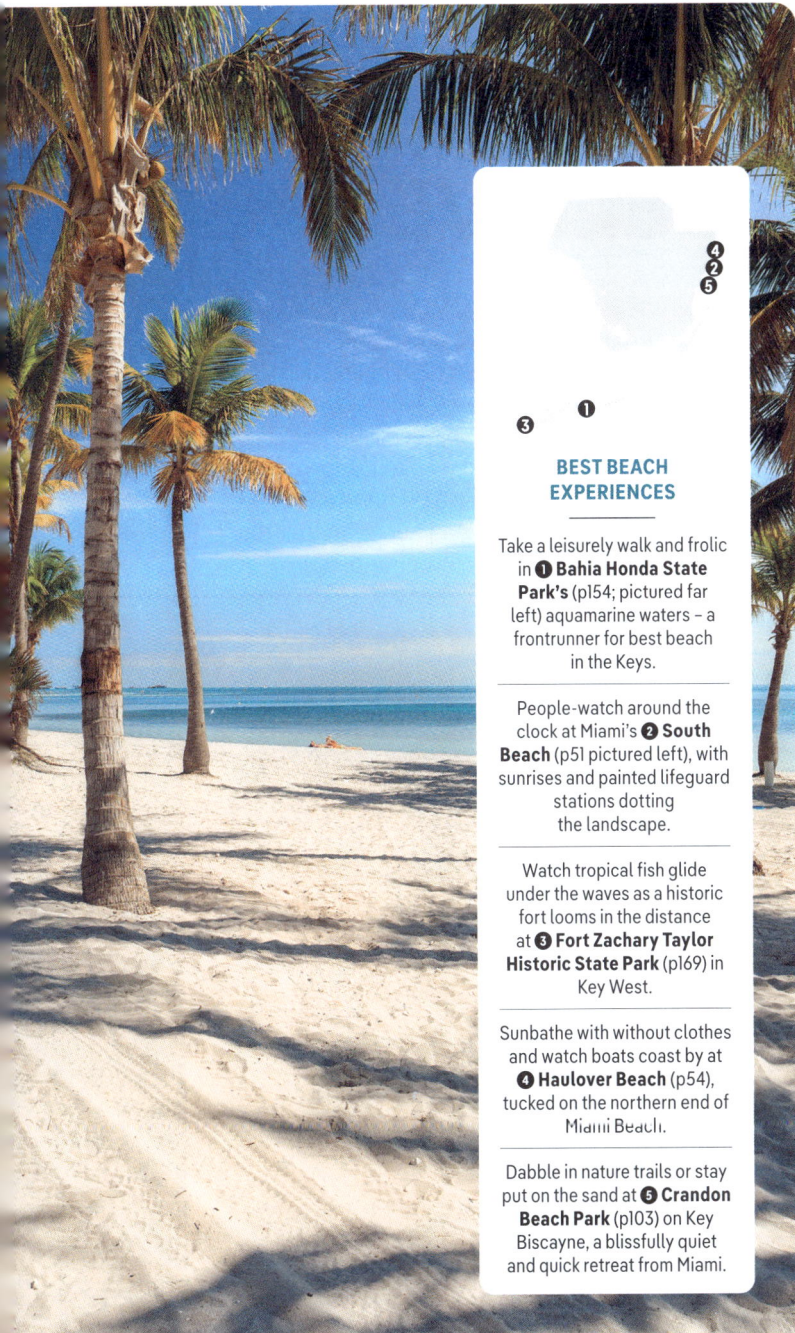

BEST BEACH EXPERIENCES

Take a leisurely walk and frolic in ❶ **Bahia Honda State Park's** (p154; pictured far left) aquamarine waters – a frontrunner for best beach in the Keys.

People-watch around the clock at Miami's ❷ **South Beach** (p51 pictured left), with sunrises and painted lifeguard stations dotting the landscape.

Watch tropical fish glide under the waves as a historic fort looms in the distance at ❸ **Fort Zachary Taylor Historic State Park** (p169) in Key West.

Sunbathe with without clothes and watch boats coast by at ❹ **Haulover Beach** (p54), tucked on the northern end of Miami Beach.

Dabble in nature trails or stay put on the sand at ❺ **Crandon Beach Park** (p103) on Key Biscayne, a blissfully quiet and quick retreat from Miami.

YOU BOAT-ER BELIEVE IT

Do you hear that? The water's always calling, whether kayaking through serene mangroves, snorkeling alongside rainbow-colored reefs or zipping across Biscayne Bay on a high-powered speedboat. Here, turquoise horizons lure paddleboarders, anglers chase trophy fish and divers discover sunken shipwrecks teeming with colorful life. The water adventures here are as endless as the tides – it's all about finding the right one to whet (or wet?) your appetite.

Paddle Paradise

Step aside, motorized vessels – exploring mangrove trails by kayak or paddleboard is where it's at. Keep your eyes peeled for colorful birdlife and even manatees as you glide.

Underwater Jewels

The Florida Keys are home to the continental US's only living coral reef. Vibrant marine life and sunken treasures are waiting to be discovered via dive or snorkel.

Dock & Dine

Many spots in the Keys and Miami offer dock-and-dine options, meaning you can cruise in by boat, tie up and enjoy fresh-caught seafood with a view.

❷
❸
❶
❹

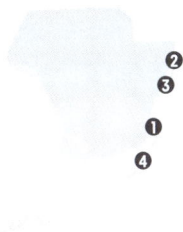

BEST BOAT EXPERIENCES

Kayak around the keys of
❶ Biscayne National Park
(p128; pictured far left), which
is 95% water, and try to spot
the prized roseate spoonbill
above water, too.

Watch eagles fly by during
a boat trip to **❷ Oleta River
State Park's** (p58)
mangrove island.

Hop on a guided pontoon
boat tour from **❸ Dinner Key
Marina** (p93) in Coconut Grove
to offshore destinations like
Stiltsville and Boca Chita Key.

Snorkel and dive at **❹ John
Pennekamp Coral Reef
State Park** (p140) in Key Largo
after a glass-bottom boat tour.

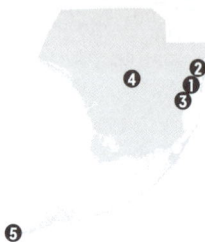

JOHN COLETTI/GETTY IMAGES

Cigar roller, Little Havana (p81)

CULTURAL MELTING POT

From indigenous communities with multi-generational lore to a new generation of Miamians stemming from every corner of Latin America, the cultural fabric of this region is as colorful as ever. Miami even has its own version of Spanglish these days, further driving home the unique ethos here, bro.

Indigenous Roots Run Deep

Long before high-rises, the Tequesta and Calusa tribes thrived. Today, the Miccosukee and Seminole Nations keep traditions alive through storytelling and crafts.

Latin Majority

More than 70% of Miami's population identifies as Latino. Reggaeton jams and *cafecito* wafts are part of the daily sensory experience in many neighborhoods.

BEST CULTURAL EXPERIENCES

Dance into the night at salsa bars along Calle Ocho in the heart of Miami's **1 Little Havana** (p81).

Browse Haitian sculptures and art, or take a folk dancing class at the **2 Little Haiti Cultural Complex** (p98).

Go on a **3 Black History Tour** (p71) with Melanin Miami, learning about key Black neighborhoods like Overtown.

Visit the grounds of South Florida's famous tribe and watch an alligator-wrestling demo at **4 Miccosukee Indian Village** (p115).

Learn all about a writing legend as six-toed cats meander outside at **5 Hemingway Home & Museum** (p166) in Key West.

12

ON ISLAND TIME

Adding another layer to the landscape of swaying palms are the region's islands. Whether keys off Miami or the entirety of the Florida Keys, islands abound, often dangling off the coast like a gem-dotted necklace. Natural beauty is a given around here, but the laid-back charm you'll find on the islands is next level.

❹ ❶ ❺ ❷ ❸

Keys by Numbers

The Florida Keys span a 113-mile archipelago with 1700 islands, many of which are connected by the Overseas Highway. The highway has 42 bridges.

An Unofficial Capital

Key Largo is globally renowned as the 'Diving Capital of the World' for its reef landscape and diving operations aplenty, catering to pros and newbies alike.

All Aboard

Accessing islands throughout the region varies, from a quick kayak trip to tiny mangrove islands to a dedicated ferry between Key West and Dry Tortugas National Park.

Hop by bridge from Miami to ❶ **Key Biscayne** (p101) for canopied trails, a nature-center tour and a selfie session at an iconic lighthouse.

Kayak to an abandoned island containing the ruins of a 19th century settlement at ❷ **Indian Key Historic State Park** (p146) off Islamorada.

Take a ferry from Key West to ❸ **Dry Tortugas National Park** (p169), tour a historic fort and stay at a campsite.

Embark on a **dolphin-spotting journey** (p118) off ❹ **Marco Island** and help researchers keep track of our finned friends.

Cruise out to ❺ **Elliott Key** within Biscayne National Park, where a 7-mile **hiking trail** (p132) awaits.

SEAFOOD WITH SOUL

From dockside dives to upscale oceanfront feasts, the seafood here isn't just fresh – it's truly a way of life and the region's industrial lifeblood. Stone crab claws cracked tableside, conch fritters straight from the fryer and mahi seared on the grill – every bite tells a story of Florida's coastal bounty. Miami and the Keys serve seafood with soul, sunshine and just the right squeeze of lime. All in all, the seafood scene here is quite the catch.

Seafood Central

Florida ranks among the top three seafood-producing states in the US. Miami, the Keys and surrounding waters haul in millions of pounds of fish and shellfish annually.

Conch Republic

Key West is known as the 'Conch Republic,' an homage to the island's deep Bahamian influence. Conch fritters and conch-dashed ceviche are local staples.

Lionfish on the Menu

Invasive and destructive to local reefs, lionfish are now a delicacy throughout South Florida. Many restaurants serve them fried or ceviche-style.

❶ ❸❹

❷

❺

BEST SEAFOOD EXPERIENCES

Feast on Everglades City's freshest stone crab and gator bites at ❶ **Camellia Street Grill** (p124), the town's ultimate no-frills seafood shack.

Start the day island-style at ❷ **Key Largo Conch House** (p142), with cracked conch eggs Benedict or Bahamian-style conch chowder.

Sip cocktails and savor fresh-caught seafood at ❸ **Rusty Pelican** (p124) while enjoying one of Miami's most breathtaking waterfront views.

Crack into world-famous claws at ❹ **Joe's Stone Crab** (p58) – a Miami institution since 1913 – and save room for the key lime pie.

Indulge in the chef's seafood-centric, nightly tasting menu at ❺ **Little Pearl** (p164) in Key West.

365 FOCUS PHOTOGRAPHY/SHUTTERSTOCK

Pérez Art Museum Miami (p66)

BRUSHES WITH BRILLIANCE

From buildings-wide murals to literal coral-stone castles (not to mention Art Basel Miami Beach), the art scene is as wild as the landscape itself. Wynwood's walls drip with color, Cuban masters grace Little Havana's galleries, and Key West creatives channel island whimsy year-round.

Warehouses Gone Wow

In the former warehouse district of Wynwood, graffiti-covered walls evolve constantly, showcasing everything from global street-art legends to local up-and-comers.

To Free or Not to Free

Larger galleries and museums throughout South Florida typically charge an entry fee. Ask ahead, though, as some may have selected free or discounted days.

BEST ART EXPERIENCES

Marvel at contemporary art and Biscayne Bay views at **❶ Pérez Art Museum Miami** (p66).

Step into Miami's vibrant outdoor gallery at **❷ Wynwood Walls** (p80), where famous street artists turn walls into urban art.

Tour the **❸ Coral Castle** (p125) in Homestead, literally handmade from coral by a single dude.

Discover fine art with a coastal flair in Key West at **❹ The Hale Gallery** (p147), with works capturing island life at its finest.

Stroll Islamorada's **❺ MoradaWay Arts & Cultural District** (p147), where live music and creative energy flow freely.

ALL THE RIGHT CHORDS

Island grooves, Latin beats, a little jazz... all designed to get that rump moving. Salsa spills onto Calle Ocho, punk and funk electrify Wynwood and tiki-lit beach bars region-wide sway to reggae beats and homegrown acoustic crooners alike. Every night here jams to a soundtrack as diverse as its crowd.

❶❹❸

❷❺

Southern Music Capital

Miami is an absolute powerhouse for Latin music, with icons like Gloria Estefan, Pitbull and Bad Bunny recording hits in the city's studios.

A Key West Soundtrack

The Keys typically embrace a laid-back, live music vibe, with frequent Jimmy Buffett tributes and acoustic duos aplenty.

Calle Ocho's Salsa Soul

Little Havana pulses with Cuban rhythms. Salsa legends like Celia Cruz and Willy Chirino paved the way for live timba, son and Latin jazz to thrive.

BEST LIVE MUSIC EXPERIENCES

Watch Broadway hits and orchestral spectacles at ❶ **Adrienne Arsht Center** (p70, Miami's performing arts hub.

Jam to live music amid an anything-goes, dive-bar vibe at ❷ **Green Parrot** (p166) in Key West.

Experience classical music reimagined, with live performances projected onto an outdoor screen, at a ❸ **New World Symphony** (p60) show.

Sip on mojitos, get moving to some salsa and perhaps dance on the bar at ❹ **Ball & Chain** (p83) in Little Havana.

Keep it cozy and cool at ❺ **Little Room Jazz Club** (p170) in Key West, an intimate hideaway for craft cocktails and saxophone solos.

17

REGIONS & CITIES

Find the places that tick all your boxes.

The Everglades & Biscayne National Park

p107

The Everglades & Biscayne National Park

MANGROVE MAZES, ISLANDS AND WILDLIFE WONDER

The Everglades and Biscayne National Park are natural spaces just removed from seemingly endless urban sprawl, ecological escapes that can appear deceivingly gentle at first blush. These waterlogged landscapes hide raw, primeval beauty – spanning alligators and countless species of birds and fish, flooded prairies and misty swamps.

p106

Florida Keys & Key West

p134

Miami

LATIN AMERICA AND THE CARIBBEAN COLLIDE

No city but Miami can so thoroughly embody the diversity and energy of Latin America and the Caribbean while wrapping that soul in a package of glamour, neon, tropical weather, beaches and sunsets. Beyond the flash, small neighborhoods thrive, where deep community ties bind enclaves from around the world.

p44

Miami
p44

Florida Keys & Key West

AMERICA'S ARCHIPELAGO RETREAT FOR OOOHS AND AAAHS

The Florida Keys float in a teal penumbra of bohemian tiki bars, quiet beaches and endless fishing destinations. Each island has its own idiosyncrasies but nowhere is as uniquely creative and infectiously quirky as Key West, the colorful terminus of the Keys' rainbow where sunsets are literally celebrated.

p134

PIDJOE/GETTY IMAGES

Art deco buildings, South Beach (p51)

ITINERARIES

A South Florida Swoop

Allow: 10 days   **Distance:** 600 miles

On this trip, you'll have a chance to explore Miami's beaches and back alleys, from white sand to classical architecture; a diverse range of neighborhoods that encapsulate the nationalities of Latin America and the Caribbean; and the unique wetland and mangrove ecosystems of the Everglades, Biscayne National Park and the Florida Keys.

① MIAMI BEACH ⏱ 2 DAYS

Take in some art deco charm with sun-soaked glamour in **Miami Beach** (p50). Stroll iconic Ocean Drive (pictured), admiring pastel-hued architecture and a mix of vintage and flashy cars cruising. Lounge on South Beach's white sands and dip into the warm Atlantic waters. Explore the shops, cafes and galleries of lively Lincoln Rd. At night, dabble in as many rooftop bars and legendary clubs as you please.

② MIAMI ⏱ 3 DAYS

Explore **Miami's** (p73) neighborhoods, each offering a distinct flavor. Little Havana (pictured) pulses with Cuban culture, from cigar shops to salsa music. Wynwood's streets double as an open-air museum of graffiti art, while the Design District beckons with high-end boutiques and trendy eateries. Visit the Mediterranean-inspired mansions of Coral Gables. End an evening with a sunset cruise on Biscayne Bay.

③ EVERGLADES NATIONAL PARK ⏱ 2 DAYS

Drive to Homestead and explore **Everglades National Park's** (p112) vast wetlands, hopping between its Homestead, Shark Valley and Gulf Coast areas. Spot alligators on an airboat tour and hike the Anhinga Trail. Visit the Shark Valley Observation Tower for panoramic views of the subtropical wilderness. At night, enjoy stargazing under the dark skies.

④
BISCAYNE NATIONAL PARK ⏱ 1 DAY

Zip by car and spend the day on the water at **Biscayne National Park** (p128). Snorkel above colorful coral reefs loaded with marine life, kayak through mangrove-fringed waters or take a boat tour to Boca Chita Key's lighthouse for memorable views. The park's remote beauty is best experienced on a guided tour – book one to get the full scoop on shipwrecks and secluded islands.

⑤
KEY WEST ⏱ 2 DAYS

Cruise to the scenic Overseas Highway, culminating in **Key West** (p161), where bohemian homes and turquoise waters await. Wander lively Duval St (pictured), packed with historic bars and art galleries. Tour the Hemingway House. Cap off the day watching performers at Mallory Sq.

⏴ **Detour:** Stop at **Bahia Honda State Park** (p154) for pristine beaches and gawk at an eerie railroad bridge. ⏱ 1 hour

Mallory Square (p166), Key West

FOTOLUMINATE LLC/SHUTTERSTOCK

Biltmore Hotel (p87)

ITINERARIES

Magic City Magic

Allow: 5 days   **Distance:** 50 miles

On this trip, you'll experience some of the best of Miami's ethnic enclaves, hobnob in some of its wealthiest neighborhoods and witness firsthand the opulence that gives Miami the nickname 'The Magic City.' This itinerary showcases the heartbeat of Miami, its history, art and leisure beyond the white sands.

❶ DOWNTOWN MIAMI ⏱ **2 DAYS**

Start in **Downtown Miami** (p64), where glittering steel and glass shadows rough alleyways and flea markets. Take a ride on the free Metromover (pictured), hopping on and off at sites such as the Pérez Art Museum Miami. At night, catch some live music at Blackbird Ordinary or enjoy Caribbean cocktails at Baby Jane. Repeat with your choice of Miami museums the next day.

🚂 **Detour:** *From Downtown,* **Miami Beach** *(p50) is a 15-minute drive over a causeway.* ⏱ *3 hours.*

❷ CORAL GABLES ⏱ **1 DAY**

The next day, head to **Coral Gables** (p86), making sure not to miss the Venetian Pool (possibly the loveliest public pool in the US; pictured), the Biltmore Hotel, and a shopping stroll down Miracle Mile. If that isn't opulent enough, see what happens when Mediterranean Revival, baroque stylings and money get mashed together at the Vizcaya Museum & Gardens.

Map of Miami area showing the itinerary route from START in Downtown Miami (1), to Coral Gables (2), Little Havana (3), and END at Key Biscayne (4).

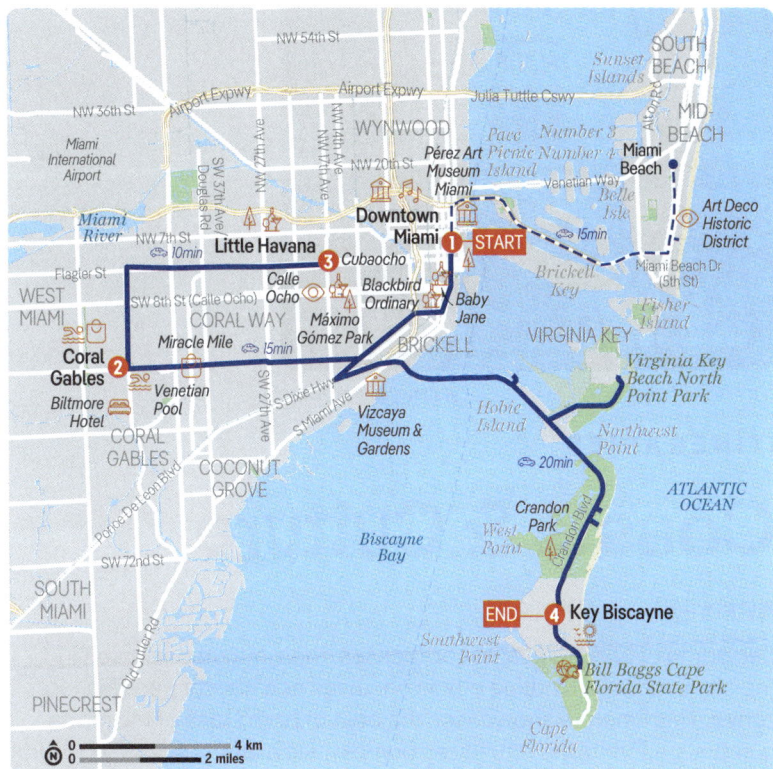

③ LITTLE HAVANA ⏱ 1 DAY

Head to **Little Havana** (p81) and stroll down Calle Ocho, stopping to watch the domino games at Máximo Gómez Park (pictured). Have a Cuban lunch, browse the local cigar and souvenir shops, then pop over to Coconut Grove, which retains its village-like charm. Grab a bite and a craft brew at a chic bar, ending the night with a live concert back in Little Havana at Cubaocho.

④ KEY BISCAYNE ⏱ 1 DAY

Spend your last day exploring **Key Biscayne** (p101), enjoying beaches and sunbathing in areas such as Bill Baggs Cape Florida State Park (pictured). Before you leave, head to Crandon Park for a stroll along the sand or an afternoon siesta. Is there a quiet, serene beach in manic Miami? You just found it, and you probably won't want to leave it.

JEFF GREENBERG/GETTY IMAGES

Wolfsonian-FIU (p51)

ITINERARIES

Coasts & Culture

Allow: 4 days   **Distance:** 25 miles

See some of Miami's glitziest addresses, then immerse yourself in the city's most fascinating ethnic enclaves and hipster gentrification zones. This itinerary showcases the best of both sides of Miami: its bumpin' beaches and equally as bumpin' – in a different way – cultural epicenters.

❶

MIAMI BEACH ⏱1 DAY

Start in **Miami Beach** (p50), using South Beach and its excellent hotels as your base. Take a walking tour with the Art Deco Museum (pictured) and Welcome Center, then visit the Wolfsonian-FIU for its excellent exhibitions on decorative arts, industrial design and architecture. Next, head for Lincoln Rd to people-watch and browse the trendy shops and restaurants. Night-cap with a cocktail at Sweet Liberty.

❷

LITTLE HAITI ⏱1 DAY

The next day, check out **Little Haiti** (p98). This is one of the most colorful foreign-feeling neighborhoods in Miami. It can be edgy at night, but by day you're fine to explore. Feast on oxtail and other Haitian treats at Chef Creole. Afterward, head to the Upper East Side for poolside drinks at the Vagabond.

FROM LEFT: BYVALET/SHUTTERSTOCK, FELIX MIZIOZNIKOV/SHUTTERSTOCK

❸ WYNWOOD & THE DESIGN DISTRICT ⏱ 1 DAY

The next day visit the galleries and shops of **Wynwood and the Design District** (p73). Start with the Wynwood Walls, an ever-changing art installation of vibrant wall-sized murals. Stop for an espresso at Panther Coffee and tacos at Coyo Taco, then head up to the Design District. Peruse public art installations, while popping in high-end galleries. At night, grab a bite and drinks at 1-800 Lucky.

❹ MID-BEACH & NORTH BEACH ⏱ 1 DAY

On your last day in town, head north along Collins Ave to **Mid-Beach and North Beach** (p54). To get there, you'll pass through what resembles condo canyons – rows of glittering residential skyscrapers, a testament to the power of real estate in Miami. In Mid-Beach, near the northern end of South Beach, you'll find an excellent boardwalk where you can stroll near the sand.

Overseas Highway Road Trip

Allow: 3 days   **Distance:** 100 miles

The Overseas Highway (Hwy 1) runs from the tip of the Florida mainland all the way to the famed Mile 0 in Key West, the end of the road and the end of America. You'll be treated to some of Florida's oddest attractions, plus the ever-inspiring view of Florida Bay on one side and the Gulf of Mexico on the other.

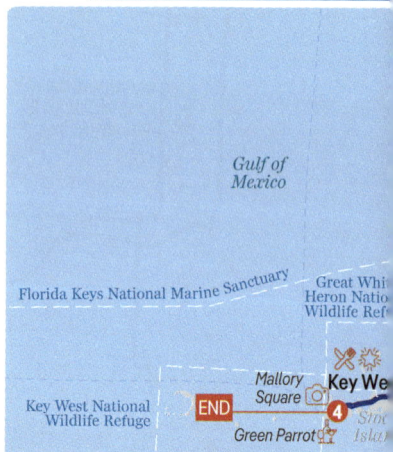

Gulf of Mexico

Florida Keys National Marine Sanctuary   Great Whi Heron Natio Wildlife Ref

Mallory Square   **Key We**

END   Sine Isla

Key West National Wildlife Refuge   Green Parrot   **4**

① KEY LARGO ⏱ HALF-DAY

You'll get to that view, but first, you have to go through the Upper Keys: larger islands where fields of scrub pine and mangroves block the water views. On northerly **Key Largo** (p140), check out the diving options at John Pennekamp Coral Reef State Park (pictured), then have lunch at a classic waterfront spot. Afterward, visit the rescued birds at the Laura Quinn Wild Bird Sanctuary.

② ISLAMORADA ⏱ 1 DAY

End the day with a seafood feast and ocean views at Lazy Days in **Islamorada** (p145). Sleep in Islamorada on your first day in the Keys. The next morning, snag a selfie with the town's iconic lobster statue (her name is Betsy) and feed the enormous tarpon at Robbie's Marina. Rent a kayak for a paddle through mangroves or out to Indian Key.

③ MARATHON ⏱ HALF-DAY

The next stop is **Marathon** (p150), the geographic center of the Keys. If you're curious about the unique ecological background of the Keys and fancy a walk in the woods, head to the Crane Point Hammock. Then learn about the Keys' best-loved endangered species at the Turtle Hospital (pictured). Eat dinner over the water and grab a beer at your choice of local tiki-inspired bars.

❹ KEY WEST ⏱ 1 DAY

The next morning, cross the Seven-Mile Bridge onto Big Pine Key, where tiny Key deer prance alongside the road. Stop for a meal at Square Grouper, one of the best restaurants south of Miami. Another hour's drive south and you're in **Key West** (p161). This island deserves its own itinerary – just don't miss the sunset show in Mallory Sq, and a night out at the infamous Green Parrot (pictured).

Seven Mile Bridge (p152)

Along the Tamiami Trail

Allow: 3 days **Distance:** 100 miles

Venture deep into the Everglades along the legendary Tamiami Trail, where alligator-filled waterways, lush cypress forests and remote fishing villages equate to an only-in-Florida wild side. This route showcases wetlands, quirky attractions and Old Florida charm. Expect close encounters with wildlife, eerie swamps and a taste of life literally at the edge of civilization.

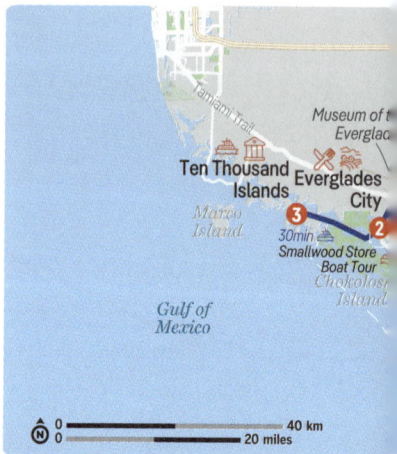

Tamiami Trail

Museum of the Everglades

Ten Thousand Islands Everglades City

Marco Island

3 30min Smallwood Store Boat Tour **2**

Chokoloskee Island

Gulf of Mexico

N 0 — 40 km
0 — 20 miles

1 EVERGLADES NATIONAL PARK ⏱ HALF DAY

From Miami, head west on Tamiami Trail (US 41) to Shark Valley, perhaps the most popular entrance to **Everglades National Park** (p112). Hop on the Shark Valley tram tour for a guided ride through sawgrass marshes, or rent a bicycle and follow the 15-mile loop, sharing the road with sunning alligators. At the observation tower, panoramic views stretch endlessly over the subtropical wilderness.

2 EVERGLADES CITY ⏱ HALF DAY

Continue west to **Everglades City** (p122), a sleepy fishing village with Old Florida vibes and access to some of the best seafood in the state. Feast on freshly caught stone crabs at a waterfront eatery while watching pelicans dive for their dinner. Stroll the quiet streets and soak up the ultra-laid-back Gulf Coast charm that feels otherworldly compared to Miami.

3 TEN THOUSAND ISLANDS ⏱ 1 DAY

Start the day with a boat tour into the labyrinth of the **Ten Thousand Islands** (p122). Spot dolphins, manatees and birds in this aquatic wilderness. Cross the causeway to Chokoloskee Island and step back in time at the Smallwood Store that showcases rugged pioneer life. On your way north, visit the Museum of the Everglades for a deeper dive into the region's history.

Map showing route from Miami START to Big Cypress National Preserve END, including Everglades National Park, Shark Valley Visitor Center, Big Cypress Gallery, Skunk Ape Research Headquarters, Fort Lauderdale, Hollywood, Biscayne National Park.

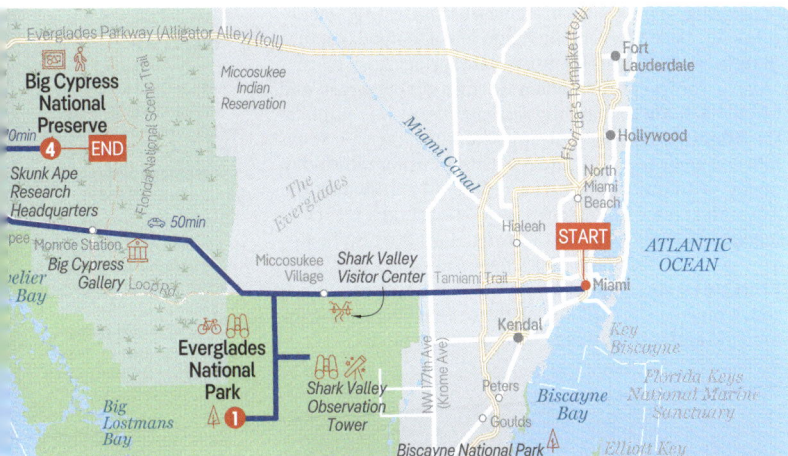

④
BIG CYPRESS NATIONAL PRESERVE ⏱ 1 DAY

On your way back toward Miami, stop at **Big Cypress National Preserve** (p119), a land of towering cypress trees and wildlife to match. Visit the offbeat Skunk Ape Research Headquarters, dedicated to Florida's own cryptid legend. Stop by Big Cypress Gallery, where black-and-white photos capture the raw beauty of the Everglades. Take a swamp walk for an immersive finale to your journey.

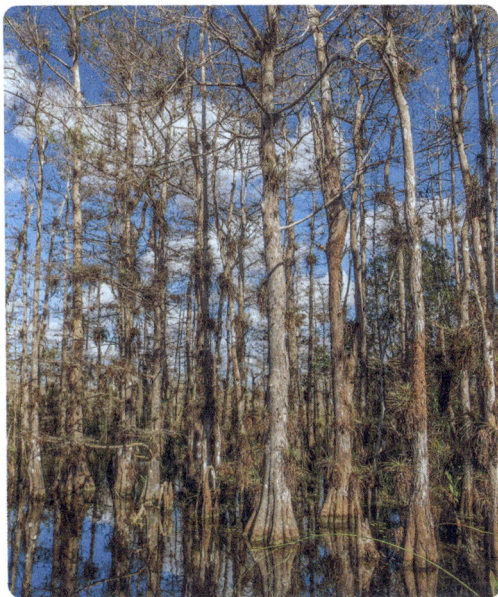

Big Cypress National Preserve (p119)

WHEN TO GO

Anytime. Snowbirds flock in the winter, summers sizzle, and cultural spectacles – both mega and quaint – enthrall year-round.

Florida's southern tip is sun-drenched each month, but knowing when to visit can unlock a whole different side of paradise. Winter lures in snowbirds and festival-goers – think Art Deco Weekend in Miami and a seafood bonanza in the Keys. But locals know that late spring (April to early June) is the sweet spot, when warmer waters gleam and island life hums at a slightly slower pace. By late summer, the Atlantic swells with drama – hurricane season keeps folks on their toes, but the rewards? A different kind of magic, with quieter stretches of beach to truly unwind. Autumn is the connoisseur's pick: stone crabs return to menus in October, sunset crowds at Mallory Sq in Key West feel just right, and more peaceful gators sun in the Everglades. And should a rogue storm darken the horizon? Consider it a call to duck into a conch house for key lime pie and a Hemingway-approved daiquiri.

⊚ **I LIVE HERE**

WINTER BLISS

Author Case Kenny lives in Miami's Edgewater neighborhood and spends the winter inspired by its striking contrasts. @case.kenny

Winter days in Miami are an abundance of duality – sweatshirts and crisp morning walks along the Venetian, plenty of SPF and warm afternoons soaking up creative ideas in Wynwood. I love the water's stillness punctuated by the hum of conversations over *cafecitos*. Energizing yet grounding. This contrast mirrors the creative essence of writing – embracing balance and shifts between calm and vibrance.

SPF ALL YEAR

Miami basks in 3200-plus hours of sunshine annually – sunburn is a year-round threat. Even in winter, UV levels rival those of peak summer in northern US cities. Whether kayaking in Biscayne Bay or spotting gators in the Everglades, SPF 50 and a wide-brimmed hat are vital.

FROM LEFT: ERIKA CRISTINA MANNO/SHUTTERSTOCK, XBROCK/SHUTTERSTOCK

Mallory Square (p166), Key West

Weather through the Year

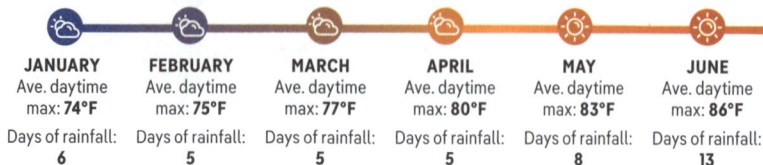

	JANUARY	FEBRUARY	MARCH	APRIL	MAY	JUNE
Ave. daytime max:	74°F	75°F	77°F	80°F	83°F	86°F
Days of rainfall:	6	5	5	5	8	13

HURRICANE SEASON

From June to November, the state of Florida stays on high alert. The most active months? August to October. Savvy travelers can track forecasts and snag great off-season deals, but staying vigilant is key – climate change and warming waters are causing storms to intensify faster than ever.

Crowd-Drawing Spectacles

Resort pools, intimate venues and mega arenas thump for **Miami Music Week** (p60). The biggest crowd-draw of all? The world-class DJ-loaded Ultra Music Festival. **March**

The Hard Rock Stadium complex and surrounds in Miami Gardens morph into a Formula One track for the **Miami Grand Prix** (p96). There's an entire week of parties, attracting global A-list celebs aplenty. **May**

A full-fledged, 10-day costumed extravaganza takes over Key West in the form of **Fantasy Fest** (p168). There are oodles of pool parties and a parade with body-painted and scantily clad revelers for blocks. **October**

Art Basel (p78) is the biggest draw of Miami Art Week. But there is so much more to it, with galleries hosting special exhibitions, parties 'round the clock and art-inspired dinners at top restaurants. **December**

The Fabric of South Florida

Ocean Drive swells with vintage charm for **Art Deco Weekend** (p60), featuring classic cars, retro fashion and parades that celebrate South Beach's 1920s and '30s architecture. **January**

Nashville meets the tropics at the **Key West Songwriters Festival** (p170). Hitmakers play intimate gigs in tiki bars and on the sand, sharing the stories behind country music's chart-toppers. Expect surprise performances and late-night singalongs. **May**

Key West pulses with Bahamian beats and Switcha (the Bahamas' national drink) for the **Goombay Festival** (p168). Junkanoo bands jam, conch fritters sizzle and the island spirit reaches another realm. **October**

Little Havana turns up the heat every third Friday of the month for **Viernes Culturales** (p84). This Cuban street party floods Calle Ocho with salsa dancers, domino games and live music, keeping Miami's Latin soul front-and-center. **Monthly**

OH, THE HUMIDITY

Miami's summer humidity is relentless. July and August see average dew points hover around 75°F, making even a morning stroll feel like a full-on sauna session. Expect heat indexes soaring above 100°F and embrace the afternoon thunderstorms – they cool things down, if only for a little bit.

JULY	AUGUST	SEPTEMBER	OCTOBER	NOVEMBER	DECEMBER
Ave. daytime max: **88°F**	Ave. daytime max: **88°F**	Ave. daytime max: **87°F**	Ave. daytime max: **84°F**	Ave. daytime max: **79°F**	Ave. daytime max: **76°F**
Days of rainfall: **13**	Days of rainfall: **14**	Days of rainfall: **14**	Days of rainfall: **11**	Days of rainfall: **7**	Days of rainfall: **6**

Cycling, Lummus Park (p58), Miam Beach

GET PREPARED FOR MIAMI & THE KEYS

Useful things to load in your bag, your ears and your brain.

Clothes

Heat-friendly fabrics Even in winter, daytime highs can reach the low 80s. You'll want to bring lightweight, breathable fabrics to stay cool and feel less sweaty.

Layers In the evenings, things can cool off, and even in the summer, it's wise to pack a light jacket for breezy walks by the water.

Rain gear Precipitation is a year-round possibility, although the biggest storms happen during the summer. Bring a lightweight rain jacket or an umbrella.

Hats A wide-brimmed hat is wise, whether for hiking or a Panama-style hat for dressier attire. Baseball hats are also popular, but you'll need to slather extra sunscreen on the back of your neck.

Manners

Most Floridians are quite cordial and will happily share insights into their local attractions, restaurants and drinking spots.

Locals tend to avoid topics like politics and instead talk sports. With local pro teams, college powerhouses and loyalties to Caribbean teams, there's always something afoot.

It's common to say hello to people you see in small towns and less busy areas such as state park trails.

📖 READ

Swamplandia! (Karen Russell; 2011) Comic, thought-provoking tale about the struggles of an alligator-wrestling Everglades family.

The Everglades: River of Grass (Marjory Stoneman Douglas; 1947) Landmark book that changed perceptions of Florida's wetlands.

Miami (Joan Didion; 1987) Deep dive into Miami's complex history and volatile identity, penned by one of the US' greatest essayists.

The Last Train to Paradise (Les Standiford; 2002) An account of Henry Flagler's dream to build a railroad to Key West.

Words

Conch (pronounced 'konk') Originally used to describe Bahamian immigrants with European ancestry. These days, it refers to a native of Key West – or the tasty sea snail.

Cracker A name given to early pioneer settlers who worked as farmers and cowhands. Some still use it today as a sign of a multi-generational connection to the Florida countryside.

Gladesmen Rough-and-ready characters who enjoy fishing, hunting and camping in the Everglades.

Hammock Not the thing you swing in, but rather an area of higher ground that contains hardwoods like oaks, hickory trees and palms.

Intracoastal Waterway A series of canals, bays, inlets, rivers and channels that provide sheltered travel by boat along both the Gulf and Atlantic Coasts.

Key From the Spanish *cayo*, a small island made of ancient remnants of coral reefs. 'The Keys' refers to the 1700-island archipelago in Florida's far south.

Old Florida The vintage Florida of yesteryear, which may include state parks, ungentrified towns or traditional seaside communities.

Mile Marker Zero The starting point of the Overseas Highway in Key West – the southernmost selfie spot in the Florida Keys.

Snowbird A person who comes to live in Florida part-time during the winter months to escape the cold weather up north.

Y'all Short for 'you all,' commonly used to address a group of people in the South.

▶ WATCH

The Birdcage (Mike Nichols; 1996; pictured) In South Beach, a gay couple try to play straight for their son's in-laws.

Scarface (Brian De Palma; 1983) Crime saga following a Cuban immigrant in the Miami underworld.

Pain & Gain (Michael Bay; 2013) Based on a true story about Miami bodybuilders caught up in a botched crime spree.

Key Largo (John Huston; 1948) Classic Bacall-Bogart film noir featuring fugitives, double-crossing and an ominous hurricane.

Dolphin Tale (Charles Martin Smith; 2011) Family favorite about a wounded dolphin given new life by a prosthetic tail.

🎧 LISTEN

Danger High Voltage (Betty Wright; 1972) Evocative grooves from Miami's trailblazing queen of soul.

Songs You Know by Heart (Jimmy Buffett; 1985) Compilation of Buffett's greatest hits including 'Margaritaville' and 'Cheeseburger in Paradise.'

Port of Miami (Rick Ross; 2006) Debut album from the Miami-born rapper, packed with lyrical odes to Magic City's streets, luxury and hustling.

The South Florida Roundup (WLRN) News radio show with a roundtable format, with local journalists commenting on South Florida issues.

MARIDAV/ALAMY STOCK PHOTO

Cuban sandwich

THE **FOOD** SCENE

A vibrant feast awaits at every turn: fresh-caught seafood, internationally inspired dishes, and bold Latin-Caribbean flavors.

An irresistible blend of bold flavors and fresh, locally sourced ingredients await at every South Florida turn. The end result can come in the form of wow-inducing bites in no-frills restaurants to Michelin-starred experiences. Coastal waters provide a bounty of just-caught seafood – think stone crab claws, spiny lobster and mahimahi that is as savory in lime-dashed tacos as it is simply grilled. The region's Latin-Caribbean influence infuses menus with the likes of zesty ceviches, smoky *lechón* (pork) and sweet, guava-filled *pastelitos* (flaky pastries).

In the Everglades, rustic outposts dish out alligator bites and frog legs, offering a taste of Florida's wilder side. Down in the Keys, conch fritters and tiki cocktails define the island-style dining experience. Whether you're feasting at a waterfront fish shack region-wide, sipping on a *cafecito* (espresso

with foam) at a *ventanita* (a walk-up window) in Little Havana, or indulging in a high-end tasting menu, the options are bountiful. Welcome to foodie heaven, and don't forget – always save room for key lime pie.

Bounty of the Sea

Grouper is by far the most popular fish throughout Florida and certainly ever-prevalent here. Grouper sandwiches can be to South Florida what the cheesesteak is to Philadelphia – a local battle of who can do it best. Finding the perfect grilled or fried grouper sandwich can be a Miami-to-Key-West quest, with locals and visitors alike hotly debating where to find the ultimate bite. The argument doesn't stop at the fish – toppings like tangy slaw, house-made tartar sauce or even a slice of fried green tomato add another layer to the debate.

Best South Florida Dishes	GROUPER SANDWICH	KEY LIME PIE	CEVICHE	ALLIGATOR BITES
	Grilled or fried local fish on a bun, typically with slaw and a sauce.	Tart, creamy dessert with a graham cracker crust and whipped topping.	Fresh fish cured in citrus with onions, peppers and, local, tropical fruit.	Crispy, seasoned chunks of Everglades alligator, often with remoulade.

Other favorites include snapper (with dozens of varieties), mahimahi (sometimes labeled as 'dolphin,' to tourists' dismay), and yellowtail, a Florida Keys staple often served blackened or in ceviche. If you're lucky, you'll hit a restaurant offering a 'hook-and-cook' experience, where you bring in your own fresh catch, and the chef prepares it how you like.

South Florida shines when it comes to crustaceans: try pink shrimp, rock shrimp, and Key West spiny lobster, which is Florida's clawless answer to its Maine cousin. Stone crab season (October to May) is a regional highlight, with massive claws served chilled and cracked tableside alongside the essential mustard dipping sauce. Blue crab, abundant in the northern parts of the state, also makes an appearance on local menus, often boiled or steamed.

For a true local experience, grab a seat at a dockside fish shack in the Keys or indulge in Miami's fresh seafood scene, where buttery lobster rolls and tangy ceviche abound. In the Everglades, wilder fare like alligator bites and frog legs share menu space with more traditional catches.

Cuban & Latin American Cuisine

Cuban food is an everyday staple in Miami, where you'll find a *sándwich cubano* – a grilled baguette packed with ham, roast pork, cheese, mustard and pickles – at nearly every corner cafe. Equally beloved is the *medianoche,* a similar sandwich served on a slightly sweet, soft yellow roll.

Essential Cuban flavors also include *mojo* (a garlicky vinaigrette), *adobo* (a citrus-garlic marinade) and *sofrito* (a mix of garlic, onion and chili peppers). Dishes emphasize hearty portions, with rice, beans and fried plantains rounding out most meals.

With its large Latin American immigrant population, Miami is a true culinary melting pot. Seek out Haitian griot (marinated fried pork), Jamaican jerk chicken, Brazilian barbecue, Central American *gallo pinto* (red beans and rice), and Nicaraguan *tres leches* ('three milks' cake).

In the morning, grab a Cuban coffee – *café cubano* (sweetened espresso) or a *cortadito* (espresso with a splash of milk). Miami's Cuban coffee culture is legendary – just stop by a *ventanita* and you'll see locals sipping *cafecito* while debating baseball, politics or the best *pastelitos.*

Fruits & Vegetables

Today, most upscale restaurants highlight local sources of their produce. South Florida's

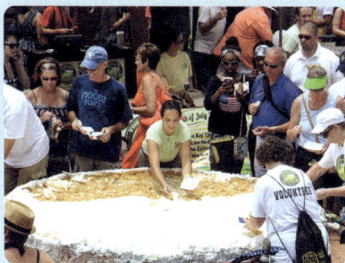

CHUCK WAGNER/SHUTTERSTOCK

FOOD & DRINK FESTIVALS

South Beach Wine & Food Festival (sobewff. org; February) A beachside feast in Miami with celebrity chefs, wine tastings and lavish culinary events. Expect exclusive dinners, hands-on cooking demonstrations and over-the-top parties hosted by some of the biggest names in food and local chefs alike.

International Mango Festival (July) A tropical celebration at **Fairchild Tropical Garden** (p94) with exotic mango varieties, tastings, cooking demos and mango-centric treats on full display. Learn about the world's rarest mangoes, sip mango cocktails and sample everything from mango salsa to mango ice cream.

Key Lime Festival (keylimefestival.com; July; pictured) A zesty homage to Florida's signature citrus with pie-eating contests, cooking classes and quirky lime-themed fun in Key West. You can sip key lime cocktails, join a pie-making workshop or compete in the wacky 'Key Lime Pie Drop' from the top of a lighthouse.

CONCH FRITTERS	CUBAN SANDWICH	STONE CRAB CLAWS	MAMEY MILKSHAKE
Golden, deep-fried batter bites packed with conch and spices.	Pressed, crispy bread filled with ham, roast pork, Swiss, mustard and pickles.	Tender crab claws cracked and served chilled, often with mustard sauce.	Thick, tropical shake made from creamy, sweet mamey fruit and milk.

tropical climate yields a bounty of exotic fruits, beyond the state's famous oranges and citrus. While Florida is the nation's largest producer of oranges, grapefruits, tangerines and limes, Miami and the Keys are all about tropical fruits you won't find elsewhere in the US – a reflection of the region's Caribbean and Latin influences. Mangoes, passion fruit, papayas, guavas and starfruit are staples, often blended into smoothies or tropical desserts.

Avocados (once called 'alligator pears'), bananas, strawberries and coconuts also thrive in South Florida's surprising farmland. The major agricultural region is around Homestead, where roadside fruit stands like the legendary Robert Is Here serve fresh produce and thick tropical milkshakes.

One fruit reigns supreme in the Keys: its namesake key limes. The tart citrus is the star of key lime pie. Variations range from a classic graham cracker-crusted slice to frozen key lime pie on a stick, perhaps dipped in several types of chocolate. For an old-school twist, look for a baked meringue topping, a nod to traditional recipes.

Specialities

Sweet Treats

Key lime pie A custard of key lime juice, sweetened condensed milk, and egg yolks in a graham cracker crust, topped with whipped cream or classic meringue.

Dare to Try

Alligator tail Tastes like a cross between fish and pork, with as much protein as chicken but half the fat.

Often fried and served with remoulade in the Everglades.

Frog legs The best ones, locals say, come from the Everglades, where they're fried crisp or sautéed in garlic butter.

Swamp cabbage Heart of palm, or 'swamp cabbage,' has a delicate, sweet crunch. Try it as a traditional Everglades side dish or in a hearty stew.

THE YEAR IN FOOD

SPRING

Farmers markets are overflowing from spring up until the summer heat arrives. Blueberries (in April and May), cantaloupe, grapefruit and oranges are all part of the largesse.

SUMMER

Indulge in the hot season's countless tropical temptations, including mangoes, papaya, passion fruit, lychees and dragon fruit. Fishing is also at its best.

FALL

Forget pumpkins and apple cider. In Florida, fall is the season of zucchini, kale, eggplants and artisanal lettuces. In mid-October, stone crab season arrives, with Floridians feasting on the scrumptious crustacean until about mid-May.

WINTER

The sweet Key West pink shrimp is available from November through June. It's strawberry season in the south; places like Knaus Berry Farm near the Everglades offer pick-your-own strawberries from late December to early April.

Oysters

HOW TO...

Eat Miami Seafood

Beyond the seafood sourced in and around Miami, the city's dynamic culinary scene attracts seafood from around the world for all to enjoy. Here's how to dig in properly.

Lobster 101

The easiest way to enjoy lobster is in a lobster roll – shredded lobster meat served in a toasted bun, either tossed with mayonnaise or warm with melted butter.

For the full experience, order a whole steamed or boiled lobster. Most South Florida restaurants provide two key utensils: a cracker (like a nutcracker) to break open the shell and a small seafood fork or pick to extract meat from narrow spaces. Lobster is meatiest in the tail and claws – use the cracker to break them open. You can often remove the tail with your hands. Don't forget the narrow legs, where you can pull or suck out small bits of meat. Lobster is best enjoyed with melted butter and a squeeze of lemon – so zest and douse away to your liking!

Sure, a steamed lobster, lobster roll, and steak upgrade (yes, you can often add a lobster tail to accompany your steak) are most prevalent on menus, but there are other ways to enjoy this popular crustacean. Typically created from a stock of lobster shells, lobster bisque is a creamy soup with shredded lobster. You might also try lobster mac 'n' cheese (baked cheesy pasta made richer with lobster meat) as well as other pastas topped with lobster, often with a spicy kick. Miami's omakase scene is booming, too, with lobster-topped sushi bites and rolls. For breakfast, you may even find a lobster-topped Benedict (tip: The Rusty Pelican (p102) has one).

Oysters

Oysters are best served fresh on ice, paired with a refreshing cocktail – perhaps a mojito, a citrusy margarita or a crisp white wine. While the finest oysters come from the cold waters of the Northeast US, Gulf and Caribbean varieties are also popular here. Many restaurants in Brickell and South Beach feature raw bars with daily selections. Look out for happy hour deals when oysters can drop to $1 or $2 each.

Global Fish Flair

Miami's seafood scene is a truly international feast. Enjoy Cuban seafood paella, Peruvian ceviche bursting with citrus, or whole snapper fried Jamaican-style with a side of plantains. Haitian *poisson gros sel*, Brazilian *moqueca*, and Caribbean conch stew are also local favorites. Don't miss the vibrant eateries in Little Havana and North Miami, where creative seafood dishes showcase Miami's diverse culinary influences, all sometimes within a single block.

Don't Miss

Peel-and-eat shrimp An old-school treat, served boiled and pink in their shells – there's always cocktail sauce nearby.
Conch fritters This giant sea snail is battered and fried – crispy on the outside, tender inside, and best enjoyed with spicy aïoli.
Stone crab claws Only one claw is taken from a stone crab – it is returned to the sea to regenerate.
Hogfish A local favorite known for its mild flavor and flaky texture, often served grilled, blackened or pan-seared. It's prized for its clean taste.
Mahimahi A yellow-green fish, with a firm texture and slightly sweet flavor when cooked. Regionally served with tropical fruit salsas or citrus sauces.

37

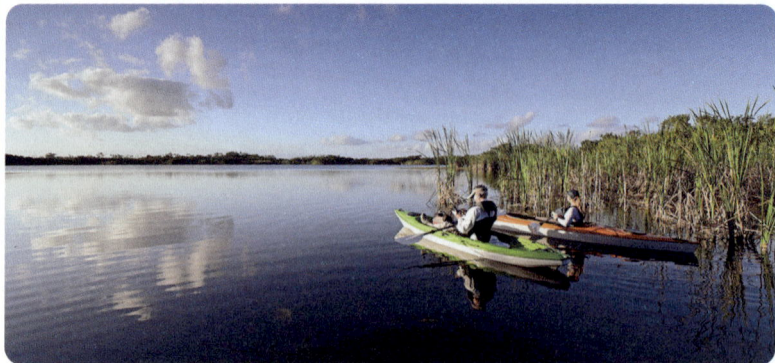

Nine Mile Pond (p117), Everglades National Park

THE OUTDOORS

A region that touches the Atlantic and Gulf coasts? Oh yes. This is an adventurer's playground, with world-class aquatic activities and flat hiking and cycling gems.

Florida has been a top destination for outdoor lovers for over a century. Hundreds of miles of sandy beaches, wildlife-rich wetlands and coastal marine preserves form the backdrop to days of adventure. Fronting two major bodies of water, this region offers stellar kayaking, snorkeling, fishing and paddleboarding. On land, you can take to scenic paths on foot or by bike or explore remote islands via boat tours in Biscayne National Park and the Florida Keys. There are plenty of less common adventures, too, from airboat rides through the Everglades to spearfishing in coral reefs region-wide.

Kayaking & Canoeing

Kayaking and canoeing are two brilliant ways to explore this watery state. South Florida's waterways offer some of the most diverse paddling experiences, from the mangrove tunnels of the Everglades to the seagrass-y meadows of Biscayne Bay.

Everglades National Park has both saltwater and freshwater paddles, including memorable forays through mangrove tunnels in Nine Mile Pond. The nearby Ten Thousand Islands offer more wilderness adventures, with endless maze-like waterways teeming with birdlife and manatees.

Other great spots for a paddle include Oleta River State Park in North Miami and Key Largo's John Pennekamp Coral Reef State Park, known for its crystal-clear waters.

Snorkeling & Diving

Two of the best spots for a dive or snorkel are John Pennekamp Coral Reef State Park in Key Largo and Biscayne National Park, south of Miami at the tip of the Florida mainland. The latter is the only national park in the US National Park Service system to exist primarily under the waves. Further along the Keys, you won't be dis-

---

Bigger Thrills

REMOTE CAMPING
Spend the night in the depths of the **Everglades** (p114) on an above-water chickee only accessible by boat.

SPEEDBOAT TOURS
Feel the need for speed on 45-minute tours of Biscayne Bay in power catamarans with **Thriller Miami Speedboat Adventures** (p67).

FISHING
Fish from shore in **Bill Baggs Cape Florida State Park** (p103) or book a sportfishing charter in **Islamorada** (p145).

FAMILY ADVENTURES

Learn about the resident dolphins off Marco Island on a naturalist-focused **boat tour** (p118).

See marine life glide below your feet on a glass-bottom boat tour or get even closer while snorkeling in **John Pennekamp Coral Reef State Park** (p140).

Spot wildlife along boardwalks off Main Park Rd in the Everglades (p115), then take a boat excursion at Flamingo (p116).

Watch massive tarpon leap from the water at **Robbie's Marina** (p145) in Islamorada as you hand-feed them. Stay for boat tours or kayaking.

Escape the crowds at the family-friendly stretch of **North Beach** (p54) in Miami, which has playgrounds.

Explore short trails and calm lagoons at **Historic Virginia Key Park** (p101). Perhaps a history lesson here, too – it was a segregated beach until the 1960s.

---

appointed at Sombrero Reef near Marathon, Looe Key or Bahia Honda State Park.

Wreck diving in South Florida is equally epic, and some sites are even accessible to snorkelers. The Florida Keys Shipwreck Trail features historic wrecks, including the famous *Vandenberg* off Key West. Biscayne National Park has an impressive underwater Maritime Heritage Trail, where divers can explore shipwrecks dating back to the 19th century.

Named for its sea turtles, Dry Tortugas National Park is well worth the effort to reach, as its pristine waters offer some of the finest snorkeling in all of Florida. Accessible only by boat or seaplane, the park features vibrant coral reefs and the 19th-century Fort Jefferson on land.

Hiking

The region's hiking trails can be challenging due to the weather, and in the Everglades, trail conditions often involve wading through knee-deep water.

South Florida swamps favor boardwalk trails, which are excellent and almost always wheelchair-accessible. Popular boardwalk hikes include the short Anhinga Trail in Everglades National Park, where alligators and wading birds are abundant, and the Gumbo Limbo Trail, which winds through a shaded tropical hardwood hammock.

For a more immersive experience, embark on a ranger-led 'wet walk' in Big Cypress National Preserve, where you'll wade through cypress domes and spot orchids, frogs, gators and...who knows what else?

While the Florida National Scenic Trail runs north from Big Cypress National Preserve, most of its long-distance hiking opportunities lie outside South Florida. Instead, hikers in the region can explore shorter scenic trails like the scenic coastal trails of Bill Baggs Cape Florida State Park.

BEST SPOTS

For the best outdoor spots and routes, see the map on p40.

Boardwalk, Everglades National Park

SURFING	**NUDE BEACHES**	**BIKING**	**AIRBOAT TOURS**
Ride the waves like a local just off **Surfside's** (p62) pristine sands.	Get rid of those tan lines while sunbathing nude at **Haulover Beach Park** (p62).	Pedal through **Pigeon Key National Historic District** (p153) or along part of the Great Florida Birding Trail on **Big Pine Key** (p157).	Feast your eyes on alligators and other wildlife as you glide across the water in the **Everglades** (p116) on an airboat tour.

ACTION AREAS

Where to find Miami & the Keys' best outdoor activities.

Animals/Wildlife

1. Jungle Island (p67)
2. Shark Valley (p112)
3. Buttonwood Canal (p116)
4. Big Cypress National Preserve (p119)
5. Turtle Hospital (p152)
6. Big Pine Key (p157)

Kayaking/Canoeing

1. Virginia Key Beach North Point Park (p102)
2. Bills Baggs Cape Florida State Park (p103)
3. Oleta River State Park (p58)
4. Everglades National Park (p114)
5. Ten Thousand Islands (p123)
6. Robbie's Marina (p145)
7. Bahia Honda State Park (p154)

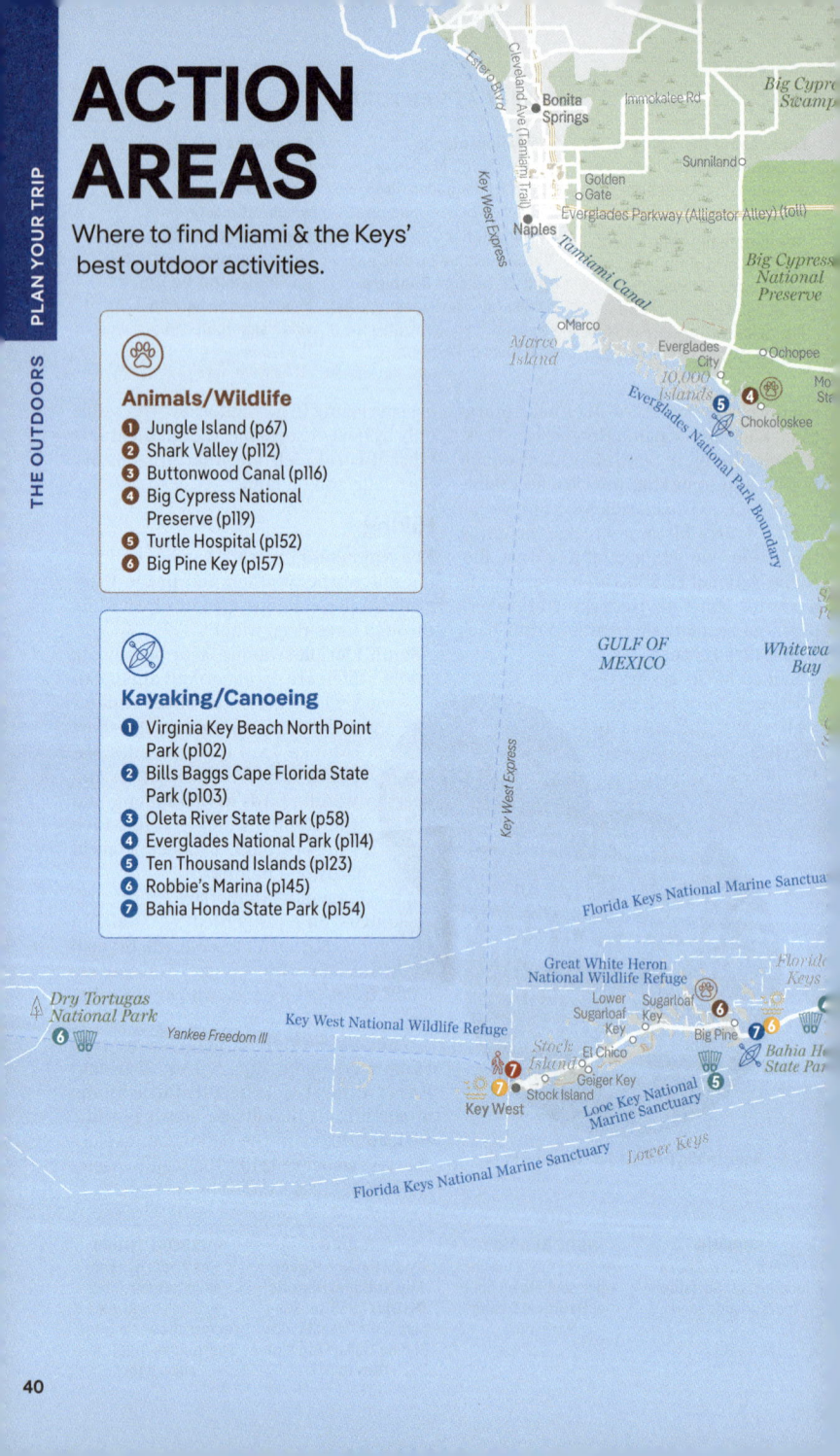

Beach

1. South Beach (p51)
2. Crandon Beach Park (p103)
3. Haulover Beach Park (p62)
4. Muscle Beach (p62)
5. Sombrero Beach (p147)
6. Bahia Honda State Park (p154)
7. Fort Zachary Taylor Historic State Park (p147)

Walking/Hiking

1. Miami Beach Boardwalk (p54)
2. Art Deco Historic District, Miami (p61)
3. Miami Riverwalk (p69)
4. Spite Highway Trail (p132)
5. Christian Point Trail (p115)
6. Mangrove Trail (p140)
7. Duval St, Key West (p167)

Snorkeling/Diving

1. Biscayne National Park (p128)
2. John Pennekamp Coral Reef State Park (p140)
3. Florida Keys Aquarium (p151)
4. Pigeon Key (p153)
5. Looe Key Reef (p156)
6. Dry Tortugas National Park (p170)

MIAMI & THE KEYS

THE GUIDE

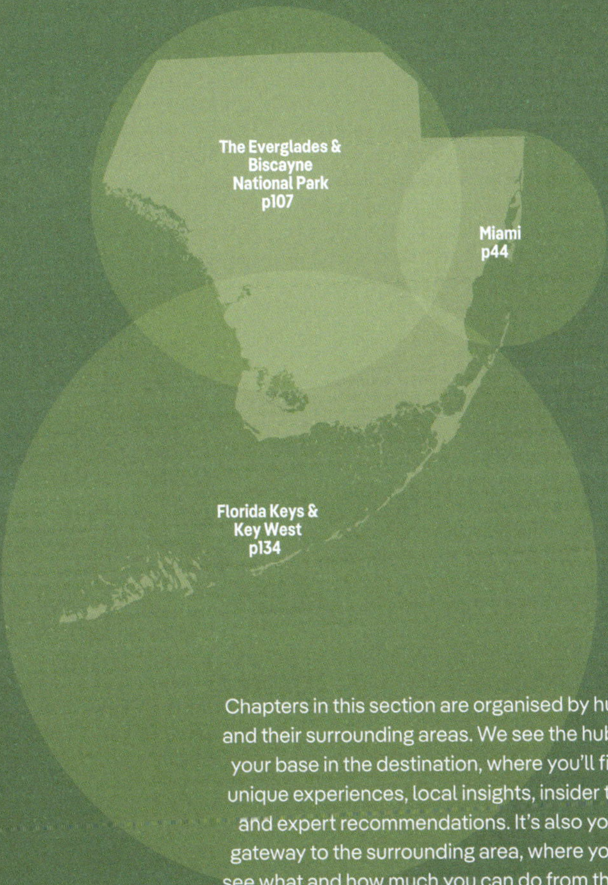
The Everglades & Biscayne National Park p107
Miami p44
Florida Keys & Key West p134

Chapters in this section are organised by hubs and their surrounding areas. We see the hub as your base in the destination, where you'll find unique experiences, local insights, insider tips and expert recommendations. It's also your gateway to the surrounding area, where you'll see what and how much you can do from there.

Bahia Honda State Park (p154)

JACQUELINE FAUST/SHUTTERSTOCK

Miami

LATIN AMERICA AND THE CARIBBEAN COLLIDE

Miami defines South Florida but stands apart from it, encompassing demographic enclaves from across the world, lashed together by the arts, creativity and sensory overload.

No city has a well-heeled foot dipped in North America, the Caribbean and Latin America, like Miami. With its diversity worn proudly on its sleeve, the city unspools a constant display of unabashed hedonism and a deep appreciation of beautiful things (and people). Art deco architecture and graffiti murals are the backdrop, Cuban coffee is the fuel, and reggaetón and clacking dominoes are the soundtrack to a city tinged with pink sunsets on a silver skyline lapped by Biscayne Bay.

One of Miami's greatest hallmarks is its creativity. From art and design to global cuisine, there is no rest for the innovative. The city's residents are constantly in search of bold new ideas. Inventive chefs blend Eastern, Western, Southern American and South American cooking styles astride open-air galleries where museum-caliber artworks cover once-derelict warehouses. The one constant in this ever-evolving city: Miami's uncanny ability to astonish.

White sandy beaches are lapped by emerald waters – perfect for a sunrise stroll along peaceful stretches of Mid-Beach or scenic paddles in search of lollygagging manatees off Virginia Key. Colorful birds can be admired along the walking trails of Oleta River State Park and tropical gardens dotting the urban metropolis. With year-round sunshine and a love for celebration, out in the open air is where Miami's biggest parties unfold – at massive music and dance festivals or neighborhood fiestas.

Even without its glorious beaches, Miami would still seduce. The gorgeous 1930s hotels lining Ocean Drive are part of the world's greatest collection of art deco buildings. Tropical motifs, whimsical nautical elements and those iconic pastel shades create a cinematic backdrop for exploring the streets of Miami Beach. When evening takes hold and the brilliant colors of a South Florida sunset fill the sky, Miami's party people spring to life. By moonlight, all the magic of the city's enigmatic nightlife is revealed. And while there's no shortage of excess, Miami has something for everyone – from backyard bars full of indie rockers to hidden dens of debauchery concealed behind neon-lit taco stands.

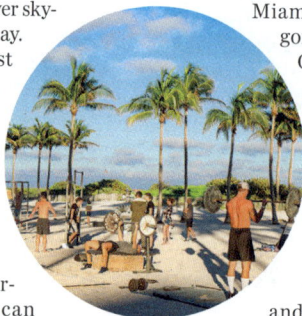

LAZYLLAMA/SHUTTERSTOCK

THE MAIN AREAS

MIAMI BEACH
Ground zero for good beachy times. **p50**

DOWNTOWN MIAMI
Electric energy along Biscayne Bay. **p64**

WYNWOOD, THE DESIGN DISTRICT & ALLAPATTAH
Art-centric neighborhoods where you'll eat well. **p73**

For places to stay in Miami, see p105

SYLVAIN SONNET/GETTY IMAGES

Left: Muscle Beach (p62); Above: Ocean Drive

LITTLE HAVANA
The core of the Cuban diaspora.
p81

CORAL GABLES & COCONUT GROVE
Lush gardens and cafe culture.
p86

GREATER MIAMI
Cultural neighborhoods and island escapes. **p96**

Find Your Way

Miami and Miami Beach are separate cities connected by a series of causeways. Greater Miami sprawls north and south, connected by highways and lots of traffic. The waterways and major highways that run through Miami are often the boundaries and borders of its neighborhoods.

LIBERTY
CITY

LIT
HA

Wynwood, the
Design District
Allapattah
p73

Margulie
Collection a
Warehou
Rubell *Warehou*
Museum
Wynwo
W

Miami
International
Airport

Greater
Miami
p96

Little
Havana
p81

Máximo
Gómez
Park
Little Havana
Art District

WEST
MIAMI

CORAL
WAY

Venetian Pool

Vizcaya
Museum &
Gardens

Coral Gables &
Coconut Grove
p86

Biscayne
Bay

SOUTH
MIAMI

PINECREST

Fairchild
Tropical
Botanic Garden

0   5 km
0   2.5 miles

*ATLANTIC
OCEAN*

NORMANDY   NORTH
SHORES   BEACH

UPPER
EAST
SIDE   NORTH
            BAY
            VILLAGE

*agabond
otel*

**Miami
Beach**
p50

*drienne Arsht
enter for the
rforming Arts*

South Beach

*érez Art
eum Miami*

Art Deco
Historic District

*Bayfront
Park*

**wntown
Miami**
p64

*Fisher
Island*

VIRGINIA
KEY

Crandon
Park

KEY
BISCAYNE

*Bill Baggs Cape
Florida State Park*

Bill Baggs
Cape Florida
State Park

FROM THE AIRPORT

You can access the usual ride apps from **Miami International Airport** at 10 locations on Arrivals Level 1. Otherwise, metered taxis are available at ground level outside baggage claim. Fares are metered – it's around $35 to $50 to Miami Beach and $25 to Downtown.

CAR & MOTORCYCLE

The most important highway is I-95, which ends at US Hwy 1 south of Downtown. If you're crossing town from around 7am to 9am or 3pm to 6pm, allow at least an extra hour (really) of travel time, especially if going to Miami Beach.

BICYCLE

Citi Bike *(citibikemiami.com)* is a solar-powered bike-share program where you can borrow a bike from more than 160 stations spread around Miami and Miami Beach. While Miami is flat, traffic can be horrendous. A variety of scooters are also available throughout Greater Miami to rent via third-party apps.

BUS

Metrobus, Miami's local bus system, can get you to most places – but it won't get you there quickly. Each bus route has a different schedule, and routes generally run from about 5am to 11pm, though some are 24 hours.

Plan Your Days

Start your day with a *cafecito* (strong, sweet Cuban espresso) and perhaps a guava and cheese *pastelito* (puff pastry) – the coffee alone ought to keep you awake and exploring for the next 48 hours!

11th Street Diner (p60)

PETER UNGE/GETTY IMAGES

Day 1

Morning

● Grab that cafecito at **News Cafe** (p59) and stroll **South Beach** (p51), stopping in the **Art Deco Museum** (p51) for information about this architectural district. Wander Ocean Dr's deco sights solo or take a guided tour with the non-profit **Miami Design Preservation League**. For more insight, visit the **Wolfsonian-FIU** (p61).

Afternoon

● Post-lunch at the **11th Street Diner** (p60) stroll Lincoln Rd's shops and restaurants. Or catch salty breezes with a jetty stroll and ocean swim at **South Pointe Park** (p58).

Evening

● Enjoy dinner at **Stubborn Seed** (p55) for New American cuisine. Along Española Way admire Spanish architecture and the nearby **Betsy Orb** (p59). Wind down with drinks at **Sweet Liberty.** (p56)

You'll Also Want to...

Leave the more popular spots behind and peel back the layers of all there is to see and do in and around Miami's beaches and neighborhoods.

BRANCH OUT WITH BEACHES

Seek out less famous beaches at **North Miami Beach** (p54) where the waters are just as blue and warm, but you have more space to stretch out on the sand.

GO BEYOND CUBAN CUISINE

Miami may be famous for Cuban food, but with so many other cultural influences here, you can find incredible cuisines from Uzbekistan (**Chayhana Oasis**) (p101) and Nicaragua (**Fritanga Montelimar**) (p101), among others.

EXPLORE THE PARKS

It's easy to focus all your attention on Miami's spectacular sands, but **Biscayne National Park** (p93) and state oases like **Oleta River State Park** (p58) are prime for bay and river views too.

Day 2

Morning
● Beeline it to Wynwood and **Enriqueta's** (p78) for a Cuban breakfast and a *cafe con leche* (coffee with milk) before checking out the murals at **Wynwood Walls** (p80) and exploring the **Rubell Museum** (p79).

Afternoon
● Spend the afternoon at **Pérez Art Museum Miami** (p69), home to some of the city's best contemporary art. Admire Biscayne Bay views from **Bayfront Park** (p68) before making your way to the Design District to browse shops and galleries on foot.

Evening
● Enjoy **Michael's Genuine** (p77) for dinner and cocktails at **The Sylvester** (p79) in the Design District. Alternatively, head to lively Little Havana to finish the fun with mojitos and Cuban food at **Cafe La Trova** (p83).

Day 3

Morning
● Decamp from Downtown Miami for the barrier island of **Key Biscayne** (p101), a residential island with great beaches and a historic lighthouse to visit at **Bill Baggs Cape Florida State Park** (p103). Have fresh grilled seafood for lunch at **Boater's Grill** (p102).

Afternoon
● Make for Coral Gables and Coconut Grove to visit the antique-filled interiors of **Vizcaya Museum & Gardens** (p92) or the lush setting of **Fairchild Tropical Botanic Garden** (p86). Perhaps sneak in a boat tour from **Dinner Key Marina** (p93).

Evening
● Feast on spicy Caribbean fare in Little Haiti and explore the nearby **Upper East Side** and **Little River** (p100), Miami's cool-kid neighborhood du jour.

DIVE INTO THE ARTS
Miami's performing arts scene is Florida's best. Catch world-class performances at the **Adrienne Arsht Center for the Performing Arts** (p70) or **New World Symphony** (p60).

GET OUT ON THE WATER
So much of what makes Miami great requires heading just offshore to enjoy: rent a board to paddle out for a surf session in **Surfside** (p62) or snorkel from Coconut Grove to see **Stiltsville** (p71).

SHOP 'TIL YOU DROP
Miami's swimwear, accessory and clothing aesthetic is in a league all its own. Factor in time for retail therapy at the billlion-dollar **Brickell City Centre** (p68) and boutiques lining Lincoln Road.

WORK IN SOME QUIRK
Miami's quirkier side is worth seeking out at spots like the **Museum of Ice Cream** (p59), the **World Erotic Art Museum** (p59) and the botanica shops in Little Haiti.

Miami Beach

GROUND ZERO FOR GOOD BEACHY TIMES

GETTING AROUND

It's a cinch to get around South Beach on foot, and it's also the most fun way to explore the area. When you need a break, however, hop aboard the free Miami Beach Trolley which brings riders from South Beach to Collins Ave, Mid-Beach and North Beach.

☑TOP TIP

From college reunions and spring break to foodie, music and art festivals, Miami Beach is ground zero for large-scale gatherings in every season. Check the calendar before arrival and prepare for a vibe dictated by the theme of whatever event is on – Miami tends to go all-in on whatever it's celebrating.

When outsiders think of Miami, it's often the wholly separate city of Miami Beach – specifically the neighborhood of South Beach – that comes to mind.

'SoBe' ticks a lot of South Florida boxes: sweeping beachfront, art deco architecture, top-end boutiques, buzzing bars and restaurants. Still, there's more to this district than velvet ropes and luxury lodging. You'll find great down-to-earth bars, good eating and cool museums, all against a backdrop of relentlessly attractive pastel deco builings and swaying palms.

The typical South Beach experience is about choosing your own adventure. Early risers might run on the beach at sunrise. You can grab breakfast at a vegan spot, do yoga in the afternoon, attend a concert at the New World Center. Night owls might start with espresso and Bloody Marys at noon, laze on the beach, shop on Lincoln Road, dine in Sunset Harbour, then hit the late-night lounges, rooftop bars and dance clubs.

Grim History   MAP P52/53

Somber space for Holocaust grief and reflection

Even for a place of Holocaust reflection, the **Holocaust Memorial Miami Beach** (*holocaustmemorialmiamibeach.org; free*) memorial is particularly powerful. With more than 100 sculptures, its centerpiece is the *Sculpture of Love and Anguish,* an enormous, oxidized bronze arm that bears an Auschwitz tattoo number – chosen because it was never issued at the camp. Terrified camp prisoners scale the sides of the arm, trying to pass their loved ones, including children, to safety only to see them later massacred, while below lie figures of all ages in various poses of suffering.

Around the perimeter of the memorial are dozens of panels detailing the grim history that led to the worst genocide of the 20th century. As you move through the memorial, consider its intent – to show the Holocaust did not simply hap-

South Beach

MIAMI BEACH'S BEST MUSEUMS & GALLERIES

The Bass: Founded in 1964, this contemporary art museum sits in a 1930s art deco building (thebass.org).

Jewish Museum of Florida-FIU: Florida Jewish history is celebrated within two art deco buildings, one a former synagogue (jmof.fiu.edu).

Wolfsonian-FIU: A museum, library and research center devoted to art and design (wolfsonian. org).

Romero Britto Fine Art Gallery: This flagship gallery of the eponymous visual artist from Brazil bursts with color, inside and out (shopbritto.com).

Art Deco Museum: Dive into the three major design styles that influenced Miami Beach, including Mediterranean Revival, Art Deco and Miami Modern. Rotating exhibits.

pen, but was the end product of structural oppression and state-sponsored hatred. This is followed by names of many – but nowhere near all – who perished. The light from a Star of David is blotted by the racist label of Jude (the German word for 'Jew'), representative of the yellow star that Jews in ghettos were forced to wear. It's impossible to spend time here and not be moved.

Lay of the Sandy Land

MAP P53/53

Beaches past South Beach

When it comes to sun, sand and surf, Miami Beach covers all the bases – and with a different vibe to look forward to depending on the stretch where you choose to unfurl your beach towel.

South Beach is without a doubt the section of sand most people think of when they hear the words 'Miami Beach,' but there's far more coast to saunter along. Unless otherwise noted, the numbered streets here all extend off Collins Ave (A1A), which runs north and south parallel to the beach itself.

continued on p54

EATING IN MIAMI BEACH: BEST BRUNCH SPOTS

MAPS P52/53, 55

Love Brunch: Casual Collins Ave favorite for omelettes, avocado toast, smoothies, New York bagels and great coffee. *8am-5pm* $

Strawberry Moon: Cheerful spot inside The Goodtime Hotel. Weekend brunch with Mediterranean flair and great baklava. *7am-4pm Mon-Thu, to 10 or 11pm Fri-Sun* $$

Serena: Latin and Mexican-inspired brunch draws many to this rooftop spot at Moxy Miami South Beach hotel. *noon-11pm Mon-Thu, to midnight Fri, 11am-11pm Sat & Sun* $$

Cafe Americano: Upscale diner-style digs along Ocean Drive. Rooftop views and American breakfast classics. *8am-10pm Mon-Thu, to 11pm Fri-Sun* $$

MIAMI BEACH

W 24th St
W 23rd St
Number 3

Bayshore Municipal Golf Course

Sunset Islands

Number 4

Sunset Dr
W 22nd St

W 21st St

BAYSHORE

Collins Canal

20th St
51
56
19
66
49
8

SUNSET HARBOUR

19th St

Collins Canal

5
9

18th St Ave

West Ave

18th St

Dade Blvd

Meridian Ct

Convention Center Dr

18th St

60

Venetian Way

Belle Isle

17th St

61
65
43
13
17
12

Lenox Ave

16
36
64
63

14
Lincoln Rd Mall
10

Lincoln Rd

Lincoln La S

62
53
52

Pennsylvania Ave

Drexel Ave

16th St

Jefferson Ave

Bay Rd

Lenox Ave

15th Tce

MIAMI BEACH

Meridian Ave

15th St
15th St

15th St
Alton Ct

Española Way

Euclid Ave

34

Flamingo Way
14th Ct

14th Pl

14th St

14th Tce

Flamingo Park

Drexel Ave

13th Tce

Lenox Ave

13th St

13th St

Biscayne Bay

12th St
25

12th St

12th St

Michigan Ave

11th St

11th St

Euclid Ave

Pennsylvania Ave

11th St
3
59

10th St

23

Jefferson Ave

Meridian Ave

10th St

47

West Ave

9th St

Euclid Ave

Collins Ct

Lenox Ave

41
8th St

Michigan Ave

8th St

45

7th St

6th St
Abbale Telavivian Kitchen (0.4mi);
Bayfront Park (4mi)

6th St

See South of Fifth (0.2mi)

57

6th St

Map labels:
- Lake Pancoast
- MID-BEACH
- 23rd St
- Collins Ave
- 21st St
- Collins Park
- Liberty Ave
- 20th St
- South Beach
- Miami Beach Boardwalk
- Atlantic Ocean
- 19th St
- 18th St
- Lincoln Rd
- 16th St
- Art Deco Historic District
- 15th St
- Ocean Dr
- Lummus Park
- ART DECO HISTORIC DISTRICT
- Promenade
- South Beach

Inset map: South of Fifth
- See Main Map (0.2mi)
- MIAMI BEACH
- 3rd St
- 2nd St
- Euclid Ave
- Washington Ave
- Collins Ct
- Collins Ave
- Ocean Ct
- Ocean Dr
- 1st St
- South Pointe Dr
- Inlet Blvd

Scale bars: 0–200 m / 0–0.1 miles; 0–100 m

HIGHLIGHTS
1 Art Deco Historic District
2 South Beach

SIGHTS
3 Art Deco Museum
4 Collins Park
5 Holocaust Memorial
6 Jewish Museum of Florida-FIU
7 Lummus Park
8 Maurice Gibb Memorial Park
9 Miami Beach Botanical Garden
10 Miami Beach Community Church
11 Museum of Ice Cream
12 New World Center
13 New World Symphony
14 Oolite Arts
15 Ophelia & Juan Js. Roca Center
16 Romero Britto Fine Art Gallery
17 SoundScape Park
18 South Pointe Park
19 Sunset Harbour
20 Temple Emanu-El
21 The Bass
22 The Betsy Orb/Poetry Rail
23 Wolfsonian-FIU
24 World Erotic Art Museum

ACTIVITIES, COURSES & TOURS
25 Flamingo Park Swimming Pool
26 Miami City Ballet
27 Spa at the Setai

SLEEPING
28 Cavalier South Beach
29 Kimpton Surfcomber

EATING
30 11th Street Diner
31 Baires Grill
32 Big Pink
33 Cafe Americano
34 Cortadito Coffee House
35 Forte dei Marmi
36 Ice Cream Factory
37 Joe's Stone Crab Restaurant
38 La Playa
39 Lilikoi
40 Lobster Shack
41 Macchialina
42 Mercato della Pescheria Miami Beach
43 MILA
44 News Cafe
45 Puerto Sagua
46 RAO's
47 Serena
48 Shepherd Artisan Coffee
49 Stiltsville Fish Bar
50 Stubborn Seed
51 True Loaf

DRINKING & NIGHTLIFE
52 Abbey Brewing Company
53 Bodega Taqueria y Tequila
54 Kill Your Idol
55 Mac's Club Deuce Bar
56 Panther Coffee
57 Strawberry Moon
58 Sweet Liberty
59 Twist

ENTERTAINMENT
60 Fillmore Miami Beach
61 Regal South Beach Theater
62 Rooftop Cinema Club

SHOPPING
63 Anthropologie
64 CB2
65 Na Lei Bhoho Clothier
66 Sunset Clothing Co

contined from p51

Mid-Beach encompasses the beaches from 23rd to 63rd Sts. It's not like the crowds out here stop preening and showing off – this is still model/influencer territory – but at least some of those influencers are past the 'post Tik-Toks of my night at the club' phase and are moving into the 'boost reels of my growing family' end of the algorithm pool. The Mid-Beach area is attached to a lot of the area's big luxury hotels, such as the **Fontainebleau** and **Faena**. On the bay side of the beach is North Bay Rd, where you can see (well, glimpse over the walls) some of the area's largest mansions. This area includes the official **Miami Beach Boardwalk** *(miamibeachboardwalk.com; free)*. It runs between 21st and 46th Sts, where Orthodox Jews often mix with social media mavens.

North Beach extends from 63rd St to 87th Tce. The beaches here are smaller and more family-friendly, although this is also where you'll find **Haulover Beach** (4.5 miles north of 71st St). The northern section of this beach park is clothing-optional and has been popular with naturists since the 1990s.

Get Divine on the Beach

MAP P53/53

Delve into churches, temples and gardens

Few people might put Miami Beach and 'quiet, worshipful reflection' in the same trip itinerary. Guess what? There are some cool worship spaces out here. In rather sharp and refreshing contrast to the uber-modern structures muscling their way into the art deco design of **South Beach** (p51), the **Miami Beach Community Church** *(miamibeachcommunitychurch. com)* puts one in mind of an old Spanish mission – elegantly understated in an area where overstatement is the general philosophy. Built in 1921, this is the oldest church sanctuary in Miami Beach, and it has a history of progressive politics, including ordaining African American men, women, and recognizing same-sex marriage. Sunday worship services are at 10:30am.

A quarter of a mile away is the smooth dome and sleek, almost aerodynamic profile of **Temple Emanu-El** *(tesobe.org),* established in 1938. The design may seem deco-esque, but it's more influenced by Byzantine and Moorish styles – although elements of deco fit that rubric too. Shabbat services are held on Fridays at 6pm and on Saturdays at 10am.

If you need a spiritual moment absent of a house of worship, head to the **Miami Beach Botanical Garden** *(mbgarden. org; free)*. This lush but little-known 2.6 acres of plantings is operated by the Miami Beach Garden Conservancy and is a veritable green haven – an oasis of palm trees, flowering hibiscus trees and glassy ponds – amid the urban jungle.

Meet Artists at Work

MAP P52/53

Getting avant-garde at Oolite Arts

Once known as ArtCenter–South Florida South Beach, this exhibition space includes dozens of artists' studios, many of

---

SOAKING UP SOUTH BEACH

Neysa King is the author of two poetry chapbooks and co-founder of Miami Poetry Club. @neysaking

South Pointe Park (p58) **at Sunset** Every day at the southernmost tip of Miami Beach is a block party with music, yoga and dancing. Bring a blanket and a bottle of wine and watch the skies change.

La Playa A convenience store and food counter where they cook up fried fish, plantains and empanadas with good tunes playing loud over the PA.

Stubborn Seed (p55) Recklessly welcoming to locals and visitors wanting to experience exquisite food and cocktails south of Fifth St (make sure you get their house negroni).

MID-BEACH

Haulover Beach Park (3.5mi);
Oleta River
State Park (5mi);
Greynolds Park (7.7mi)

NORMANDY SHORES

NORTH BEACH

La Gorce Country Club

Indian Creek

MID-BEACH

Biscayne Bay

South Beach

ATLANTIC OCEAN

Indian Creek

BAYSHORE

Sunset Islands

Number 2
Number 3

Lake Pancoast

Boardwalk

SIGHTS
1 Boardwalk
2 Eden Roc Renaissance
3 Faena District
4 Faena Forum
5 Fontainebleau
6 Mammoth Garden
7 Mid-Beach

SLEEPING
8 Faena Hotel Miami Beach
9 Fontainebleau
10 Freehand Miami
11 Generator Miami

EATING
12 Arlen Beach Restaurant
13 Love Brunch

DRINKING & NIGHTLIFE
14 Bob's Your Uncle
15 Broken Shaker
16 North Beach Bandshell

which are open to the public. **Oolite Arts** (oolitearts.org) also offers a slate of sought-after residencies, which are reserved for artists who do not have major exposure, making this a good place to spot up-and-coming talent. Monthly rotating exhibitions keep the presentation fresh and pretty avant-garde. Along with the art you can view, there is a printshop on hand,

EATING IN MIAMI BEACH: OUR PICKS
MAP P52/53

Lilikoi: Head to this laid-back, indoor-outdoor spot for healthy, mostly organic, veg-friendly dishes. *8am–3pm* $$

Macchialina: This buzzing, rustic-chic Italian trattoria has all the right ingredients for a terrific night out. *6–11pm Mon–Thu, from 5pm Fri–Sun* $$

Abbalé Telavivian Kitchen: Mediterranean-inspired weekend brunch. *8am–10pm Mon–Thu, to 11pm Fri, 10am–11pm Sat, to 10pm Sun* $$

Baires Grill: Argentinean parrillada (barbecue) for two just like in Buenos Aires. *noon–11pm Sun–Thu, to 11.30pm Fri & Sat* $$

MILA: With an omakase-style rooftop bar, this swanky concept restaurant takes guests on a culinary odyssey from the Med to Japan. *hours vary* $$$

Stubborn Seed: Won a Michelin star and a James Beard award for its haute-American cuisine. Reserve. *6–10pm Sun–Thu, to 11pm Fri-Sat* $$$

RAO's: Italian restaurant in Loews Miami Beach Hotel. Raw bar, antipasti and southern Neapolitan cuisine. *5.30–10pm Sun–Thu, to 11pm Fri & Sat* $$$

Forte dei Marmi: With a two Michelin-starred chef, this Italian restaurant occupies a building that conjures a Tuscan villa. *hours vary* $$$

DV EDWARDS/SHUTTERSTOCK

DISCOVERING LINCOLN ROAD

Sheena Goldhagen, owner of **Na Lei Boho Clothier** on Lincoln Rd and a Miami Beach resident. *@naleibohoclothier*

When it comes to dining, **MILA** (p55) remains my top spot. It's the perfect rooftop lounge in Miami – chic, always packed, and offering amazing performances, drinks, and food. World-famous DJs perform weekly – it's electric. For a memorable date night, hit the iconic **Regal South Beach Theater** (indoor) or the **Rooftop Cinema Club** (outdoor) – you won't find anything like this in any other city.

Before or after the movies, I recommend the **Ice Cream Factory**, a delicious kosher staple that's been around for years.

open by appointment *(email printshop@oolitearts.org)*, and the facility hosts virtual and in-person art classes.

Faena Fun   MAP P55

Architectural dreams on Miami Beach

The area of Mid-Beach from 32nd St to 36th St, known as the **Faena District** (*faena.com; free*), was named for an Argentine businessman and developer and is Miami Beach's answer to the Wynwood District and **Wynwood Art Walk** (p78) on the mainland. Park your car or arrive on foot to spend a morning exploring this design-focused district where urban character grows out of the intersection of the arts and attached commercial retail. The area is anchored by the **Faena Forum**, an architectural dream that hosts performances, exhibitions, lectures and other events in a circular Rem Koolhaas-designed building.

Nearby is **Faena Hotel Miami Beach**, characterized by heavy use of animal print fabrics, coral and seashell decorative touches. Damien Hirst's iconic **Mammoth Garden** sculp-

---

🍸 DRINKING IN SOUTH BEACH: OUR PICKS ─────── MAP P52/53

Mac's Club Deuce: The oldest bar in Miami Beach, the Deuce is a seedy neighborhood dive par excellence. *8pm-5am*	**Kill Your Idol:** This lovable hipster spot has graffiti and shelves full of retro bric-a-brac covering the walls. *8pm-4am*	**Sweet Liberty:** Friendly bartenders whip up excellent cocktails amid flickering candles and a long wooden bar. *4pm-5am*	**Broken Shaker:** This well-equipped bar produces expert cocktails, mostly consumed in a beautiful, softly lit garden. *hours vary*

Faena Forum

ture here is a timeless social media darling. And each room
has butler service – because this is Miami, damn it. Finally,
high-end shoppers should check out **Faena Bazaar.** Housed
inside a historic hotel, it has four floors of expensive home-
wares and furniture for the visitors who happen to have lots
of space in their checked bags.

Get Outdoors Already

MAP P55

Breathe deep in North Beach

Miami's beaches and the fun-loving crowds they attract might
steal the spotlight. But there are other ways to immerse yourself in nature in these parts. If you're looking to get outdoors
in that sweet Miami tropical weather, the northern stretches
of Miami Beach have you covered.

With a playground, green fields, an intact hardwood hammock, mangrove forest and views of the Oleta River, 249-
acre **Greynolds Park** is a nice spot to savor fresh air and let
the kids run around. The big outdoor attraction around here

🍸 DRINKING IN MIAMI BEACH: BEST BARS

MAP P52/53

Abbey Brewing Company: South Beach's oldest brewpub is friendly and packed. *3pm-5am Mon-Fri, from 1pm Sat, from noon Sun*

Twist: DJs and drag queens mean there's never a dull moment at this two-story gay club with seven different bars. *3pm-5am*

Bodega Taqueria y Tequila: Popular taco joint with a food truck on-site, known for its happy hour and tequila drinks. *11.30-1am Sun-Wed, to 3am Thu-Sat*

Bob's Your Uncle: Casual, friendly neighborhood bar with cocktails, beer, old-school games and some of Miami Beach's most chilled-out vibes. *3pm-3am*

MIAMI BEACH'S BEST URBAN PARKS

Lummus Park
Spans a 10-block stretch of South Beach between the Atlantic Ocean and Ocean Drive.

Collins Park
Relax in this small green space with manicured lawns and a giant baobab tree, located between the Holocaust Memorial and the beach.

Flamingo Park Swimming Pool
People come to swim, as well as for courts and fields offering tennis, handball, racquetball, basketball, soccer and more.

SoundScape Park
A 2.5-acre urban park next to the New World Symphony center hosting family-friendly films and WallCast concerts.

South Pointe Park
Gorgeous green space and beach on the southern tip of Miami Beach; playground, walking trails and picnic areas.

FOTOLUMINATE LLC/SHUTTERSTOCK

Fontainebleau

can be found at **Oleta River State Park** (*floridastateparks.org/OletaRiver; vehicle $6*). The park itself is a treat. Tequesta people were boating the Oleta River estuary as early as 500 BCE, so you're following a long tradition if you canoe or kayak here.

At almost 1,000 acres, it's the largest urban park in the state and one of the best places in Miami to escape the maddening crowds. Boat out to the local mangrove island, watch the eagles fly by, or just chill on the pretension-free beach. How to access the aforementioned mangroves and inlets? An onsite outfitter offers both guided and self-directed adventures. If you're into the latter, you can rent kayaks, canoes, stand-up paddleboards and mountain bikes for exploring this stretch of North Biscayne Bay on your own.

Bounce to the Bayfront

MAP P52/53

South Beach's quieter corner

Away from Ocean Dr and close to Lincoln Rd, palm-lined promenades and a bayfront shopping enclave draw a mix of local residents and savvy travelers who are less into flash, clubs and couture, and more attracted to indie stores, galleries, outdoor cafes and bakeries. All those and more give the **Sunset Harbour** neighborhood on the bay side of Miami Beach plenty of character.

EATING IN MIAMI BEACH: BEST SEAFOOD

MAP P52/53

Stiltsville Fish Bar: Coconut shrimp, ceviche and red snapper fly off the menu at this breezy restaurant. *noon-10pm Mon-Thu, to 11pm Fri, 11am-11pm Sat, to 10pm Sun* **$$**	**Lobster Shack:** With a Lincoln Rd beachfront location, this spot reels them in for piled-high lobster rolls made with the good stuff from Maine. *11am-midnight* **$$**	**Joe's Stone Crab:** Try seasonal crab claws local to Florida at this South Beach staple (mustard sauce obligatory). *5-10pm Mon & Tue, 11.30am-10 or 11pm Wed-Sun* **$$$**	**Mercato della Pescheria Miami Beach:** Italian seafood market vibes, with fresh fish and delicious steaks. *11.30am-11.30pm Sun-Thu, to 12.30pm Fri & Sat* **$$$**

Start the day with fresh pastries at **True Loaf Bakery** (*trueloafbakery.square.site*). This well-regarded bakery is a breadbox-sized space where you can pick up heavenly croissants, tarts and *kouign amman* (Breton-style butter cake that is simply to die for).

Just around the block, **Sunset Clothing Co** (*facebook.com/SunsetClothingCo*) is a great little fashion boutique for stylish gear that won't cost a fortune (though it isn't cheap either). You'll find well-made shirts, soft cotton T-shirts, lace-up canvas shoes, nicely fitting denim (including vintage Levi's), warm sweaters (not that you need them here) and other casual gear.

Maurice Gibb Memorial Park is a five-minute walk away. This small palm-fringed green space overlooking the water has a playground, benches and grassy areas. It's a favorite destination for dog walkers, runners and families with kids. Against a backdrop of bobbing sailboats and the Venetian Causeway, it's worth stopping by to admire the view.

Going Grand Amid Brash Buildings   MAP P55

Millionaire's Row unwrapped

As you proceed north on Collins Ave, leaving the deco of South Beach for the high-rises of Mid-Beach, the condos and apartment buildings grow in grandeur and embellishment until you enter an area nicknamed **Millionaire's Row**. One of the brightest jewels in this crown is the **Fontainebleau** (*fontainebleau.com*). If you've never been here in person, you may have visited cinematically – the hotel was the setting for the classic final show down in Brian de Palma's *Scarface*.

Well, sort of. This iconic 1954 leviathan is a brainchild of the great Miami Beach architect Morris Lapidus, but it has undergone many renovations; in some ways, it is utterly different from its original form. Then again, it undoubtedly retains a sense of overblown glamour.

The same can be said of the **Eden Roc** (*nobuedenroc.com*), the second ground breaking resort from Morris Lapidus, a five-minute walk from the Fontainebleau. The Eden Roc has also undergone renovations, but better retains the architectural aesthetic known as MiMo (Miami Modern); while some of Lapidus' style has been eclipsed, the building is still an iconic piece of Miami Beach architecture and an exemplar of the brash beauty of Millionaire's Row. Speaking of brash, historical sidenote: this was the hangout for the 1960s Rat Pack – Sammy Davis Jr, Dean Martin, Frank Sinatra and crew.

MIAMI BEACH'S BEST OFFBEAT ATTRACTIONS

World Erotic Art Museum (WEAM) Ogle erotica that includes ancient sex manuals, explicit pre-Columbian sculptures and works by Picasso.

Museum of Ice Cream Unlimited ice cream, play spaces and colorful exhibits celebrate all things ice cream.

The Betsy Orb Near Española Way, this giant white, beach ball-ish sculpture is squashed into an alley between Ocean Dr and Collins Ave.

Poetry Rail This metal wall etched with the words of 12 poets tributes Miami's multicultural population and unique geography.

Obstinate Lighthouse In **South Pointe Park** (p59), this 55-foot tall lighthouse by German artist Tobias Rehberger is made of aluminum and frosted glass.

🍸 DRINKING IN MIAMI BEACH: BEST COFFEE   ——————— MAP P52/53

Panther Coffee: Specialty coffee shop in Sunset Harbour known for small-batch roasting and industrial-chic decor. *7am-5pm*	**Shepherd Artisan Coffee:** Collins Ave favorite for beautiful breakfast pastries and strong brews; all-day breakfast. *7am-8pm*	**News Cafe:** An Ocean Dr landmark for sitting with a cappuccino or grabbing a latte to-go in an ambiance evocative of European cafe culture. *8am-10.45pm*	**Cortadito Coffee House:** With locations on Lincoln Rd and Washington Ave, this is the spot for legendary strong, sugary Cuban coffee shots. *7am-10pm*

MIAMI BEACH'S BEST FESTIVALS

Miami Beach Pride
A two-day festival and parade in April, with more than 185,000 attendees celebrating the LGBTQ+ community and cultural arts *(miamibeachpride. com).*

South Beach Wine & Food Festival
SOBEWFF for short, this February event draws the world's best chefs for four days of fun *(sobewff.org).*

Art Deco Weekend
January weekend devoted to celebrating all things art deco in South Beach *(artdecoweekend.org).*

Art Basel Miami Beach
The Americas' premiere art show in December draws leading galleries from five continents *(artbasel.com/ miami-beach).*

Miami Music Week
Bayfront Park (p68) Downtown Miami and smaller venues across town bring the sound for March's Miami Music Week and Ultra Music Festival *(miamimusicweek.com).*

Ballet, Symphony, Comics & More MAP P52/53

Embrace the performing arts

For lovers of the performing arts who prefer to bide most of their time out at the beaches, there's no need to cross a bridge to downtown Miami to get your cultural fill. You may want to begin by dipping your toes into the arts at the Frank Gehry-designed **New World Center**, home to the **New World Symphony** *(nws.edu)* and the premier concert hall in Miami Beach. Here, scores of young musicians are on fellowships that last three years and a year-round event calendar hosts classical concerts, dance and much more. In a historic art deco space, **The Fillmore Miami Beach at the Jackie Gleason Theater** *(fillmore-miami.com)* hosts comedians, ballet troupes, singer-songwriters and more. And the **Miami City Ballet** *(miamicityballet.org)* is also at home in Miami Beach at the 63,000-sq-ft **Ophelia & Juan Js. Roca Center** which hosts regular performances by the troupe, one of the most renowned ballet companies in the US.

The Fillmore Miami Beach at the Jackie Gleason Theater

EATING IN MIAMI BEACH: BEST DINERS ——————— MAPS P52/53, 55

Puerto Sagua: This beloved Cuban eatery has been slinging *ropa vieja* (shredded, seasoned beef) in huge portions since 1962. *7am-11pm* $

Arlen Beach Restaurant: Ticks a lot of boxes in one stop. *9.30am-9pm Sun-Mon, to 3pm Tue, 10am-9pm Wed & Thu, 9.30am-10pm Fri & Sat* $

11th Street Diner: Dine on shrimp, grits and sandwiches in a gleaming retro Pullman car imported in 1992 from Wilkes-Barre, PA. *7.30am-midnight Sun-Thu, 24hrs Fri & Sat* $$

Big Pink: Come for gourmet comfort food and retro vibes where the daily specials are served on a stainless steel tray. *8am-midnight* $$

ART DECO AMBLE

Spend a morning walking around South Beach to admire the world's largest collection of 1920s and 1930s art deco buildings.

START	END	LENGTH
Art Deco Museum	Wolfsonian-FIU	1 mile; 1 hr

Some 800 deco buildings here are listed on the National Register of Historic Places, and you'll happen upon many of them – whether you set out on a purposeful stroll between bold facades and whimsical tropical motifs or not.

Start at the ❶ **Art Deco Museum** for a backgrounder and exhibits on art deco style. Stroll north along Ocean Drive between 12th and 14th Sts to spot examples of the area's more famous art deco hotels. ❷ **The Leslie** is known for its boxy shape and eyebrows (cantilevered sunshades) wrapped around the side of the building; ❸ **The Carlyle** has modernistic styling; and the graceful ❹ **Cardoza**, built by Henry

Hohauser and owned by Gloria and Emilio Estefan, can be recognized by its sleek, rounded edges.

When you arrive at 14th St, take a peek inside the ❺ **Winter Haven Hotel** to admire its fabulous terrazzo floors, made of stone chips set in mortar and polished when dry. Then turn left and head down 14th St to Washington Ave and the ❻ **US Post Office**, at 13th St, distinguished by its curvy block of white deco and stripped classical style.

Finish your amble nearby at the ❼ **Wolfsonian-FIU**, an excellent design museum, formerly the Washington Storage Company. Wealthy snowbirds of the '30s stashed their pricey belongings here before heading back up north.

Look up once inside the **US Post Office** to admire a period lighting feature resembling the sun.

After dark, cross the street from **Winter Haven Hotel** into Lummus Park to snap an iconic photo of the neon-lit deco facades.

The **Cardoza** hotel was named after Benjamin Cardoza, a Jewish Supreme Court justice.

○ **HELP ME PICK:**

Miami's Many Beaches

Maps refer to the area above South Beach as Miami Beach, but locals use the jargon "Mid-Beach" (around the 40th streets) and "North Beach" (70th St and above). Communities like Surfside and Sunny Isles are farther north. And North Miami Beach (as opposed to the region of Northern Miami Beach) is not technically on the spit of land known as Miami Beach – it's on the mainland. Confused? There's a beach for everybody here.

Where to go if you love...

Surf Culture

In the residential neighborhood of **Surfside**, you'll spot local surfers padding barefoot through town toward the sand, boards in tow. It feels far more like a laid-back surf town here than in busier parts of Miami Beach to the south. The beach break here is usually nice and mellow, but make sure to wear a leash with your board as it's a popular place for families to frolic too. Cold fronts from November to May tend to bring the biggest waves. Rent boards from **Island Water Sports** (*$15/hr*).

Haulover Beach Park (p54)

Family-Friendly Waters

Families feel safe with little kids splashing in the sheltered waters of the man-made atoll beach at **Matheson Hammock Park** (p95) just south of Coconut Grove. Keep in mind that the shallow water heats up quickly, especially during the sultry summer months when it won't feel refreshing at all. Lifeguards lining Miami Beach and shops selling snacks never far from the sand make it a real favorite among families.

Nude Swimming

Those with few inhibitions can sunbathe and swim in their birthday suit (read: nude) at **Haulover Beach Park** (p54) on the northern end of Miami Beach. If you're wondering which part of the beach is the naked one and where to park nearby, Google Maps has it clearly marked so you'll make no mistake. Keep in mind that all genders mingle here; there are no designated zones for different sexes. Bathrooms and shower facilities are available by the beach, but you need to put clothes on before stepping off the sand to use them.

Flexing

Muscle Beach is Miami's answer to California's Venice Beach. Come to show off the proof of all your workouts at an outdoor fitness park on the sand, open year-round between 10th St and 12th St in the heart of South Beach. There are exercise bars and you can lift weights right on the sand, using the free outdoor gym equipment. When you work up a sweat, the Atlantic Ocean is just a few steps away to cool off.

A Natural Backdrop

The neon art deco of South Beach is a pretty backdrop for a swim. But if you're seeking something more natural, it's impossible to top the dune-backed bliss of the 1.2-mile-long stretch of undeveloped beachfront within **Bill Baggs Cape Florida State Park** (p103) on Key Biscayne. The park takes up nearly the entire southern third of Key Biscayne and feels like a true island paradise in the middle of a busy city.

CAROL CITY

Intercoastal Waterway

Ives Dairy Rd

Golden Beach

Southern Memorial Park

Island Water Sports

Palmette Expwy

OPA-LOCKA

Haulover Beach Park

Biscayne Bay

NW 119th St

Surfside

HIALEAH

Indian Creek

Pelican Harbor Park

NW 79th St

Indian Creek

NW 62nd St
NW 54th St

South Beach

NW 36th St

Miami International Airport

NW 20th St

Muscle Beach

Miami River

NW 7th St
Flagler St
SW 1st St
SW 7th St

Causeway Island

Brickell Ave Bridge

SW 8th St (Calle Ocho)

Coral Way

Virginia Key

Virginia Key Beach North Point Park

Dinner Key Marina

Northwest Point

West Point

Crandon Park

Atlantic Ocean

SOUTH MIAMI

SW 72nd St

Southwest Point

KENDALL

Biscayne Bay

Bill Baggs Cape Florida State Park

Matheson Hammock Park

Key Biscayne

Cape Florida

PINECREST

0   5 km
0   2.5 miles

Prepping for the Perfect Beach Day

A little advanced planning for a day of the beach can take your time on the sand from simply decent to memorably delicious.

For starters, consider how long you plan to be out there enjoying the beach in the Miami sun. If you're just heading down to the sand for a quick swim, you'll probably only need to pack a small beach bag with sunscreen, a towel and reusable water bottle.

But if you're planning to settle in for longer, you'll likely want a few extra accessories to make yourself comfortable. Not all beaches have chairs and umbrellas for rent, so if that's important to you, you'll probably want to stick around South Beach, where rentals are abundant.

A rolling or backpack-style cooler is a lot more efficient for transporting picnic supplies from your car down to the beach than other bulkier ones. It's a good idea to bring a dry bag for your phone, too, both to keep it from getting wet and to keep sand at bay, too.

And while you can never put on enough sunscreen (water- and sweat-proof is best), there are other beach hazards to consider too. Never let children dig holes in the sand that are deeper than their knee height when standing up. Tragic accidents have led to suffocating deaths when deep holes collapsed. Forewarned is forearmed.

Downtown Miami

ELECTRIC ENERGY ALONG BISCAYNE BAY

GETTING AROUND

You don't need a car here – free public transport can whisk you around, and parts of Downtown (like Bayfront Park and the riverside) are well worth exploring on foot. The city's free trolley service stops near Bayside Marketplace, and the free elevated Metromover runs three loops around Downtown.

☑TOP TIP

Dress to sweat. Downtown Miami is a palm-fringed concrete jungle and doesn't capture quite the ocean breezes of points east. Even during the winter, slather on the sunscreen and wear a sun hat for protection if you plan to spend any time walking around.

Downtown Miami, the city's financial and banking center, is a mash-up of old indoor shopping arcades, shiny new condos and vertiginous luxury hotels with glittering water views. At night, these towers are illuminated in hot pinks and cool blues, and the effect is magical. Bordered on nearly all sides by Biscayne Bay and the Miami River, there's water, water everywhere, adding to the dazzling views.

Construction around downtown Miami carries out at a near-constant thrum, but there are still creative pockets of iconoclastic identity, and one of the city's best museums to boot. You could easily spend a few days taking in local attractions and cooling off in your hotel pool before catching a show at a performing arts venue and venturing across the bridges to the beaches. Make time to sample the rooftop bars, plush nightclubs and creative eateries that have sprung up to cater to waves of well-heeled condo-dwellers who happily call downtown Miami home.

Free Downtown Tour Up High

Metromover groovin'

What's that train whirring overhead throughout some of Miami's densest built-up real estate? The answer is the **Metromover** *(miamidade.gov/global/transportation/metromover .page; free),* an elevated, electric monorail that was meant to provide mass transit and alleviate the traffic woes of Downtown and Brickell. The Metromover did not succeed in doing this, as anyone who has driven in South Florida can attest. But it is a beloved, complete rail line that moves thousands of people a month through Downtown – for free! It also happens to be a pretty cool way of seeing central Miami from on high, which is a nice thing, given the urban geography out here is basically skyscraper canyons.

The Metromover opened in 1986 and channels that distinctive, so-modern-it-looks-dated appearance of public works from that period. There are three different lines (the Omni

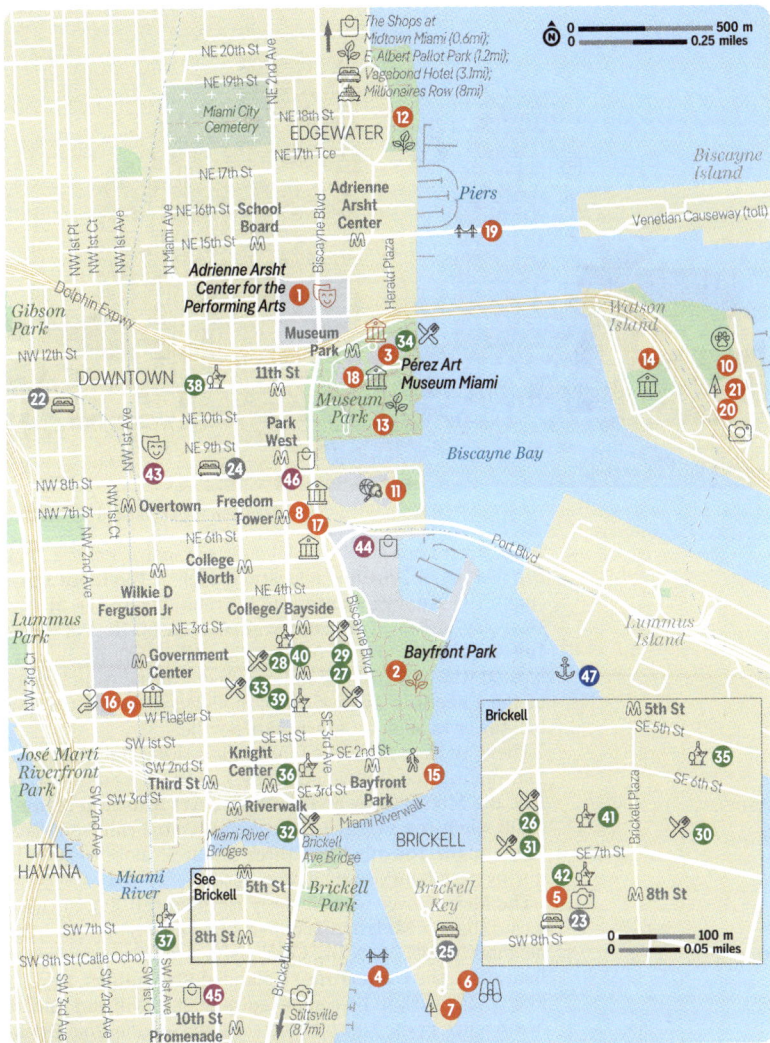

The Shops at
Midtown Miami (0.6mi);
E. Albert Pallot Park (1.2mi);
Vagabond Hotel (3.1mi);
Millionaires Row (8mi)

Venetian Causeway (toll)

Biscayne
Island

Watson
Island

Lummus
Island

Biscayne Bay

Pérez Art
Museum Miami

Museum
Park

Bayfront Park

Brickell
Key

Brickell

José Martí
Riverfront
Park

Miami
River

Stiltsville
(8.7mi)

HIGHLIGHTS
1 Adrienne Arsht Center for
the Performing Arts
2 Bayfront Park
3 Pérez Art Museum Miami

SIGHTS
4 Brickell Avenue Bridge
5 Brickell City Centre
6 Brickell Key
7 Brickell Key Park
8 Freedom Tower
9 HistoryMiami
10 Jungle Island
11 Kaseya Center
12 Margaret Pace Park

13 Maurice A. Ferré Park
14 Miami Children's Museum
15 Miami Riverwalk
16 Miami-Dade Cultural Center
17 Museum of Art & Design
18 Patricia & Phillip Frost
Museum of Science
19 Venetian Causeway
20 Watson Island
21 Watson Island Park

SLEEPING
22 Dunns Josephine
23 EAST Miami
24 Gale Miami Hotel &
Residences

25 Mandarin Oriental Miami

EATING
26 Bonding
27 CVI.CHE 105
28 NIU Kitchen
29 Pollos & Jarras
30 Quinto
31 River Oyster Bar
32 Riverview Bar & Grill
33 Soya e Pomodoro
34 Verde

DRINKING & NIGHTLIFE
35 Baby Jane
36 Black Market
37 Blackbird Ordinary

38 Elleven Miami
39 Lost Boy
40 Mama Tried
41 Rosa Sky
42 Sugar

ENTERTAINMENT
43 Black Archives - Historic
Lyric Theater

SHOPPING
44 Bayside Marketplace
45 Mary Brickell Village
46 Miami WorldCenter

TRANSPORT
47 Port of Miami

65

ALEXANDER SPATARI/GETTY IMAGES

Freedom Tower (second from left)

Loop, Inner Loop and Brickell Loop) that span 4.4 miles. They connect major Downtown locations such as **Bayfront Park** (p68), the **Kaseya Center** (p71) arena (where the Miami Heat play) and the **Adrienne Arsht Center for the Performing Arts** (p70), among others. The mover is a particularly good way of seeing the full architectural span and beauty of the **Freedom Tower** (p70), modeled after the Giralda bell tower in Spain's Cathedral of Seville.

The high rises of Brickell make for a shiny sight from the Metromover too, and you can enjoy great views of Biscayne Bay, the Miami River and the **Pérez Art Museum Miami** (p69) when you ride the Omni Loop. Trains run from 5am to midnight, roughly every three minutes (more frequently during rush hour), seven days a week.

The Metromover isn't the only elevated rail line in these parts. Miami's **Metrorail** connects Downtown to residential neighborhoods, including Coral Gables and Coconut Grove. Beneath it, the **Underline** – a planned $146 million, 10-mile long linear park to be completed in 2026 – will run underneath much of the Metrorail's tracks; the section from Brickell to Vizcaya station was unveiled in 2024. You'll find weekly community yoga classes staged on the Underline, an outdoor gym, a meditation garden and, of course, a walking and biking path to explore.

✗❍ EATING IN DOWNTOWN MIAMI: OUR PICKS

Quinto: Sexy rooftop in the EAST Miami hotel with tropical greenery everywhere, incredible cocktails and fusion fare. *hours vary* $$

Niu Kitchen: Stylish restaurant serving delectable, often shareable Catalan cuisine and a killer wine list. *5.30-10pm Tue-Thu & Sun, to 10.30pm Fri & Sat* $$

Verde: Inside the Pérez Art Museum Miami, this is a local favorite for tasty market fresh dishes in an atmospheric setting. *11am-4pm Fri-Mon, to 8pm Thu* $$

River Oyster Bar: A few paces from the Miami River, this buzzing little spot whips up excellent plates of seafood. *noon-10.30pm* $$

Get Out on the Water

Cruise on Biscayne Bay

The Atlantic Ocean might be a causeway away from Downtown Miami, but you can still get out on the area's sparkling waterways from Downtown's shoreline when you head out on a boat tour with one of the companies operating from **Bayside Marketplace**.

For a serious rush, **Thriller Miami Speedboat Adventures** *(thrillermiami.com; $45)* offers 45-minute 'Miami Vice-style' tours (Don Johnson sightings not guaranteed) aboard its fleet of three power catamarans that take you across Biscayne Bay and past the mansions of Fisher Island and Star Island.

Island Queen Cruises *(islandqueencruises.com; $35, $25 for kids 4-12, $5 for kids 3 and under)* offers a slower-paced, 90-minute sightseeing jaunt on a private ship with an open upper deck and air-conditioned salon during which you'll cruise past sites like **Millionaire's Row**, Miami Beach and the **Port of Miami.**

On both tours, it's impressive to catch sight of Downtown Miami's shoreline and skyscrapers from the turquoise waters, showcasing just how truly tropical the city is.

Ziplines & Capybaras, Why Not?

Jungle Island escapes

Located on **Watson Island**, a blip on the radar between downtown Miami and South Beach, **Jungle Island** *(jungleisland. com; adult/child $44/28)* is a South Florida landmark and eco-adventure park. It's the kind of attraction you'd really only expect to find in a place like Miami. Those capybaras that have gone so viral on social media of late? You'll find them living their next-best lives here, alongside a veritable Noah's ark array of other creatures that include tropical birds, alligators, chimps, lemurs, alligators, sloths and so much more. In short, Jungle Island is a good bit of smelly fun. It's one of those places kids (justifiably) beg to go to, so just give up and prepare for some bright-feathered, bird-poop-scented enjoyment in this artificial, self-contained jungle.

Also on offer: rope bridges among the trees, a flight generating wind tunnel, an escape room and Adventure Bay – an area with rock-climbing walls and kid-friendly bungee jumping. Do all of these activities cost a fair amount extra? You better believe it. You can even head out on a **Treetop Trekking** course, South Florida's only aerial adventure park.

BEST JOGGING ROUTES IN DOWNTOWN MIAMI

Sarah Greaves-Gabbadon, travel writer and on-screen host *@jetsetsarah*
There are so many great water routes for running around Miami. I love to jog to **Brickell Key** from my house in downtown Miami. I follow the water the whole way and if I'm lucky I'lll see dolphins and manatees. I also love a run to South Beach from downtown Miami across the **Venetian Causeway**. You end up in the Sunset Harbour neighborhood of South Beach. A city route I like downtown is to **E. Albert Pallot Park** along Biscayne Boulevard, passing shops, condos and restaurants. There's a huge statue of dominoes and from the park you can see the barrier island and South Beach across the bay.

🍸 DRINKING IN DOWNTOWN MIAMI: PARTYING PICKS

Rosa Sky: Rooftop cocktail bar in Brickell with jaw-dropping views of the Downtown Miami skyline. *4.30pm-2am Tue-Sat, 2pm-1am Sun*

Blackbird Ordinary: Late-night drinking spot in Brickell with excellent cocktails that draw a neighbourhood crowd. *3pm-5am*

E11even: Multi-level club and 'social playground' spread across 20,000 sq ft, promising an immersive experience. Great cocktails and huge party vibes. *hours vary*

Sugar: Come for creative cocktails and Biscayne Bay views on the tropical rooftop deck of the EAST Miami hotel. *hours vary*

JHSILVA/GETTY IMAGES

Brickell City Centre

Neon Nights & Crowded Condos

Gawk at glass towers in Brickell

Concrete, neon and the dense space where these two elements blend characterize much of Downtown Miami. The association is only amplified in **Brickell** *(brickell.com)*, perhaps the ritziest neighborhood in Miami (which is saying something). Located just south of Downtown, Brickell has a reputation as the financial heart of South Florida (and a fair chunk of the southern US). That identity remains, but it's been glittered over by a glut of restaurants, bars and nightclubs. Walk around here in the evenings, and you'll see a crowd that's arguably as sexy, beautiful and well-off as any gaggle of models you can spot around South Beach.

The Miami River forms the northern border of Brickell, spanned by the lovely **Brickell Ave Bridge**, which sits between SE 4th St and SE 5th St. At the edge of the bridge is a bronze statue of a Tequesta (Native American) warrior aiming his arrow at the sky; the bridge itself is accented with reliefs that honor Miamians like Everglades conservationist Julia Tuttle. Walking here is the best way to see the sculptures, and will also allow you to avoid one of the most confusing traffic patterns in Miami.

Brickell Key is an island that is technically part of Brickell proper. It looks more like a floating porcupine, with glass

🍸 DRINKING IN DOWNTOWN MIAMI: BEST BARS

Baby Jane: Part-cocktail house, part-noodle bar, Baby Jane is a neon-lit Brickell mainstay where good times roll. *noon-3am Sun-Thu, to 5am Fri & Sat*

Mama Tried: Moody 1970s-style bar with a speakeasy feel, giant metallic light fixtures and retro-chic aesthetic. *4pm-5am Mon-Fri, from 5pm Sat & Sun*

Lost Boy: Vintage Cuban furniture, exposed brick and old wood come together in this enormous pub. *hours vary*

Black Market: Quintessential sports bar with HD TVs on every conceivable surface, frosty beers and American pub grub on tap. *hours vary*

towers for quills, than an island. To live the life of Miami glitterati, come here, pretend you belong and head into a patrician hangout like the ultra-luxe **Mandarin Oriental Miami** hotel, where the lobby and intimate lounges afford sweeping views of Biscayne Bay.

Channel Creativity by the Coast

Catch an art exhibit at PAMM

You'll want to spend at least half a day devouring one of Miami's most impressive spaces from every angle. Designed by Swiss architects Herzog & de Meuron, this museum integrates foliage, glass, concrete and wood – a melding of tropical vitality and fresh modernism that fits perfectly in Miami. **Pérez Art Museum Miami** (PAMM; pamm.org; adult/child $18/14) stages some of the best contemporary exhibitions in the city, with established artists and impressive newcomers. The permanent collection rotates through unique pieces every few months, drawing from a treasure trove of work spanning the last 80 years.

The temporary shows and retrospectives bring major crowds (past exhibitions have included the works of artist Ai Weiwei and kinetic artist Julio Le Parc). The outdoor space has hanging gardens that took an entire two months to install.

If you need a little breather amid all this contemporary culture, PAMM has a first-rate cafe. Or you can simply hang out in the grassy park, or lounge on a deck chair enjoying views over the water.

This art institution inaugurated **Museum Park**, a patch of land that oversees the broad blue swath of Biscayne Bay.

A Current Through Downtown's Past

Stroll the Miami Riverwalk

Tequesta Indians built the first human settlement here where the Miami River meets Biscayne Bay, although the land has undergone as drastic a transformation as possible over the centuries. There is a walkway that shapes itself around this vital geography: a shoreline promenade traces the northern edge of the river as it bisects Downtown, leading past high-rise condos and battered warehouses. On the water, a few small tugboats pull along its glassy surface, fisherfolk float in with their daily catch, and fancy yachts make their way in and out of the bay.

At night, admire the Brickell skyline's lights, close up and in person. You can follow the **Miami Riverwalk** along the

DOWNTOWN MIAMI'S BEST SPOTS TO SHOP

Mary Brickell Village: Open-air shopping complex in Brickell with two levels of upscale boutiques, restaurants and bars.

Brickell City Centre: Four levels of luxury shopping and innovative dining, anchored by an ultra-modern 107,000-sq-ft Saks Fifth Avenue.

Bayside Marketplace: Popular waterfront shopping complex with a range of retailers and restaurants in Downtown Miami.

Miami WorldCenter: Flagship brands and local-favorite boutiques bloom along tree-lined avenues in this shopping district that's still rolling out near the Kaseya Center.

The Shops at Midtown Miami: Big box and factory stores in one place for finding anything you need.

🍴 EATING IN DOWNTOWN MIAMI: INTERNATIONAL EATS

Pollo & Jaras: Peruvian spot serving outstanding barbecued chicken (and chicken crackling, ie deep-fried skin, oh yes!). *hours vary* **$$**

Bonding Thai: Multiple Asian cuisines, including Thai, Japanese and Korean, come together in a modern and trendy setting. *hours vary* **$$**

Soya & Pomodoro: Feels like a bohemian Italian retreat, where you can dine on fresh pasta surrounded by vintage posters. *hours vary* **$$**

CVI.CHE 105: Beautifully presented ceviches go down nicely with a round of specialty Peruvian cocktails. *noon-10.30pm Sun-Thu, to 11.30pm Fri & Sat* **$$**

IMMIGRATION ICON AMIDST SKYSCRAPERS

Impossible to miss along Biscayne Boulevard, the richly ornamented **Freedom Tower**, completed in 1925, is one of two surviving towers modeled after the Giralda bell tower in Spain's Cathedral of Seville. As the 'Ellis Island of the South,' it served as an immigration processing center for almost half a million Cuban refugees in the 1960s.

Placed on the National Register of Historic Places in 1979, the tower houses the **Miami Museum of Art & Design** (MOAD; moadmdc.org), with exhibits ranging from contemporary sculpture to historical photography. The tower and MOAD were scheduled to reopen to the public in 2025 with a reimagined visitor experience celebrating the tower's 100th anniversary.

northern bank of the Miami River, often spotting manatees and dolphins frolicking in the middle of this most unlikely and hectic urban locale. Stop under the shade of tropical trees to admire the views. For something cool to drink or a meal that blends American and Latin cuisine, pop into the **Riverview Bar & Grill** in the Hyatt Regency Miami hotel.

Stay Entertained

Museums, performing arts and sports

For day-into-night cultural and sporting entertainment, you can spend all your time during an action-packed week in just a few blocks of Downtown Miami and hardly get bored. The city's beloved performing arts center and downtown architectural darling, the **Adrienne Arsht Center for the Performing Arts** (arshtcenter.org; ticket prices vary) has balconies that rise in a spiral and resemble a sliced-open seashell. The acoustics, as you'd expect, are phenomenal, and the venue – home to the Florida Grand Opera Miami and Miami City Ballet – hosts some 300 performances a year.

A 10-minute stroll away, the **Patricia & Phillip Frost Museum of Science** (frostscience.org; adult/child $30/25) lures families to its 250-seat planetarium and three-level aquarium. Exhibitions range from weather phenomena to creepy crawlies, feathered dinosaurs and vital microbe displays, while Florida's fascinating Everglades and rich coral reefs play starring roles.

The **Miami Children's Museum** (miamichildrensmuseum.org; $26) is full of imaginative areas where you can let the kids make music, embark on undersea adventures, make wall sketches, explore little castles made of colored glass or simply run off some excess energy on outdoor playgrounds. A 400-seat theater in a renovated 1913 space, **Black Archives – Historic Lyric Theater** (bahlt.org), once hosted Duke

Black Archives – Historic Lyric Theater

Ellington and Ella Fitzgerald. Today it welcomes shows and exhibitions exploring African American heritage in Miami and beyond. Sports fans and mass concert-goers flock to the **Kaseya Center** *(kaseyacenter.com),* formerly the FTX Arena, to see everything from *reggaeton* and salsa stars to the city's beloved NBA team, the Miami Heat.

Unfolding the Florida Story

Learn about the past at HistoryMiami

Making sense of today's Miami means taking a look at South Florida's multifaceted and fascinating past. This land of escaped enslaved people, guerrilla Native Americans, gangsters, pirates, tourists and alligators has a special history – and it takes a special place to capture that narrative. A Smithsonian Affiliate, **HistoryMiami Museum** *(historymiami.org; adult/child $15/8)* inside the **Miami-Dade Cultural Center** does just that.

The museum weaves together the stories of the region's successive population waves, from Native Americans to Nicaraguans. Interactive exhibits show life among the Seminoles and early Florida industries like sponge diving. Other areas touch on the history of Jewish and African American communities in South Beach; Cuban refugees, complete with a rustic homemade boat, that managed to survive the Florida crossing; and cultural expression in public spaces (highlighting traditions such as street art, parades, protests and even vehicle customizing).

Specials tours and events scheduled throughout the year include themed family fun days (like Cuban Carnival) and even cruises with a museum historian to visit **Stiltsville** (a community built on stilts in the middle of Biscayne Bay). You'll walk away from this place with a better understanding of the people who made Miami what it is today.

MIAMI'S BEST TOURS

Melanin Miami: Black History Tour: Immersion in the culture, history and soul food of Miami's Black community in neighborhoods like Overtown *(key2mia. com/melanin-miami).*

Jewish Miami Beach Tour: Offered on demand, this tour explores the rise and fall of the Jewish population of Miami Beach over the past century *(mdpl.org/ tours/jewish-miami-beach-tour).*

Tours 'R' U.S. Miami: Join local guide George Neary in Miami's many cultural neighborhoods, including Overtown, Little Bahamas and Little Overtown.

Big Bus Tours Miami: South Beach, Wynwood, Midtown, Little Havana, Downtown and beyond are on the docket during hop-on, hop-off tours aboard open-air buses *(bigbustours.com/en/ miami).*

Bobby's Bike Hike Miami: Cycling and food tours around Miami Beach *(bobbysbikehike.com/ miami/).*

🚶 **AMBLING DOWNTOWN MIAMI**

Downtown Miami is constantly reinventing itself. Put your finger on the pulse of what's trending while treading the city as locals do.

START	END	LENGTH
El Sitio Coffee Bar	Cantina La Veinte	2.5 miles; at least 2 hrs

Start your stroll past the city's shiniest corners on a mellow note with breakfast – of Venezuelan arepas and café con leche – at ① **El Sitio Coffee Bar**. Afterwards, walk to ② **Bayfront Park** and onwards to the ③ **Miami Riverwalk**; walk from the south end of Bayfront, beneath bridges and along the waterline, until it ends just west of the SW 2nd Ave Bridge (10 minutes/0.4 miles).

Crossing the Miami River, the ④ **Brickell Avenue Bridge**, between SE 4th St and SE 5th St, affords even better views of the Downtown skyline. Note the 17ft-high bronze statue by Cuban-born sculptor Manuel Carbonell of a Tequesta Indian

warrior, atop the towering Pillar of History column.

Continuing just east, arrive at ⑤ **Miami Circle National Historic Landmark**. Listed on the National Register of Historic Places, it's an ancient archaeological site of earth-midden deposits. They were discovered in the late 1990s prior to downtown riverside construction at the mouth of the Miami River, in the middle of downtown Miami. Marveling at the modernity all around, it's impossible not to feel awed by the passing of time. Finish with lunch nearby at ⑥ **Cantina La Veinte**, a waterfront spot in Brickell with authentic Mexican fare.

Mini empanadas and arepas make up the sampler platter at **El Sitio Coffee Bar.**

Covering 32 acres, **Bayfront Park** was first established in 1924.

Stone axes and bone and shell implements were among the artifacts unearthed at **Miami Circle National Historic Landmark.**

Wynwood, the Design District & Allapattah

ART-CENTRIC NEIGHBORHOODS WHERE YOU'LL EAT WELL

Whatever is on trend in the world is emulated – if not started – on the streets of Wynwood, in the shadow of public art and Instagrammable food halls. The Design District is a high-end shopping area and neighboring Allapattah is a cultural swirl all its own.

Wynwood was once a working-class, Spanish-speaking area before rapid-onset gentrification roared in. The area is busy by day, but truly comes alive at night when creatives mingle in candlelit brewpubs and backyard music joints. You can easily explore the more refined Design District in a day, hitting the shops and galleries during daylight hours – lovely, if stratospherically priced, objects fill its main shopping strip – then sticking around (or returning) for evening dining and nightlife.

Be sure to make a foray into neighboring Allapattah, one of Miami's most diverse neighborhoods and a melting pot of all things Caribbean and Latin American. It's home to more street art and a serious art-world heavy hitter too.

Art & High Design

Beauty unbound in the Design District

The Design District is compact but it overflows with galleries, high-end designer boutiques and places to eat, and you could easily spend the better part of a morning and afternoon diving in. You'll also find some lovely contemporary architecture throughout, along with intriguing outdoor installations that bring the art out of the gallery and into the public sphere. Even the parking garages go all-in on the design theme here. The main drags are along NW 39th and 40th Sts.

Locust Projects *(locustprojects.org; free)* has become a major name for emerging artists in the contemporary gallery scene and is the city's longest-running, non-profit experimental art space. Run by artists since 1998, Locust Projects has exhibited work by more than 250 local, national and international

continued on p76

GETTING AROUND

You can ride the MetroBus and Miami Trolley from downtown to reach Wynwood. If you're coming with your own car, there's ample metered parking on the streets. It's easy enough, if not overly scenic, to walk the mile or so between Wynwood and the Design District, just north, during the day, but opt for a taxi or rideshare after dark. Allapattah, to the west of both, is a short ride away (again, taxi or rideshare is the way to go).

☑TOP TIP

Wynwood covers a large area, with attractions spread across many blocks. However, you'll find the densest concentration of sights on or near NW 2nd Ave. A handy approach is to head north from 23rd St to about 29th St, dipping in and out of intersecting streets along the way.

73

WYNWOOD, THE DESIGN DISTRICT & ALLAPATTAH

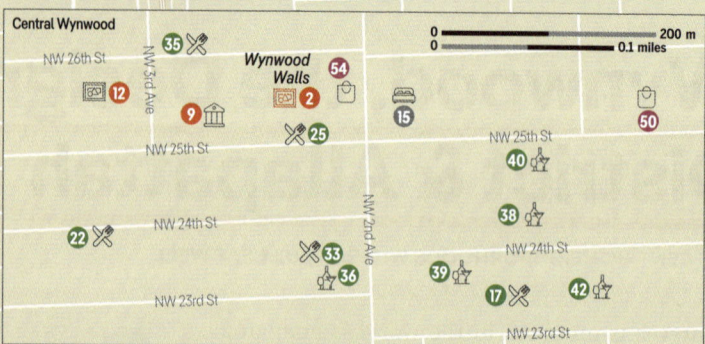

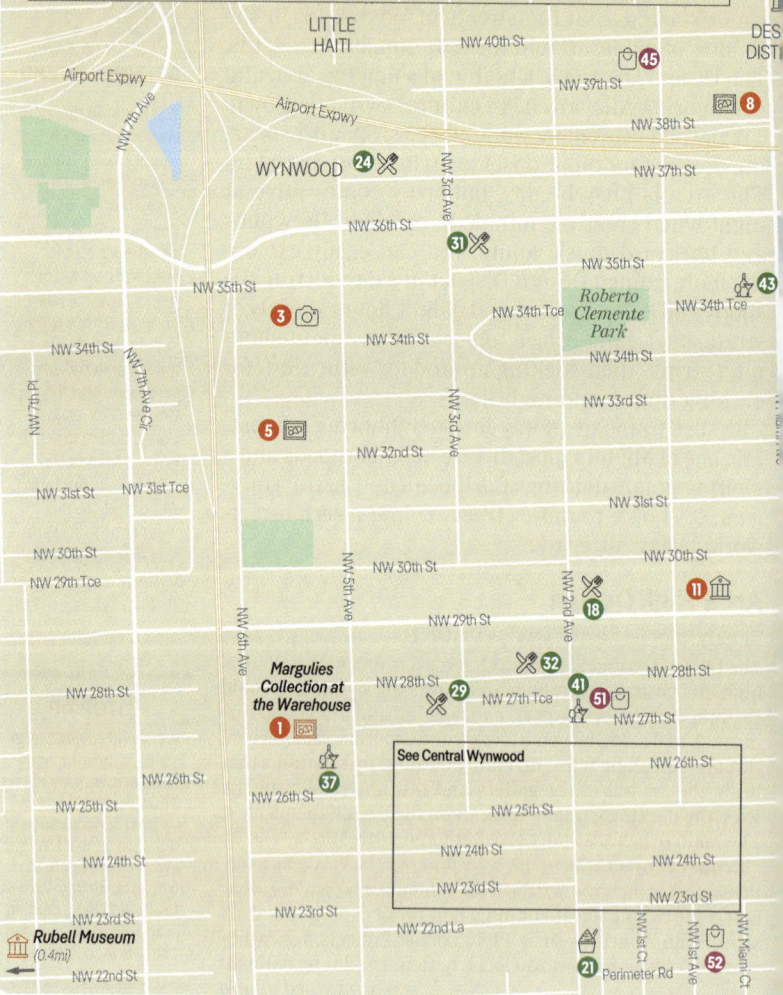

Central Wynwood

NW 26th St
35

**Wynwood
Walls**

54

12

9

NW 25th St

NW 25th St

NW 26th St

0 _____ 200 m
0 _____ 0.1 miles

NE 47t

2

25

15

50

40

38

22

NW 24th St

NW 24th St

33

39

36

17

42

NW 23rd St

NW 23rd St

LITTLE
HAITI

NW 40th St

45

Airport Expwy

NW 39th St

NW 38th St

8

Airport Expwy

WYNWOOD

24

NW 37th St

NW 36th St

31

NW 35th St

Roberto
Clemente
Park

NW 34th Tce

43

3

NW 35th St

NW 34th Tce

NW 34th St

NW 34th St

NW 33rd St

5

NW 32nd St

NW 31st St

NW 31st St

NW 31st Tce

NW 31st St

NW 30th St

NW 30th St

NW 30th St

NW 29th Tce

18

11

NW 29th St

NW 29th St

32

**Margulies
Collection at
the Warehouse**

NW 28th St

29

41

51

NW 28th St

NW 28th St

1

NW 27th Tce

NW 27th St

37

See Central Wynwood

NW 26th St

NW 26th St

NW 26th St

NW 25th St

NW 25th St

NW 24th St

NW 24th St

NW 23rd St

NW 23rd St

NW 23rd St

NW 23rd St

NW 22nd La

🏛 **Rubell Museum**
(0.4mi)

NW 22nd St

21

Perimeter Rd

52

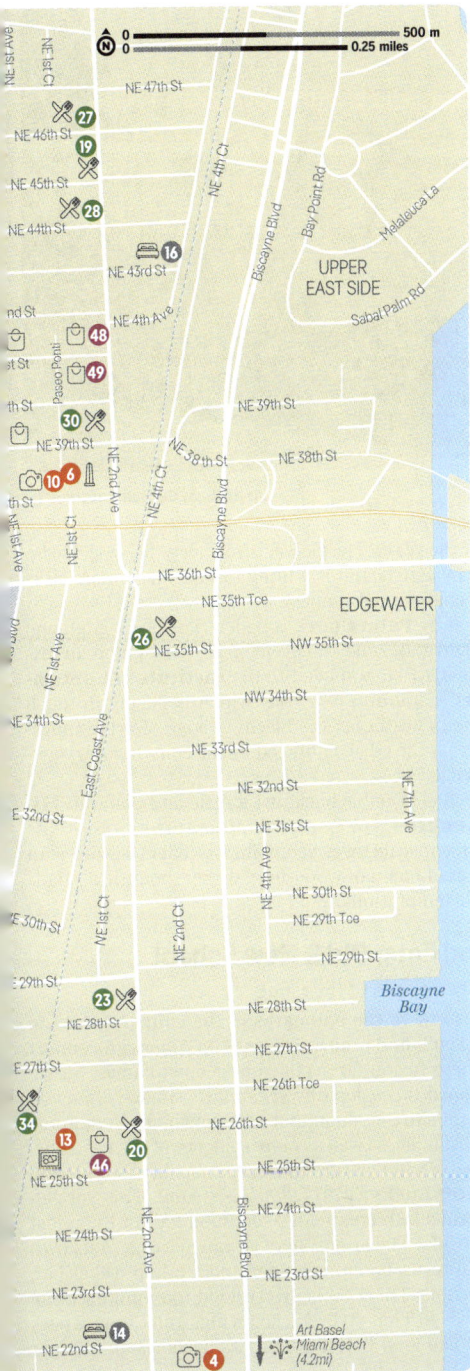

HIGHLIGHTS
1 Margulies Collection at the Warehouse
2 Wynwood Walls

SIGHTS
3 Allapattah
4 Bacardi Building
5 Bakehouse Art Complex
6 Fly's Eye Dome
7 Institute of Contemporary Art
8 Locust Projects
9 Museum of Graffiti
10 Palm Court
11 Rubell Family Art Collection
12 Walt Grace Vintage
13 Wynwood Art Gallery

SLEEPING
14 Arlo
15 Moxy Miami Wynwood
16 The Hotel at the Moore

EATING
17 1-800 Lucky
18 Bakan
19 Buena Vista Deli
20 Cerveceria La Tropical
21 Dasher & Crank
22 Doya

23 Enriqueta's
24 Hometown BBQ
25 Kyu
26 La Latina
27 Lemoni Café
28 Mandolin Aegean Bistro
29 Miam
30 Michael's Genuine
31 Monchy's
32 Morgan's
33 Panther Coffee
34 Piegari
35 Zak the Baker

DRINKING & NIGHTLIFE
36 Coyo Taco
37 Dante's HiFi
38 Dirty Rabbit
39 Gramps
40 La Casa de Rubia
41 R House
42 Selvatico
43 The Sylvester

SHOPPING
44 Acne Studios
45 Alice+Olivia
46 Capelle
47 GANNI
48 Golden Goose
49 Maison Francis Kurkdjian
50 Ofy
51 Osme
52 Sole Garden
53 The Wynwood Shop
54 Wynwood Walls Shop

UPPER EAST SIDE

EDGEWATER

Biscayne Bay

Art Basel Miami Beach (4.2mi)

NE 47th St
NE 46th St
NE 45th St
NE 44th St
NE 43rd St
NE 4th Ave
NE 39th St
NE 38th St
NE 36th St
NE 35th Tce
NW 35th St
NE 35th St
NW 34th St
NE 34th St
NE 33rd St
NE 32nd St
NE 31st St
NE 30th St
NE 29th Tce
NE 29th St
NE 28th St
NE 27th St
NE 26th Tce
NE 26th St
NE 25th St
NE 24th St
NE 23rd St
NE 22nd St

Biscayne Blvd
Bay Point Rd
Malaleuca La
Sabal Palm Rd
Pasco Ponti
East Coast Ave
NE 1st Ave
NE 2nd Ave
NE 7th Ave

0   500 m
0   0.25 miles

KENSOCAL7/SHUTTERSTOCK

Institute of Contemporary Art

contined from p73

artists over the years. The gallery often hosts site-specific installations by artists and is willing to take a few more risks than more commercial venues.

Next, stroll by **Palm Court**, a pedestrian plaza, high-end and designer retail zone and event space which more or less anchors the district, and head to the **Institute of Contemporary Art** *(icamiami.org; free)* which is deeply in touch with the area's aesthetic: the bleeding edge of arts innovation, or at least the edge embraced by the contemporary-art-criticism scene.

Need to refuel? Double back just a little and pop into **Michael's Genuine** (p77) *(michaelsgenuine.com)*. This long-running upscale tavern combines excellent service with a well-executed menu of wood-fired dishes, bountiful salads and raw bar temptations.

Wynwood Eats: Old & New School

Treat your tastebuds to the range

Creativity is one of the hallmarks of the culinary scene in Wynwood. You'll find innovative takes on American comfort food, Japanese fusion fare cooked over open flames, imaginatively topped tacos, healthy vegan fare, single-origin coffee, paradigm-shifting doughnuts and much, much more.

A perfect example, as well as more evidence of Wynwood becoming a sort of adult playground for cosmopolitan world wanderers: **1-800 Lucky** (p78) *(1800lucky.com)*. This sprawling eatery aims to recreate an Asian food hall in the midst of South Florida. The atmosphere is transporting in its own right: red lanterns, booming lounge and hip-hop, a slick bar, beautiful people. The food is pretty good too, ranging from sashimi bowls to Thai-style chicken wings and Chinese pork belly buns. The food hall more or less becomes an outdoor bar as the night wears on, and is as popular as the most packed Miami club.

Where did people eat before successive waves of gentrification washed away old Wynwood? One institution stands out, and it drips with character: **Enriqueta's** (p78) (*enriquetas. com*), an outpost of old Miami in the heart of that city's (arguably) flashiest neighborhood. At this roadhouse diner, local Spanish speakers looking for a filling, affordable feed (as opposed to international installation artists looking for the latest artisanal whatever) rule the roost. Head here for truly excellent coffee, *pan con bistec* (steak sandwiches), *croquetas* (deep-fried rolls), Cuban sandwiches, daily specials such as *picadillo* (spiced ground beef) and *lechón asado* (roast pork), and lots of good-natured Spanish gossiping among regulars.

Culture, Coffee, Cheers, Repeat
Sip, clink glasses and salute creativity

Wynwood is Miami's unofficial capital of art and all things avant-garde. Its mural-lined streets are one giant canvas – albeit one that's ever changing – and the gallery scene is unrivaled.

Kick things off by putting some expresso-laced fuel in your tank at **Panther Coffee** *(panthercoffee.com),* a beloved local roaster that is fast becoming internationally known for its quality caffeine. From here, walk up NW 2nd Ave, then turn left onto 26th St and head to NW 3rd Ave. In this area you'll be strolling past some truly staggering mural 'galleries.' At the corner of NW 27th St is the zebra-striped Wynwood Building, which functions as a creative office and retail space. You'll also find **Miam** *(miamcafe.com),* another fine coffee spot.

From here you can turn right down 27th St. Two blocks on, you'll reach the **Margulies Collection at the Warehouse** (*margulies.com; adult/student $10/free*). It's well worth the admission as this vast gallery houses an incredible collection of contemporary art. It's a quick walk from here to **Cerveceria La Tropical** *(cervecerialatropical.com),* a craft brewery that originally came into being in Cuba that has sports bar vibes inside and a gorgeous alfresco tropical garden for raising a frosty glass al fresco.

Soak Up the Community Art Scene
Wynwood block parties and art walks

One of the best ways to take in the Miami art scene is to join in the **Wynwood Art Walk Block Party** *(wynwoodartwalkblockparty.com),* held on the second Saturday of every month.

THE DESIGN DISTRICT'S BEST SHOPS

Acne: Italian leather and Japanese denim are among the elite raw ingredients in this cult Swedish atelier's stable.

Alice+Olivia: Women's clothing boutique known for designer denim and beautiful print dresses.

Golden Goose: There are sneakers and then there is this beloved high-fashion Italian brand, known for its emblematic star.

Maison Francis Kurkdjian: Pop in for a signature scent from this luxury French perfumery. Candles and scented body lotions round out the offerings.

GANNI: If it's cool enough for Copenhagen's cool girls, you'll find the Scandinavian fashion favorite here.

EATING IN WYNWOOD & THE DESIGN DISTRICT

Michael's Genuine: A tavern-turned-temple to New American cuisine with a great raw bar, wood-fired dishes and buzzing crowds. *11.30am-11pm Mon-Sat, 11am-10pm Sun* **$$$**

Mandolin Aegean Bistro: It's all Mediterranean whites and blues at this Greek restaurant. Grilled bass, lamb, kabobs and more. *noon-11pm* **$$$**

Doya: Meze plates from Greece and Turkey are ideal for sharing at this lively Aegean-inspired restaurant in Wynwood. *noon-midnight* **$$$**

Kyu: Go all in on umami at this sublime Wynwood Asian restaurant that's mastered the art of Japanese wood-fired grilling. *5-10pm Mon & Tue, noon-10pm Wed-Sun* **$$$**

LOCAL LANDMARK

The former Miami headquarters of **Bacardi** at 2100 Biscayne Blvd is a masterpiece of tropical architecture, and holds a spot on the National Register of Historic Places. The main event is a beautifully decorated jewel-box-like building, built in 1973, that seems to hover over the ground from a central pillar supporting the entire structure. One-inch-thick pieces of hammered glass cover the exterior in a wild Mesoamerican-style pattern modeled after a mosaic designed by German artist Johannes M Dietz. Also on-site is the older 1963 building: a tower covered with blue-and-white handmade tiles – some 28,000 – in a striking ceramic pattern designed by Brazilian artist Francisco Brennand.

FELIX MIZIOZNIKOV/GETTY IMAGES

Art Basel

Many galleries around Wynwood host special events and art openings, with ever-flowing drinks (not always free), live music, food trucks and special markets.

Another way to see the neighborhood is the similarly named **Wynwood Art Walk** (p56) (*wynwoodartwalk.com; from $25*). This 'walk' is actually a 90-minute guided tour to some of the best gallery shows of the day, plus a look at some interesting street art around the 'hood. It also offers other tours, like a golf cart trip around the area's best graffiti.

Jive with the Jetset Art World

Go all-in with Art Basel

Art Basel (*artbasel.com/miami-beach*) is one of the biggest international art shows in the world, and one of the most Miami things to ever take place in Miami. It's all there: influencers on overload, nonstop people watching and preening, conspicuous consumption (often blended with a dash of either activism or

EATING IN WYNWOOD & THE DESIGN DISTRICT: OUR PICKS

Enriqueta's: No-frills Cuban diner with daily specials and great Cuban sandwiches and coffee. *7am-3pm Mon-Fri, to 2pm Sat* $	**1-800 Lucky:** Miami's take on an Asian hawker market, with tons of street food and Wynwood neon to boot. *noon-1am Mon-Thu, to 3am Fri-Sun* $	**Lemoni Café:** European cafe vibes and delicious French toast, paninis and pancakes with pleasant outdoor seating. *10am-8pm* $	**Zak the Baker:** Artisan and kosher bakery; known for its ridiculously good pastries and BLTs on croissants. *7am-5pm Sun-Fri* $
Dasher & Crank: Quite literally churns out ice cream, ranging from passion fruit sorbet to (of course) mojito. *noon-11pm* $	**La Latina:** Popular with both locals and transplants who dig into arepas, pulled pork and Venezuelan favorites. *9am-10pm Sun-Thu, to 4pm Sat & Sun* $	**Bakan:** Live the good ceviche and aguachile life at this lively Mexican restaurant. Fab Mezcal selection. *noon-11pm Sun-Wed, to 2am Thu-Sat* $$	**Piegari:** Upscale Italian spot near Wynwood, known for freshly made pastas. *12.30-11pm Sun-Thu, to 11.30pm Fri & Sat* $$$

intellectualism), and parties that only stop long enough to up-load the next viral snapshot. Even if you're not a billionaire collector, there's plenty to enjoy at this festival, with open-air art installations around town, special exhibitions at many Miami galleries and outdoor film screenings, among other goings-on.

While a lot of the action is in Miami Beach, Wynwood is a huge Basel center of gravity, hosting a mural festival and temporary venues for drinking, eating and general hedonism. **Wynwood Art Gallery** *(wynwoodartgallery.com)* is always a good place to find your bearings here during Art Basel before following the crowds to other pop-up events and installations around town.

Allapattah's Art World Icon

The next big thing at Rubell Museum

Don and Mera Rubell started collecting art from the beginning of their marriage in 1964 and, over the decades, earned an enviable reputation for identifying the next big things. Since then, the Rubell family's private art collection has helped make Miami synonymous with the contemporary-art scene, and their Wynwood museum helped set the stage for that neighborhood's gentrification. In 2019, the family museum relocated to **Allapattah**, a neighborhood just northwest of Downtown Miami to the west of Wynwood, which had by then entered a sort of supercharged era of gentrification. The new **Rubell Museum** *(rubellmuseum.org; adult/child $15/10)* – six industrial buildings since converted into a frosty, yet inviting museum space – was redesigned by Selldorf Architects into one of the largest private contemporary art institutions in North America.

The institution consists of some 53,000 sq ft of soaring exhibition space divided into 40 galleries. Artists on display include Kehinde Wiley, Jeff Koons, Cindy Sherman and Cady Noland. While many art museums of this size may be sustained by temporary exhibitions, at the Rubell the split is roughly 65% long-term holdings and 35% special (ie temporary) shows.

The Rubell is noted for presenting work with thematic consistency and exhaustive context; curators here are very good at their jobs, and proud of the art they're presenting to the public.

RETAIL & DESIGN UNITE

At the epicenter of the Design District is **Palm Court** (p76), a lavish courtyard with tall palm trees, reflecting mirrors, two floors of swanky retailers and one particularly eye-catching sculpture sitting at the center of everything: the **Fly's Eye Dome**. Designed by Buckminster Fuller, this geodesic dome appears to float in a small reflecting pool surrounded by slender, gently swaying palm trees, themselves often decorated with temporary art exhibitions. The 24-ft-tall sculpture was dubbed an 'autonomous dwelling machine' by Fuller when he conceived it back in 1965; now it's a backdrop to high-end shopping, and a covered entry-exit point connecting the below-ground parking lot with Palm Court.

DRINKING IN WYNWOOD & THE DESIGN DISTRICT: BEST BARS

Dirty Rabbit: Colorful cocktails, edgy if cute art and live music attracts all the cool kids. *hours vary*	**Dante's HiFi:** Have an excellent cocktail in a laid-back lounge that doubles as a vinyl listening room. *hours vary*	**Gramps:** Everyone loves this super laid-back spot for its beer, cocktails, live DJs and Thursday drag shows. *noon-1am Sun-Thu, to 3pm Fri & Sat*	**La Casa de Rubia:** Craft beer, Latin vibes, salsa and salsa nights, and fútbol watch parties sum up the fun at this Wynwood brewpub. *hours vary*
The Sylvester: Mixes Design District vibes with contemporary art and lots of beautiful people, especially on weekends. *hours vary*	**Coyo Taco:** Wynwood's secret bar hidden behind a taco stand. DJs draw the crowds when Afro-Cuban funk is spinning. *hours vary*	**R House:** A favorite for drag brunches, served up with lots of revelry and bottomless white wine sangrias and mojitos. *hours vary*	**Selvatico:** Jungle-inspired balls near Wynwood Walls. Sneak off into a secret forest to sip herbaceous mojitos. *7pm-3am Thu-Sat*

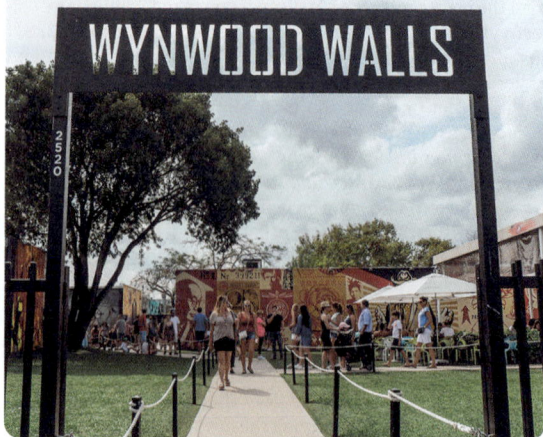

PI03/SHUTTERSTOCK

Wynwood Walls

MORE ART MUSTS

Bakehouse Art Complex: Creative incubator with studios and workspaces for local artists.

Institute of Contemporary Art: Free bastion of contemporary art in the Design District, with changing exhibitions and programs.

Museum of Graffiti: Dive into the history of this particular art form seen on so many surrounding blocks. Hit the gift shop for pop art presents.

Margulies Collection at the Warehouse: Vast, not-for-profit exhibition space in Wynwood housing a 4000-piece art collection, including sculptures, sound installations and room-sized works.

Walt Grace Vintage: Wynwood has a hundred galleries, but this is the only one showcasing classic cars and classic guitars.

Color Pop & Shop

Walk the Wynwood Walls

One of the most photographed locations in Miami (if social media hashtags are anything to go by), **Wynwood Walls** *(thewynwoodwalls.com; free)* is a collection of murals and paintings laid out over an open courtyard that bowls people over with its sheer exuberant colors and commanding presence. What's on offer tends to change with the coming and going of major arts events, such as Art Basel, but it's always eye-catching, interesting stuff, and the energy that congregates around the Walls is buzzy and exciting. Depending on your worldview, the Walls are either a triumph of Wynwood's unwritten mission of bringing street-generated contemporary art to the masses...or a triumph of the commercial forces that have taken the creative energy of the street and repackaged it for conspicuous consumption. Are we thinking too hard about it? Maybe, but that's the point of art, right? In any case, if you want to take a little piece of the Walls home, pop into the on-site shop. You can also learn the spray paint basics and create your own piece of graffiti here with the **Wynwood Graffiti Experience** *(wynwoodartwalk.com; adult/child $42/34)*.

🍽 EATING IN ALLAPATTAH & THE DESIGN DISTRICT

Buena Vista Deli: Come in the morning for bakery temptations and, later in the day, big slices of quiche at this Design District hideaway. *7am-5pm* $

Monchy's: Find no-frills Dominican fare and great fried chicken on the menu in Allapattah. *9am-9pm Mon-Sat, from 10am Sun* $

Hometown BBQ: Ribs, slaw, mac 'n' cheese in a melt-in-your-mouth brisket are the tip of the BBQ iceberg at this Allapattah go-to. *11.30am-9pm Sun-Thu, to 10pm Fri & Sat* $

Morgan's: Newly relocated to Allapattah, Morgan's serves comfort fare like Greek feta fries and chicken and waffle sandwiches. *8am-10pm* $$

Little Havana

THE CORE OF THE CUBAN DIASPORA

The Cuba-ness of Little Havana may be exaggerated for visitors, but it's still an atmospheric area to explore, with the clack of dominoes, the scent of cigar smoke in the air and salsa beats spilling onto the streets. This is the best-known Cuban American neighborhood in all of the US, and was officially declared a national treasure in 2017 by The National Trust for Historic Preservation.

As you walk around, keep an eye out for art murals: older ones often reference the Cuban Revolution, while newer pieces contain contemporary references to things like hip-hop and the Miami Heat. Little Havana's main thoroughfare, Calle Ocho (SW 8th St), is the heart of the neighborhood – most vibrant by day (preferably weekends). See wise-cracking old timers chattering over games of dominoes in Máximo Gómez Park and ponder modern art in galleries. Shop for souvenirs and cigars, pausing for strong coffee along the way.

Stroll Through Living History

Visit the Cuban Memorial Boulevard Park

Cuban Memorial Boulevard Park is a testament to the enormous cultural significance of an island that thousands of Miamians have never set foot on, yet remains, in a vital way, a place they consider integral to their identity.

Taken on its own, it's a skinny public space occupying the median of SW 13th Ave and taking up four blocks of real estate. There are statues and memorials popping up every few feet, and it takes some cultural or historical context to appreciate many of them. You'll see many Cuban American families among the curious tourists stopping to take pause.

The **Eternal Torch of Brigade 2506** is dedicated to those soldiers who gave their lives in the 1961 Bay of Pigs Invasion of Cuba. Anti-communism is also given a nod in a bronze **Statue of Nestor 'Tony' Izquierdo**, a Bay of Pigs veteran who went on to fight for Nicaragua's right-wing Somoza regime.

GETTING AROUND

Get around Little Havana the way most Cubans do in their home country – on foot. All of the attractions along Calle Ocho are within a manageable stroll of each other, and being on the street with the people – Cubans, newly minted Cuban Americans, long-ago arrivals and tourists alike – is part of the draw.

☑ TOP TIP

Exploring Little Havana is less about ticking off a litany of sights and more about soaking up the atmosphere in this place totally unique in the US. Be on the lookout for the **Cuban Walk of Fame**, a series of sidewalk stars emblazoned with the names of Cuban celebrities that runs up and down most of 8th St.

LITTLE HAVANA

La Plaza de la Cubanidad

Little Havana Art District

CORAL WAY

Máximo Gómez Park

Versailles (1.5mi)

Little Havana Art District

See Art District

Café La Trova (0.3mi); San Pocho (0.4mi)

CORAL WAY

Eternal Torch of Brigade 2506 (0.6mi); Xixón (1mi)

HIGHLIGHTS
1 Little Havana Art District
2 Máximo Gómez Park

SIGHTS
3 Cuban Memorial Boulevard Park
4 Statue of Nestor 'Tony' Izquierdo

EATING
5 Azucar
6 El Cristo
7 La Camaronera Seafood Joint and Fish Market
8 La Vasca Deli
9 Lung Yai Thai Tapas
10 Old's Havana Cuban Bar & Kitchen

11 Sala'o Cuban Restaurant & Bar
12 Sanguich de Miami
13 Yambo

DRINKING & NIGHTLIFE
14 Ball & Chain
15 Bar Nancy

16 Los Pinareños Frutería

ENTERTAINMENT
17 Cubaocho
18 Tower Theater
19 Viernes Culturales

SHOPPING
20 Little Havana Visitors Center

The World's Most Famous Cuban Restaurant

Dine and drink coffee at Versailles

Few Little Havana sights make the stomach rumble as much as the green-and-white sign of **Versailles** (p83) *(versailles-restaurant.com)*. The self-proclaimed 'most famous Cuban restaurant in the world' (and, to be fair, that boast is hard to argue with) has been around since 1971. Generations of Cuban Americans, along with Miami's Latin political elite, rub elbows here in this dining room, over plates of black beans, *ropa vieja, croquetas* (croquettes) and countless cups of sweet, strong Cuban coffee. The mainstays are all here, but you can also find more involved, regional cuisine from the island, up to and including a seafood paella, shredded dry beef (unlike the sauce-y *ropa vieja*), and grilled liver steak. For a quick shot of caffeine, hit **La Ventanita** (p83) – the restaurant's to-go window selling strong shot-like coffees called *cortaditos* and *coladas*.

Beats of the Diaspora

Making music in Little Havana

Music is at the heart of the Cuban diaspora, and several businesses in Little Havana tap into the island's soul via songs.

The jewel of the **Little Havana Art District**, **Cubaocho** (*cubaocho.co; prices vary*) is renowned for its concerts, with excellent bands from across the Spanish-speaking world. It's also a community center, art gallery and research outpost for all things Cuban. The interior resembles an old Havana cigar bar, yet the walls are decked out in artwork that references both the classical past of Cuban art and its avant-garde future.

With its wood accents, immaculately dressed bartenders and faded Havana-esque walls, **Cafe La Trova** (*cafelatrova.com*) nails the 'Old Cuba' concept (how you feel about said concept is, of course, another question). Regular live shows featuring classic Cuban dance music accompanied by a crowd decked out in their best dresses and *guayaberas* is insanely fun; if the scene here doesn't get you dancing, we're not sure what will. **Ball & Chain** (*ballandchainmiami.com*) is known for music all day and salsa dancing that often spills out onto the street.

But music in Little Havana doesn't always have to evoke the old island, and locals don't always need a conga accompaniment to shake their tail feathers. At craft-cocktail-centric **Bar Nancy** (*nancy305.com*), millennial and Gen Z Cuban Americans (among others) dance to hard rock, punk, Southern blues, Latin trap, chiptune and whatever the heck else catches their fancy.

Comer, Beber y Ser Feliz

Beyond Cuban fare in Little Havana

Sure, you can do that all over Miami. But in Little Havana you can eat your way around the Spanish-speaking world over the course of a few scant blocks. We do mean the world, too – Cuban cuisine is only a small slice of Little Havana's pan-Latin palate. There are menus from all over el Sud, from Ecuador to El Salvador and Mexico to Mendoza, Argentina. And while locals say you have to go further afield than Calle Ocho for the best *comida latina* (Latin food), you'll rarely go wrong when you stroll into ethnic eateries in this part of town.

You don't even need to stick to the Western Hemisphere. Take a little gem of a restaurant like **Lung Yai Thai Tapas** (p85) (*lungyai.com*) – at places like this, you realize the whole concept of sharing lots of little snackish plates on a humid

LOOKING UP TO THE TOWER

Think all the best South Florida deco is in South Beach? Come to the **Tower Theater** *(towertheater miami.com)* on Calle Ocho and think again. This renovated, 1926 landmark has a proud deco facade and a handsomely renovated interior. In its heyday it was the center of Little Havana social life and, via the films it showed, served as a bridge between immigrant society and American pop culture. Today, it frequently shows independent and Spanish-language films (sometimes both). The theater also hosts varied art exhibitions in the lobby. It's also just a lovely neighborhood anchor, a landmark and point of reference that generations have grown up with and fought to preserve and protect.

EATING IN LITTLE HAVANA: BEST CUBAN FOOD

| Sanguich de Miami: Gourmet takes on classic Cuban sandwiches have 'em lining up at this cult neighborhood spot owned by first-gen Cuba Americans. *10am-6pm* $ | Old's Havana Cuban Bar & Cocina: Snag a table in the pretty tropical garden of this hot spot. *11am-11pm Sun-Thu, to midnight Fri & Sat* $$ | Sala'o Cuban Restaurant & Bar: Live music every night and specialties like *rabo encendido* (oxtail). *noon-midnight Sun-Wed, to 2am Thu, to 3am Fri & Sat* $$ | Versailles: Miami's not-to-miss famous Cuban restaurant on Calle Ocho, famed for sit-down feasts and walk-up window *cafecitos. hours vary* $$ |

afternoon is not exclusive to the Spanish-speaking world (by the way, the chicken wings here will blow your mind).

All that said, nothing says refreshment on a sultry Miami afternoon like a cool glass of fresh juice or *batidos* (milkshakes) from **Los Pinareños Frutería**, a fruit and veggie stand beloved by generations of Miamians. Sip a *guarapa* (sugar-cane extract) *batido* while roosters cluck and folks gossip and argue in Cuban-accented Spanish; this is as Miami as it gets, short of being in a Pitbull song.

The Soundtrack Goes Clickety-Clack

Doing Domino Park

Perhaps Little Havana's most evocative reminder of street life from Cuba is **Máximo Gómez Park** (*miami.gov; free*). More commonly called Domino Park, it's a tree-shaded, gated oasis on Calle Ocho. The big iron gates are open between 9am and 6pm daily. Regulars file in from around the neigh-

EATING IN LITTLE HAVANA: OUR PICKS

Azucar: One of Little Havana's oldest ice-cream parlors serves sweet treats like *abuela* used to make. *11am-9pm Mon-Wed, to 11pm Thu-Sat, to 10pm Sun* $

La Camaronera Seafood Joint and Fish Market: Come for the *pan con minuta* (fried fish sandwich with the tail on). *11.30am-5.30pm Sun-Thu, to 8.30pm Fri & Sat* $

Xixón: Modern Spanish tapas joint with excellent *bacalao* (cod) fritters, sizzling shrimp and baby eel. *noon-10pm Sun-Thu, to 1pm Fri & Sat* $$

El Cristo: Down-to-earth El Cristo has options from all over the Spanish-speaking world, but the fish dishes stand out. *hours vary* $$

BRIAN LOGAN PHOTOGRAPHY/SHUTTERSTOCK

Máximo Gómez (Domino) Park

borhood and across Miami, and the competitive banter and strategizing gets going as cups of Cuban coffee are sipped. The sound of seasoned players trash-talking over games of dominoes is harmonized with the quick clack-clack of slapping tiles – though photo-taking tourists do give an odd spin to the experience, not that the players pay them any heed. In fact, they don't seem to mind people watching them at all – if anything, they feed off the crowd's energy.

The heavy cigar smell and a sunrise-bright mural of the 1994 **Summit of the Americas** add to the atmosphere. You might spend a few minutes here passing through or get sucked into watching a game for longer. The walkways around the park are decorated with domino-inspired tiles and there are benches where you can sit for a spell to soak up the ambiance of it all in the shade. The neighborhood's cult ice creamery **Azucar** (p84) *(azucaricecream.com)* is right across the street if all the spectating makes you peckish.

EATING IN LITTLE HAVANA: BEYOND CUBAN FARE

Sanpocho: For a quick journey to Colombia, head here for hearty, meat-heavy dishes that fill you up for a week. *7am-11pm Sun-Wed, to 1am Thu, to 4am Fri & Sat* $

Yambo: Dine around the clock on Nicaraguan *carne asada* (grilled beef), sweet plantains and piles of rice and beans. *24hrs* $

La Vasca Deli: Unassuming restaurant and bodega with authentic specialties from Spain, like *fabada* (bean stew), Galician soup and of Iberico ham. *hours vary* $$

Lung Yai Thai Tapas: Shareable Thai small plates make for spicy snacks that pair perfectly with the Calle Ocho street scene. *hours vary* $$

Coral Gables & Coconut Grove

LUSH GARDENS AND CAFE CULTURE

GETTING AROUND

Flat terrain makes it easy to explore Coconut Grove and Coral Gables on foot. There's a Metrorail station about a mile from Coconut Grove, and you can catch the free Coconut Grove trolley from there to the heart of the action. Once there, explore on foot or grab an inexpensive **Citi Bike** (citibikemiami.com) to pedal around. The Metrorail also goes to Coral Gables, where you'll find another free trolley service with two routes for getting around.

Coral Gables, filled with a pastel rainbow of mansions, feels a world removed from the rest of Miami. Here you'll find pretty banyan-lined streets and a walkable village-like center so lush and pedestrian-friendly that it's easy to linger for hours, soaking it all in. Much of the Gables is defined by unique urban planning and aesthetics, reminiscent of an old Mediterranean village. Boutiques, cafes and upscale eateries are scattered along (and near) the so-called Miracle Mile.

Coconut Grove was once a hippie colony, but these days its demographic is boat-loving Miamians (this is Miami's sailing capital, after all) alongside laid-back college students and wealthy residents, making for a fun mix. It's a compact place with intriguing shops and cafes, and is particularly appealing in the evenings when residents fill outdoor tables at its many bars and restaurants. The Grove backs onto the water, so you're never far from those salt-and-skyline breezes that make Miami so magical.

Botanical Legacy

Bask in the Fairchild Tropical Botanic Garden

A true natural jewel of Coral Gables, **Fairchild Tropical Botanic Garden** (*fairchildgarden.org; adult/child $25/12*) is one of America's great tropical botanical gardens, and you'll want to devote at least a morning to enjoying it. A butterfly grove, a tropical-plant conservatory and gentle vistas of marsh and keys habitats, plus frequent art installations from artists such as Roy Lichtenstein, all contribute to the beauty of this peaceful, 83-acre garden.

The garden was founded in 1936 by businessman and tropical plant aficionado Robert Montgomery, and named for explorer and scientist David Fairchild, who played a pivotal role in the garden's creation. He donated many of the plants, including the large African baobab growing by the gatehouse. He also went on official plant-collecting expeditions for the

MARIAKRAY/SHUTTERSTOCK

Fairchild Tropical Botanic Garden

garden, sailing a Chinese junk around the Indonesian archipelago just before the outbreak of WWII.

At **Wings of the Tropics**, hundreds of butterflies flutter freely through the air, the sheen of their wings glinting in the light. One behind-the-scenes highlight is the **Vollmer Metamorphosis Lab** where visitors can watch in real time as butterflies emerge from chrysalises. The butterflies are then released into the Wings of the Tropics exhibit several times a day.

Amid the lushly lined pathways of the **Tropical Plant Conservatory** and the **Rare Plant House** is a glass sculpture with colorful tendrils unfurling skyward like flickering flames. Created by American artist Dale Chihuly, the **End of Day Tower** sits in a small pond, with African cichlids swimming about the base of the sculpture.

Beauty at the Biltmore

Take a free tour of a grande dame

In the most opulent neighborhood of one of the showiest cities in the world, Coral Gables' **Biltmore Hotel** (p105) *(biltmorehotel. com)* has a classic beauty that seems impervious to the passage of years. Sure, you could book a room at the hotel to fully bask in its beauty. Or you could save some pennies and reserve a spot on one of the free tours of this National
continued on p90

☑**TOP TIP**

Want to soak up local life? The **Coconut Grove Saturday Organic Farmers Market**, held every Saturday from 10am to 7pm at the corner of Grand Ave and Margaret St, is the spot to load up on seasonal and pesticide-free fruits, exotic durian and jaboticaba, vegan foods, organic breads and more.

🍸 DRINKING IN CORAL GABLES & COCONUT GROVE: OUR PICKS

Taurus: Cool mix of wood paneling, smoky-leather chairs, about 100 beers to choose from and a convivial vibe. *5pm-3am*

Titanic: Brewpub near the University of Miami that's bound to be going off any night of the week. Daily happy hour specials. *11.30am-midnight Sun-Thu, 11.30-1am Fri & Sat*

Seven Seas: Nautical-themed neighborhood dive in Coral Gables where you're sure to rub shoulders with many walks of life. *noon-3am*

Monty's: Raw bar and tiki hut alongside the marina, with a happy hour that reels in salty dogs and more buttoned-up types. *11.30am-10pm*

CORAL GABLES & COCONUT GROVE

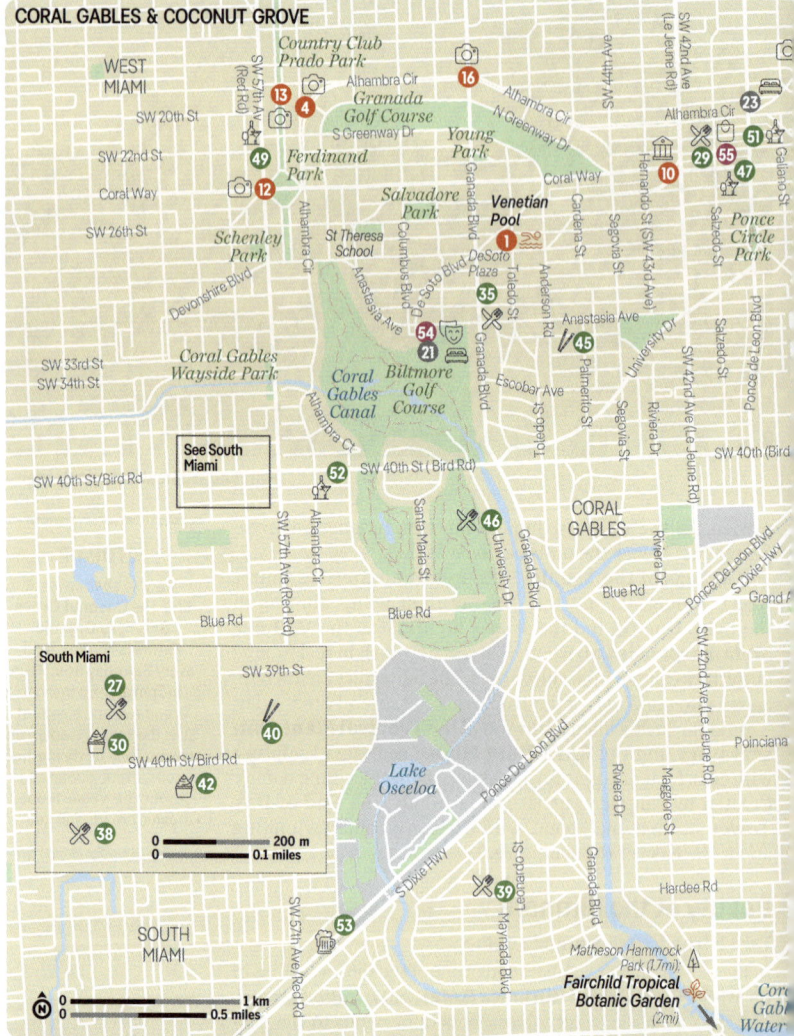

WEST
MIAMI

SW 20th St

SW 22nd St

Coral Way

SW 26th St

Country Club
Prado Park

Alhambra Cir

Granada
Golf Course

S Greenway Dr

Ferdinand
Park

Young
Park

Alhambra Cir

N Greenway Dr

Coral Way

Venetian
Pool

Schenley
Park

St Theresa
School

Salvadore
Park

DeSoto
Plaza

Ponce
Circle
Park

Coral Gables
Wayside Park

SW 33rd St
SW 34th St

See South
Miami

Coral
Gables
Canal

Biltmore
Golf
Course

Coral
Gables
Canal

SW 40th St/Bird Rd

Devonshire Blvd

SW 40th St (Bird Rd)

CORAL
GABLES

Blue Rd

Blue Rd

Blue Rd

SW 40th (Bird

Grand A

South Miami

SW 39th St

SW 40th St/Bird Rd

Lake
Osceloa

Polinciana

200 m
0.1 miles

SOUTH
MIAMI

Hardee Rd

1 km
0.5 miles

Matheson Hammock
Park (1.7mi)

Fairchild Tropical
Botanic Garden
(2mi)

Core
Gabl
Water

HIGHLIGHTS
1 Venetian Pool
2 Vizcaya House &
Gardens

SIGHTS
3 Alhambra Entrance
4 Alhambra Water Tower
5 Barnacle Historic
State Park
6 Biscayne Bay Yacht
Club

7 Biscayne National
Park Institute
8 Coconut Grove
Library
9 Coconut Grove
Sailing Club
10 Coral Gables City
Hall
11 Coral Reef Yacht
Club
12 Coral Way Entrance

13 Country Club Prado
14 Dinner Key Marina
15 Ermita de la Caridad
16 Granada Entrance
17 Kampong
18 Peacock Park
19 Plymouth
Congregational Church
20 U.S. Olympic Sailing
Center

SLEEPING
21 Biltmore Hotel
22 Hotel Arya
23 Hotel St Michel
24 Mr C
25 Mutiny Hotel

EATING
26 Ariete
27 Bachour
28 Barracuda Taphouse
& Grill

Coconut Grove

Grand Ave

Thomas Ave

William Ave

Charles Ave

Franklin Ave

0 _____ 200 m
0 _____ 0.1 miles

Commodore Plaza

Fuller St

McFarlane Rd

Peacock Park

Barnacle Historic State Park

Via Abitare Way

Munroe Dr

SW 12th Ave

Bill Baggs Cape Florida State Park (8mi); The Cleat (8mi)

S Bayshore Dr

Vizcaya House & Gardens

S Miami Ave

Biscayne Bay

uglas rk

SW 27th Tce

SW 27th La
SW 28th St

Coconut Ave

S Dixie Hwy

SW 30th St (Bird Ave)

McDonald St

Day Ave

Day Ave

Kirk Monroe Park

Calusa St
Lucaya St
Jefferson St
Washington St
Aviation Ave
S Miami Ave

Kennedy Park

S Miami Ave

SW 27th Ave
Main Hwy

Myres Bayside Park

Dinner Key Marina

See Coconut Grove

Peacock Park

Main Hwy

etery

Biscayne Bay

OCONUT GROVE

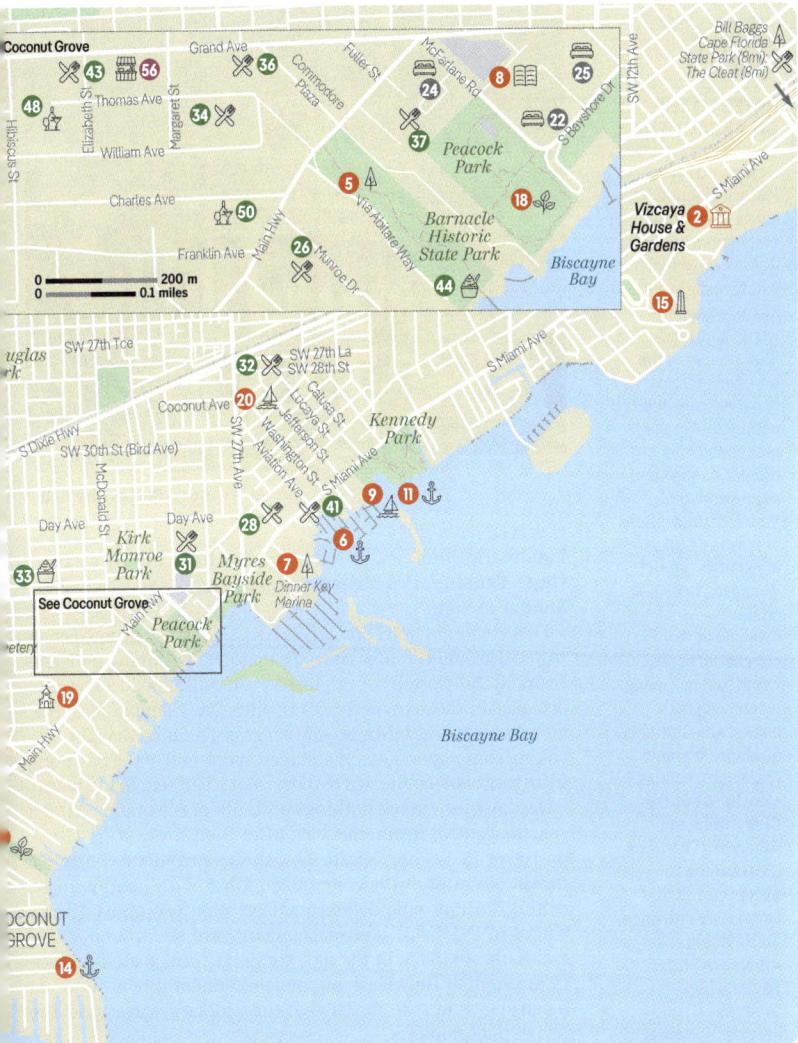

29 Caffe Abbracci
30 Chocolate Fashion
31 Chug's Diner
32 Coral Bagels
33 Danielle Gelato
34 Fireman Derek's Bake Shop
35 L'Artisane Bakery & Bistro

36 LoKal
37 Los Félix
38 Luca Osteria
39 Madruga Bakery
40 Matsuri
41 Monty's Raw Bar
42 Morelia las Paletas
43 PLANTA Queen
44 Salt & Straw
45 Shingo

46 Threefold Cafe

DRINKING & NIGHTLIFE
47 Copper 29
48 Happy Wine in the Grove
49 Seven Seas
50 Taurus
51 The Bar
52 The Globe

53 Titanic Brewing Company

ENTERTAINMENT
54 GableStage

SHOPPING
55 Books & Books
56 Coconut Grove Saturday Organic Farmers Market

FOTOLUMINATE LLC/SHUTTERSTOCK

Designer George Merrick planned a series of elaborate entry gates to Coral Gables, but a real estate bust meant many projects went unfinished. It's a shame, as the gorgeous Gables deserves over-the-top entrances. On the other hand, the project's unfinished nature adds a timeless atmosphere, or maybe speaks to humanity's hubris? Whatever, they look cool.

Among the completed gates worth seeing – many resembling and named after entrance pavilions to grand Andalusian estates – are the **Country Club Prado**, the **Alhambra Entrance**, the **Granada Entrance** and the **Coral Way Entrance**. Also notable is the **Alhambra Water Tower**, where Greenway Ct and Ferdinand St meet Alhambra Circle, which resembles a Moorish lighthouse.

Coral Gables City Hall

continued from p87

Landmark Hotel. Tours, led by guides from the **Dade Heritage Trust** *(dadeheritagetrust.org; free),* take place every Sunday at 2pm.

This elaborate hotel spreads across 150 acres encompassing tropical grounds, tennis courts, a massive swimming pool and restored 18-hole golf course. Inside, you could spend a few days occupied by the many activities on offer. One example: local theater company **GableStage** *(gablestage.org)* puts on thought-provoking contemporary works, staged at one end of the Biltmore, in an intimate setting where there's not a bad seat in the house.

Design-wise, there's nothing subtle about the grande dame's soaring central tower, modeled after the 12th-century Giralda tower in Seville, Spain. The showy grandeur continues inside, starting in the colonnaded lobby with hand-painted ceiling, antique chandeliers and Corinthian columns. It continues in the lushly landscaped courtyard set around a central fountain. Back in the day, gondolas transported celebrity guests like Judy Garland and the Vanderbilts around via a private canal system. Though the waterways are gone, the lavish pool remains.

Are there ghosts? The mobster Thomas 'Fatty' Walsh was gunned down by another gangster on the 13th floor and some say his spirit still roams the hallways.

EATING IN CORAL GABLES & COCONUT GROVE: LOCAL FAVES

Coral Bagels: They are bagels, and they are cheap, and they are also very, very good at this family-owned shop. *7am-3pm* $

PLANTA Queen: This bright, beautiful queen is a vegan's dream, serving plant-based Asian-inspired fare. *hours vary* $$

Matsuri: Miami doesn't want for trendy sushi spots, but this strip mall hideaway trades in the real deal. *hours vary* $$

Threefold Cafe: Cheerful cafe with Down Under vibes, strong espresso drinks, divine eggs Benedict and a memorable salmon salad. *7.30am-3pm Mon-Thu, to 4pm Fri-Sun* $$

Dip into Coral Gables' Historic Wonder

Frolic in the Venetian Pool

There are pools and then there are *pools*, and you can leave it to Miami to serve up the latter on a silver platter. The Mediterranean Revival-style **Venetian Pool** (*coralgables.com/ attractions/venetian-pool; adult/child $22/17*), reopening in May 2025 following renovations, is one of the very few swimming pools listed on the National Register of Historic Places.

We need to emphasize what a palatial, over-the-top swimming experience this is: a wonderland of rock caves, cascading waterfalls, a palm-fringed island and Venetian-style moorings. If Miami – and, particularly, Mediterranean Coral Gables – could morph itself into a swimming space, this would be it. Plan to spend a morning or afternoon (or even an hour, if that's all you can squeeze in) swimming, lounging around and following in the footsteps of stars like Esther Williams and Johnny 'Tarzan' Weissmuller to name some of the many celebrities who've waded in here.

Back in 1923, rock was quarried for the completion of Coral Gables, leaving an ugly gash – a sort of nasty scar to balance out the 'City Beautiful.' Of course, if you're the sort of urban planner who is going to develop a place you nickname 'City Beautiful', you're not going to let a pit like that remain. Cleverly, it was laden with mosaic and tiles, and filled up with water. Back in the day, actual gondolas plied the water, and every now and then the pool would get drained so the Miami Symphony Orchestra could perform and take advantage of the natural acoustics.

The orchestra doesn't perform anymore and the gondolas are gone, but the Venetian Pool still looks like a Roman emperor's aquatic playground (there's even a grotto that stretches 12ft deep). The water ranges in depth from 4ft to a bit over 8ft, and there's a 2ft-shallow kiddie area.

Bureaucracy with Style

Iberian-Mediterranean romance at City Hall

It's a little funny to think of the often tedious grind of city council business being conducted in a building as grand as the **Coral Gables City Hall** (*coralgables.com; free*). It was built largely from local limestone and opened in 1928. And, architecturally at least, the building suggests romance and power as opposed to parking ordinances and other bureaucratic bits and bobs.

That's precisely the idea, though: the Corinthian colonnade, stucco exterior and central clock tower are all meant to evoke

GHOSTS OF THE PAST

Completed in 1963, the photogenic **Coconut Grove Library** (*mdpls. org/branch-coconut-grove; free*) has limestone walls and a steep roof paying homage to the original 1901 library that stood here. Inside, there's a small, well-curated reference section on South Florida.

Tucked into a small gated area nearby, you'll find the humble headstone of **Eva Munroe**. Eva, who died in Miami in 1882, lies in the oldest American grave in Miami-Dade County (a sad addendum: local African American settlers died before Eva, but their deaths were never officially recorded). Eva's husband Ralph entered a depression, which he tried to alleviate by building The Barnacle, now one of the oldest homes in the area.

EATING IN CORAL GABLES & COCONUT GROVE: BEST BAKERIES

L'Artisane Bakery & Bistro: Come for French-style pastries, quiche and sinfully good Biscoff cookie butter croissants. *hours vary* $

Bachour: Pastries almost too beautiful to pick apart and eat delight the senses at this industrial-aesthetic bakery. *7am-7pm* $

Madruga Bakery: Come for craft breads made with just three ingredients (water, flour and salt), divine chocolate or hazelnut croissants. *hours vary* $

Fireman Derek's Bake Shop: Killer key lime pie, coconut guava rum cake, empanadas and more sugar tooth types to the Grove. *hours vary* $

BOOKSTORE NE PLUS ULTRA

The most renowned indie bookstore in South Florida has branches across town, but the Coral Gables outpost of **Books & Books** (booksandbooks.com) is its flagship and a special sort of place. Think of the images that spring to mind when you imagine a wonderful old library, then place that temple of literature in the tropics and wash it with golden Miami sunshine. We're not the only ones taken with this brick and mortar temple to all things paper and ink; it feels like every writer who ever visited Florida trots across the store's stage. Books & Books was founded by Mitchell Kaplan, a teacher-turned-founder of **Miami Book Fair International** (miamibookfair.com), an event that has no small presence at this store.

the grace of Iberian-Mediterranean design. Wander around City Hall to admire design influences from a swirl of cultures, among them Italian, Spanish, French, Arabian and Moorish. Check out Denman Fink's *Four Seasons* ceiling painting in the tower, as well as his framed, untitled painting of the underwater world on the 2nd-floor landing. The Coral Gables City Hall is open weekdays only, from 8am to 5pm.

The Magic City's Magic Mansion

Go full golden age at Vizcaya

Back in 1916, industrialist James Deering started a Miami tradition of making a ton of money and building ridiculously grandiose digs. He employed 1000 people (then 10% of the local population) and stuffed his home with Renaissance furniture, tapestries, paintings and decorative arts.

You'll want at least a few hours to see all there is to see at **Vizcaya Museum & Gardens** (*vizcaya.org; adult/child $25/10*; p102). The Coconut Grove mansion fronts Biscayne Bay and is a classic of Miami's Mediterranean Revival style. The largest room is the informal living room, sometimes dubbed 'Renaissance Hall' for its works dating from the 14th to 17th centuries. The music room is intriguing for its beautiful wall canvases from northern Italy, while the banquet hall's regal furnishings evoke the grandeur of European imperial dining rooms. On the south side of the house, a series of gardens modeled on the formal Italian gardens of the 17th and 18th centuries form a counterpoint to the wild mangroves beyond. Sculptures, fountains and vine-draped surfaces give an antiquarian look to the grounds, and an elevated **Garden Mound** terrace provides a fine vantage point over the greenery. You can access a very informative and free audio tour by downloading the Vizcaya app on your phone.

A Date with a Higher Power

Admire a Mission-style church

Originally founded in 1897 as the small Union Chapel, the **Plymouth Congregational Church** in Coconut Grove is one of the most striking houses of worship in Miami. The current structure, built in 1917, has solid masonry and a hand-carved door from a Pyrenees monastery that looks like it should be kicked in by Antonio Banderas carrying a guitar case full of explosives and with Salma Hayek on his arm. That's all to say: even in a city blessed with many fine Spanish Mission-style churches, architecturally this is an exceptional example. The

EATING IN CORAL GABLES & COCONUT GROVE: OUR PICKS

LoKal: Hits the spot when you just want a damn good craft beer and burger in a good-vibes-only setting. *11.30am-10pm Sun-Wed, to 11pm Thu-Sat* $

Chug's Diner: Mix an American diner and a Cuban cafeteria and you've got Chug's, serving things like short rib *boliche* (pot roast) and cast iron pancakes. *hours vary* $$

Barracuda Taphouse & Grill: You'll never go wrong with a snapper or grouper sandwich at this beloved spot in the Grove that stays true to its original, rustic roots. *hours vary* $$

Caffe Abbracci: Fine Italian outpost offering delicious pasta, seafood and meat dishes in an upscale sidewalk cafe setting in Coral Gables. *hours vary* $$$

Vizcaya Museum & Gardens

church opens rarely, though all (and truly 'all' – this is an LGBTQ+ friendly congregation) are welcome at the organ- and choir-led service on Sunday at 10am.

Channel Your Inner Salty Dog

Hit the water in Miami's sailing capital

Many a salty dog has set sail from Coconut Grove, aka 'the sail- ing capital of Miami,' for waypoints in the Caribbean and well, well beyond. To feel the wind in your virtual sails, and per- haps spark a desire to get out on the water here, all it takes is a stroll around sail-centric spots clustered here: **Biscayne Bay Yacht Club**, Coconut Grove Sailing Club, **Coral Reef Yacht Club** and the **US Olympic Sailing Center** among them.

To snorkel patch reefs and shipwrecks within **Biscayne Na- tional Park**, consider setting sail on guided tours aboard pon- toon boats with the **Biscayne National Park Institute** (*biscayne nationalparkinstitute.org; variable*) from **Dinner Key Mari- na** in Coconut Grove. Other boat trips on offer include historic tours to **Boca Chita Key**, just offshore, and **Stiltsville** (p71).

You can sign up for sailing lessons with the **Coconut Grove Sailing Club** (*cgsc.org; one-day Sunfish sailing courses from $325 per person*) or paddle out for more basic fun by renting a kay- ak or paddleboard from the self-service rental ststions at **PADL** (*padl.co; from $25/hr*) in the Grove's **Peacock Park** (p95).

A CHURCH WITH TIES TO THE ISLA

The Catholic diocese purchased some bayfront land from Deering's Villa Vizcaya estate and built a shrine here for its displaced Cuban parishioners. Built in 1967, **Ermita de la Caridad** is a beacon, facing the homeland, 290 miles due south, as well as a lighthouse for those Miamians who long for a land they may never have visited. This isn't the only way this church – full title: Santuario Nacional de Nuestra Señora de la Caridad – engages with Cuba. A mural depicts the island's history and a Spanish-language presence is the norm for the congregation. Outside the church is a grassy stretch of waterfront that makes a fine picnic spot.

DRINKING IN CORAL GABLES & COCONUT GROVE: LOCAL SPOTS

The Bar: With a name like The Bar, you can count on this spot to be divey, laid-back and big on cold brews and burgers. Very affordable too. *3pm-3am*

Copper 29: Retro Coral Gables gastropub on the Miracle Mile, with DJs, craft cocktails and bottle service for those who wouldn't have it any other way. *hours vary*

The Globe: A lively bar, Euro-cafe undertones and Saturday night live jazz make The Globe a perennial pick. *hours vary*

Happy Wine in the Grove: Happy hour tapas at this convivial neighborhood spot go down even better when you have hundreds of wine labels on offer. *hours vary*

WHY I LOVE KEY BISCAYNE

Terry Ward, Lonely Planet writer

It's impossible not to get swept up in the rush of a thrilling night out or simply awed by another over-the-top hotel lobby in Miami. But sometimes I really just crave a reset from it all in the form of ocean breezes and a something more chill. So I cross the Rickenbacker Causeway from downtown Miami to Virginia Key and Key Biscayne for a beach day at **Bill Baggs Cape Florida State Park** (p103). Come sunset something frosty in hand and a bowl of smoked fish dip on the table is all I need at **The Cleat** (p103), my favorite beach bar in all of Florida (it's actually located inside the state park, fronting a gorgeous little stretch of No Name Harbor).

Peacock Park

Shake-A-Leg Miami is a noble and civic-minded water sports center that provides activities for people with physical, developmental and financial challenges.

Beyond-Beautiful Backyards

Two gardens of wonders

In between journeys all over the world seeking beautiful and profitable plant life, David Fairchild – the Indiana Jones of the botanical world and namesake of Coral Gables' **Fairchild Tropical Botanic Garden** (p86) – would rest and relax at his winter residence, Kampong, on the shores of Biscayne Bay in Coconut Grove.

As a pioneer of tropical botany, Fairchild was no slouch when it came to his own tropical backyard back home in Miami. He bought **Kampong** *(ntbg.org; self-guided/guided tour $7/27)* meaning 'village' in Malay or Indonesian, with his wife and the couple played host to guests like Thomas Edison, Henry Ford and Dwight Eisenhower. Today the house and its lush gardens are listed on the National Register of Historic Places, while the fecund grounds serve as a classroom for the National Tropical Botanical Garden. Both self-guided and guided tours are by appointment. Keep an eye out for the peanut butter fruit (a real thing!), the ylang-ylang flower and jackfruits (the trees and the actual fruit).

EATING IN CORAL GABLES & COCONUT GROVE: SWEET TREATS

Danielle Gelato: Artisan gelato tempts your tastebuds. Pistachio, passion fruit and other flavors. *noon-11pm Sun-Thu, to midnight Fri & Sat* $

Salt & Straw: Small-batch ice creams with lots of vegan offerings. Don't miss the Freckled Mint Chocolate Chip. *noon-midnight Mon-Fri, from 11am Sat & Sun* $

Morelia Ice Cream Paletas: With outposts in the Grove and Gables, this local chain's gourmet pops are kosher and made with natural ingredients. *hours vary* $

Chocolate Fashion: Treat yourself to macarons, tiramisu cake, tarts and more at this artisanal Coral Gables bakery. *7am-3pm Mon-Sat, from 8am Sun* $

Bayfront History & Fresh Air

Kick it in the Grove's Urban Park

City parks always provide a window into the true pulse of a neighborhood, and Coconut Grove's beloved **Peacock Park** (*miami.gov; free*) is no exception. Extending to the edge of Biscayne Bay and open from 7am to 10pm, it serves as the great open backyard of Coconut Grove. Young families stop by the playground and join the action on the ball fields, and power-walkers take in the view while striding along the waterfront. The boardwalk trail by the bay offers some of the cleanest, most peaceful views of Biscayne Bay on the mainland side.

What's in a name? You'd think gaudy birds roamed the grounds, but no. This 9-acre plot of land was once the site of the Bayview Inn, owned by Charles and Isabella Peacock (she later renamed the hotel to the Peacock Inn). The Peacocks employed Bahamian workers, who came from the Bahamas via Key West to Miami, and they proceeded to form the core of the oldest black community in Miami. The knowledge those workers brought with them to this corner of Miami from the islands – about tropical plants, agriculture, building in this environment and beyond – turned out to be essential to the development of Coconut Grove.

The County's Oldest Residence

Tour Barnacle Historic State Park

In the center of Coconut Grove village is Miami-Dade County's oldest residence – the former home of pioneer Ralph Munroe, Miami's first honorable snowbird. The house, built in 1891 in **Barnacle Historic State Park** (*thebarnacle.org; $2*), is open for guided tours several times a day (the only way to actually enter inside for a look) and you can picnic in its grounds. The 5-acre park, which Munroe originally bought for $400 after moving to South Florida from New York, sits in a shady oasis that's ideal for strolling and is a great spot to let the kids run off some energy.

The Barnacle's name comes from its irregularly shaped rooms, including one in the form of an octagon. Its engineering is quite interesting too. Munroe got his design inspiration from traditional Caribbean home construction and elements of boat design. Considering the property has so far withstood storms like Hurricane Andrew, it's safe to say the man knew what he was doing. The Barnacle hosts frequent events, from sailing regattas to yoga classes and moonlight concerts, usually featuring jazz or classical music. As far as outdoor venues for this sort of chilled-out music go, this place is just a chef's kiss.

A PARK WITH AN ATOLL

The first park in Dade County and thus Miami's oldest park, **Matheson Hammock Park** is a green dream: 630 acres of hungry raccoons, fragrant lawns, banyan trees, palms, dense mangrove swamps, a marina with sailing school and (pretty rare) alligator-spotting, all just south of Coral Gables. The park originally opened in 1930 after a land donation from the Matheson family of 85 acres of tropical hardwood hammock forest.

Besides the gorgeous trees and landscaping to admire here, keep an eye out for a human-made atoll pool, which rises and falls with the tide of nearby Biscayne Bay. It's a popular swimming hole for local families and a lovely place to refresh on a hot Miami day.

EATING IN CORAL GABLES & COCONUT GROVE: WORTHY SPLURGES

Shingo: Omakase spot in Coral Gables with just 14 seats. Almost all the fish is fresh from Japan. *6-11pm Tue-Sat* $$$

Ariete: Michelin star-recipient in the Grove, merging Latin traditions, French techniques and South Florida ingredients. *5.30-11pm* $$$

Los Félix: The maiz is ground daily at this Coconut Grove Mexican spot where indigenous traditions inspire the menu. *hours vary* $$$

Luca Osteria: A Chopped winner helms this Italian restaurant, known for pasta and negronis, in a pedestrian zone of Coral Gables. *hours vary* $$$

Greater Miami

CULTURAL NEIGHBORHOODS AND ISLAND ESCAPES

GETTING AROUND

You're best off renting a car or using taxis or rideshares to cover the most ground across Greater Miami's southern and northern reaches. A car is also the best way to get around Key Biscayne, although you can reach the barrier island from the Brickell Metrorail/Metromover station along the Rickenbacker Causeway and Crandon Boulevard. Should you prefer to explore Key Biscayne on two wheels, rent a bike inside Crandon Park.

☑TOP TIP

If you're into auto racing, don't miss being here for the electric atmosphere of the **Formula 1 Miami Grand Prix**, held at the Miami International Autodrome in Miami Gardens in May (with a 10-year contract with the city that runs through the 2031 event).

Little Haiti and the Upper East Side are at the northern edge of mainland Miami. Little Haiti is North America's largest Haitian community, and while it feels as Caribbean as the rest of Miami, it is also undeniably distinct: the kreyòl language dominates, as do Haitian businesses and community institutions. Further east, the Upper East Side is best known for the so-called 'MiMo on Bibo' or Miami Modern on Biscayne Blvd – a spread of photogenic buildings running from 50th St to 77th St. Just west, up-and-coming Little River has gone from former warehouse district to still-unpretentious neighborhood brimming with culture and art.

To the south, Key Biscayne and neighboring Virginia Key – easy getaways from Downtown Miami – boast magnificent beaches, lush nature trails in state parks and aquatic adventure. Sights are spread along two islands, with one of the biggest highlights, the Bill Baggs Cape Florida State Park, anchoring the south end of Key Biscayne.

Architecture, Art & Urban Oases   MAP P97

Upper East Side surprises

Northeast of Wynwood, the Upper East Side is stuffed with creative shops, art studios and cafes, many of which have opened in the past few years. There are plenty of pleasant surprises here, from mid-20th-century architecture to cutting-edge arts collectives.

An icon in the **MiMo Biscayne Boulevard Historic District**, the **Vagabond Hotel** (p105) is a 1953 motel and restaurant where Frank Sinatra, Sammy David Jr, Dean Martin and other Rat Packers hung out in the 1950s. Today it's been reborn as a boutique hotel, and has lost none of its allure. It also has a great bar, and the seafood and mezcal restaurant Ensenada which dishes up delicious raw fish dishes from south of the border like *aguachiles* (raw fish or shrimp marinated in citrus and chilis) and ceviche.

GREATER MIAMI NORTH

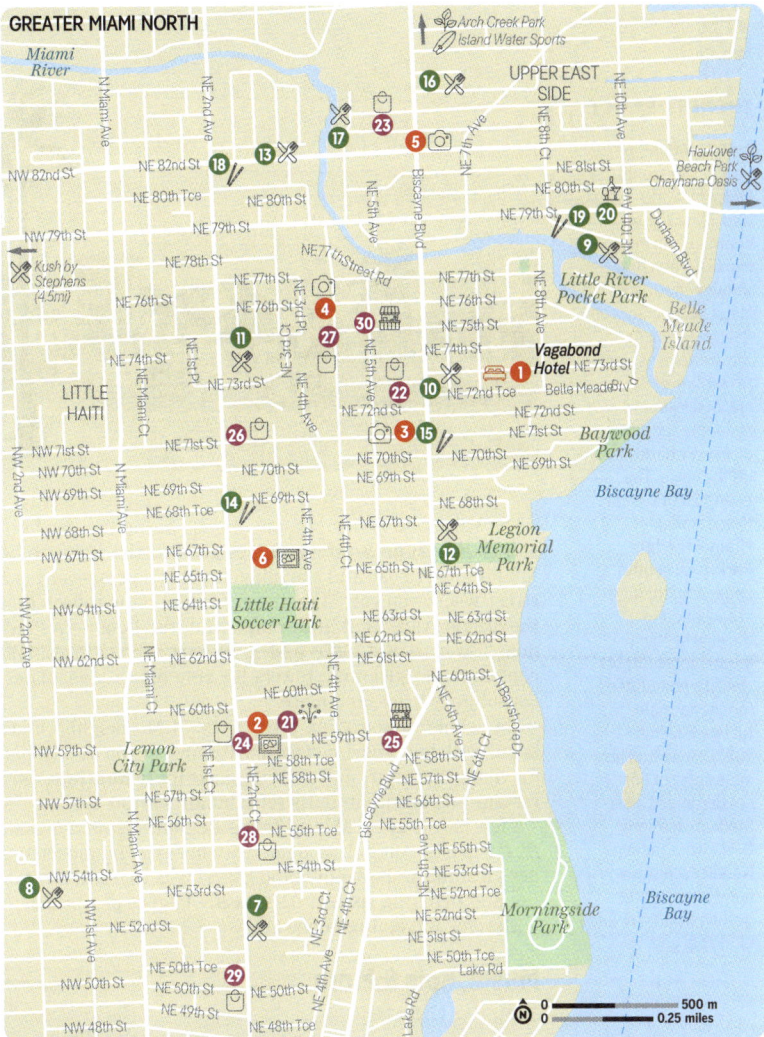

Arch Creek Park
Island Water Sports

UPPER EAST SIDE

Miami River

Haulover Beach Park
Chayhana Oasis

Kush by Stephens (4.5mi)

LITTLE HAITI

Little River Pocket Park

Vagabond Hotel

Belle Meade Island

Baywood Park

Biscayne Bay

Legion Memorial Park

Little Haiti Soccer Park

Lemon City Park

Biscayne Bay

Morningside Park
Lake Rd

0   500 m
0   0.25 miles

HIGHLIGHTS

1 Vagabond Hotel

SIGHTS

2 Little Haiti Cultural Complex
3 Little River
4 Miami Ironside
5 MiMo Biscayne Boulevard Historic District
6 Pan American Art Projects

EATING

7 Boia De
8 Chef Creole
9 Half Moon Empanadas
10 Jimmy's Eastside Diner
11 La Natural
12 Legion Park Farmers Market
13 Magie
14 Ogawa

15 Phuc Yea
16 Pinch Kitchen+Bar
17 The Citadel
18 Tran An
19 Wabi Sabi

DRINKING & NIGHTLIFE

20 Boteco

ENTERTAINMENT

21 Sounds of Little Haiti

SHOPPING

22 éliou
23 Fly Boutique
24 Libreri Mapou
25 Mache Ayisyen
26 Mids Market
27 Rose Coloured
28 Sweat Records
29 Upper Buena Vista
30 Walter's Mercado

OLGA V KULAKOVA/SHUTTERSTOCK

THE MESSI EFFECT

In 2023, Argentine soccer star Lionel Messi of World Cup-fame signed a contract with Inter Miami CF that runs through the 2025 Major League Soccer (MLS) season. And the excitement – not to mention pink and black jerseys suddenly sprouting up everywhere – was off the scale. The team's 25,000-seat Miami stadium, **Miami Freedom Park**, is currently under construction in a location to the east of Miami International Airport. Until it's completed (projections are for late 2025 or 2026), Messi and his mates play at Fort Lauderdale's Chase Stadium, formerly DRV PINK Stadium. Needless to say, you'll need some *suerte* getting tickets for any of the big games.

The Vagabond is one of many motels lining the northern end of **Biscayne Boulevard**, designed in the 1920s to be Miami's most beautiful shopping street. The boulevard is a street where you can Miami's very evolution is reflected in the architecture. Buildings range from the Boom-era Freedom Tower to mid-1930s and 1940s' art deco edifices, and contemporary gleaming towers housing offices, consulates, consultancy firms, and more.

The whole surrounding area of the MiMo neighborhood brims with boutiques, consignment shops (if you hit just one for vintage furniture and clothing, make it **Fly Boutique**) and restaurants inside similarly retro buildings, too.

A few blocks away, **Miami Ironside** (*miamiironside.com; free*) is a pleasant hub of creativity where you'll find art and design studios, showrooms and galleries as well as a few eating and drinking spaces. It's a lushly landscaped property, with some intriguing public art.

Music, Epis & More
MAP P97

Exploring Little Haiti

Little Haiti has been a major nexus of the Haitian diaspora since the late 1970s. Within the neighborhood, the **Little Haiti Cultural Center** (*miami.gov; free*) serves as both a cornerstone and an access point for outsiders. It hosts an art gallery

---

🍴 EATING IN LITTLE RIVER: OUR PICKS
MAP P97

La Natural: Come for natural wines and wood-fired pizza, served in a gorgeous tropical garden. *hours vary* **$$**	**Tran An:** Delicious pho, banh mi and bún chà are the menu at this stylish Vietnamese spot. *11.30am-9pm Tue-Thu, to 10pm Fri-Mon* **$$**	**Magie:** Low-key wine bar goes big on *vino* from Spain, Portugal and Italy, with charcuterie and other small plates. *4pm-1am Thu-Sun, to 11.30pm Wed* **$$**	**Ogawa:** Swanky 12-seater for outrageously good sushi and small plates. *6pm-9pm Tue-Sat* **$$$**

Vagabond, Biscayne Boulevard

with thought-provoking exhibitions from Haitian painters, sculptors and multimedia artists. You can also find dance classes, drama productions and a Caribbean-themed market (that's where you might find *epis* – the traditional Haitian seasoning base made from peppers, garlic and herbs, that's an essential ingredient in most Haitian cuisine). The building itself is a confection of bold tropical colors, steep A-framed roofs and lacy decorative elements. Next door is the Caribbean Marketplace or **Mache Ayisyen**, a 9000-sq-ft venue that replicates the Iron Market in Haitian capital Port Au Prince. It's a lively place to browse Haitian arts and crafts and try goat dishes from the island.

Little Haiti is a sprawling neighborhood where street crime is a concern. If you're looking to visit the neighborhood, it's easy enough to start at the Cultural Center and Mache Ayisyen. Probably the best time to visit that space is during the **Sounds of Little Haiti**, a music- and food-filled fête held on the third Friday of every month from 6pm to 10pm. The celebration is rife with music, Caribbean food and kids' activities.

EATING IN LITTLE HAITI & THE UPPER EAST SIDE: OUR PICKS ——— MAP P97

Jimmy's Eastside Diner: A classic greasy spoon that's excellent for big breakfasts, or burgers and such later in the day. 7am-3.30pm **$**	**Chef Creole:** Delicious Caribbean food. Head here for stewed conch, fried pork and oxtail. 11am-9pm Mon-Wed, to 10pm Thu-Sat **$**	**Half Moon Empanadas:** Walk-up window hawking Argentine-style empanadas. 7am-11pm **$**	**Boteco:** Miami's Brazilian community comes out for live shows, caipirinhas and snacks. *noon-midnight Mon-Thu, to 2am Fri & Sat* **$$**
Wabi Sabi: Donburi, poke bowls, sushi and temaki are on the menu at this authentic Japanese spot. *noon-3pm & 6-9.30pm Tue-Sat* **$$**	**Pinch Kitchen+Bar:** Great for burgers and Spanish-inspired shared plates like *croquetas*, *gambas al ajillo* (shrimp with garlic). *hours vary* **$$**	**Boia De:** Ridiculously tasty, contemporary Italian fare cooked and served by a punk-rock crew. 5.30-10.30pm **$$**	**Phuc Yea:** A little Latin, a little Cajun, a lot Vietnamese and always delicious. hours vary **$$$**

Another can't miss in the neighborhood is **Pan American Art Projects** (panamericanart.com; free). Formerly in Wynwood, PAAP made the move up to Little Haiti in 2016 – a growing trend as gallerists were priced out of the neighborhood they helped popularize. Inside the space, you'll find excellent contemporary work by emerging and established artists.

Sweat, Books & Banyans   MAP P97

Shopping with true place

A few businesses – some at the edge of Little Haiti, and one in the heart of the neighborhood – speak to the roots of the neighborhood, and the rapidly changing cityscape of the Upper East Side.

Sweat Records (sweatrecordsmiami.com) might feel like a new kid on the block, but it's been in Little Haiti for well over a decade. This is almost a stereotypical indie record store – there's funky art and graffiti on the walls, tattooed staff arguing over LPs and EPs you've never heard of, and a general air of vigorous musical knowledge married to iconoclastic hipness. It's great.

Libreri Mapou (mapoubooks.com) is arguably the center of literary life in Little Haiti. This bookstore specializes in English, French and Creole titles and periodicals, and features thousands of great titles and literary events. The owner, Jan Mapou, is a writer and political thinker of some distinction.

As for the newer gentrification game, it's hard to get fancier, or more beautiful, than **Upper Buena Vista** (upperbuenavista. com). We've never thought we could describe a mall as being 'banyan-chic,' yet that is the vibe here: enormous trees shade a series of outdoor shopping kiosks linked by pleasant breezeways. It's downright, dare we say, cozy. The retailers are all local boutique-level vendors, mainly selling clothes, home goods and jewelry, too. An utterly lovely, alfresco place to while away some relaxed retail hours.

Little River on the Rise   MAP P97

Warehouse district gone hip

There's always a new neighborhood on the make in Miami. And the cool kid du jour is **Little River** – a former warehouse district-turned-buzzy neighborhood bordered to the south by Little Haiti that takes its name from the river streaming through its northern reaches. Spend a morning or afternoon (then stay for lunch or dinner), browsing boutiques like **éliou** (eliou.com) for creative jewelry, popping into food and fashion market **Walter's Mercado**, and feasting on global cuisines at the marketplace-food hall **The Citadel**.

Secondhand hounds should check out **Mids Market** (midsmarket.com) for bargain basement finds; there's even a 'rework station' here where you can get creative with embellishments for your purchases. At the inspiring and women-led floral design studio **Rose Coloured** (rosecolouredfloral.com), cobble together your own affordable and unique-in-the-world bouquet to bring home (or better yet, gift to a an unsuspecting stranger).

Legion Park

Grab a Picnic

MAP P97

Park and market with soul

Hungering to eat alfresco? Picnic lovers rejoice, and stop by **Legion Park** for a bustling **local farmers' market** *(facebook .com/LegionParkFarmersMarket)*. Held every Saturday from 9am to 2pm, it strikes a balance between representing neighborhood old-timers and fresh-faced newcomers. It's got all the produce (especially tropical fruits), cheese and breads you'd need for a good picnic. As with most markets of this ilk, it's also a nice place to wander and soak up the community vibe. A fun fact about the park is that it was created when the American Legion sold 36 acres of land to the City of Miami in 1966 after realizing its declining and aging membership couldn't sustain the maintenance of the land. The waterfront park is now a community favorite and has picnic tables, a playground, tennis courts, a dog park and outdoor gym equipment for a human workout with fresh air and Vitamin D.

Beach-Hop & Bask in Green

MAP P102

Get natural on Key Biscayne

Floating like a glittering residential jewel in the bay it is named for, Key Biscayne and neighboring Virginia Key are a quick and easy getaway from Downtown Miami. Once you

A PARK'S DARK PAST

With its small pretty beachfront and kids playgrounds, the **Historic Virginia Key Park** *(virginiakey beachpark.net),* a short drive or bike ride from Downtown Miami, is great for a dose of nature. In the dark days of segregation however, this beachfront – initially accessible only by boat from downtown along the Miami River – was a segregated beach for African Americans, Cubans, Haitians and others from Latin America. It was both a beloved place for an urban getaway and a sacred site for religious ceremonies. City beaches were only desegregated in the early 1960s. Today, happily, you'll see people from all over the city and all walks of life enjoying the beautiful setting, occasional open-air concerts and ecology-minded family picnics.

EATING IN GREATER MIAMI: CHEAP & CHEERFUL

Islas Canarias: We won't dare say 'best Cuban food in Miami,' but this restaurant is certainly a contender. *7am-10pm Sun-Thu, to 11pm Fri & Sat* **$**	**Kush by Stephen's:** Damn, if the pastrami isn't a religious experience at the oldest deli in Miami. *hours vary* **$**	**Fritanga Montelimar:** This beloved spot serves up huge portions of Nicaraguan favorites (grilled pork, chicken stew etc). *8am-9pm* **$**	**Chayhana Oasis:** A gorgeous Silk Road-esque outpost for Uzbek cuisine like pilaf and steamed lamb dumplings. *noon-10pm* **$$**

HIGHLIGHTS
1. Bill Baggs Cape Florida State Park

SIGHTS
2. Crandon Park
3. Historic Virginia Key Park
4. Marjory Stoneman Douglas Biscayne Nature Center
5. Muscle Beach
6. Stiltsville
7. Virginia Key Beach North Point Park
8. Vizcaya Museum & Gardens

SLEEPING
9. Silver Sands Beach Resort

EATING
10. Boater's Grill
11. Clasica Victoria
12. Flour & Weirdoughs
13. Gramps Hideaway
14. Kebo
15. La Boulangerie Boul'Mich
16. Piononos
17. Rumbar
18. Rusty Pelican
19. The Cleat
20. The Golden Hog
21. The Sandbar

GREATER MIAMI SOUTH

pass some scenic causeways you'll feel like you've left Miami for a floating suburb that skews somehow even more tropical, thanks in large part to the lush greenery everywhere. This is a place to sit by the water on a stunning beach, or get out onto the water, too, whether for a dip or aboard something you can paddle to explore. The stunning skyline views of Miami alone are worth the trip out, but you can easily spend all day here.

Virginia Key Beach North Point Park is an attractive green space with several small, pleasing beaches and short nature trails. Pretty waterfront views aside, the big reason for coming is to get out on the water and explore; hire kayaks or bikes from PADL at Virginia Key Beach Club.

🍴 EATING IN KEY BISCAYNE: OUR PICKS

MAP P102

The Golden Hog: The place in Key Biscayne to grab picnic fare before hitting the beach or state parks. *7am-9pm* $

Boater's Grill: Follow the seafood paella with a slice of key lime pie and you'll be set at this waterfront. *11am-8pm Sun-Wed, to 10pm Thu-Sat* $$

Kebo: Spanish outpost on Key Biscayne serving excellent grilled prawns and Galician octopus. *noon-10pm Tue-Sun* $$$

Rusty Pelican: On the Rickenbacker Causeway with great views of Biscayne Bay. Come for the fresh seafood as much as fine vistas. *hours vary* $$$

Marjory Stoneman Douglas Biscayne Nature Center (*biscaynenaturecenter.org; vehicle $7*) is a child-friendly space and a great all ages introduction to South Florida's unique ecosystems, with hands-on exhibits as well as small aquariums full of local marine life. You can also stroll a nature trail through coastal hammock (hardwood forest) or enjoy the beach in front.

Finally, head to 1200-acre **Crandon Beach Park**, a serene clump of dense coastal hammock, mangrove swamps and a 2-mile-long beach, which is clean and often uncluttered, and faces a lovely sweep of teal goodness. In a city well-known for its beaches, this is one of the best.

Dune-Backed Beach Bliss
MAP P102

A taste of the Keys at Bill Baggs

If you don't make it to the Florida Keys, **Bill Baggs Cape Florida State Park** (*floridastateparks.org; vehicle $8*) is the next best way to get a taste of its unique island ecosystems. The 494-acre space is a tangled clot of tropical fauna and dark mangroves – look for the 'snorkel' roots that provide air for half-submerged mangrove trees – all interconnected by sandy trails and wooden boardwalks, and surrounded by miles of pale ocean.

A concession shack rents out kayaks, bikes, in-line skates, beach chairs and umbrellas. Head to the western side of the park for some excellent shore fishing. Or if that's not your thing, head there for hiking, cycling or skating – there are trails running throughout this side of the island, including some concrete paths. A mile- and-a-quarter of Atlantic-side beach here is also open to swimming. Bear in mind that there are no lifeguards on duty, so you swim at your own risk.

Prehistoric Burial Mounds & More
MAP P102

Dive into Deering Estate at Cutler

South of downtown along Miami's Palmetto Bay coast, **Deering Estate at Cutler** (*deeringestate.org; adults/kids $18/$10*) is sort of 'Vizcaya lite,' which makes sense as it was built by Charles, brother of James Deering (of **Vizcaya** (p92) mansion fame). The 150-acre grounds are awash with tropical growth, and a slew of activities are generally on offer, including moonlight kayak trips into the surrounding mangroves and tours of the surrounding nature preserve.

Also on the estate is the **Cutler Burial Mound**, one of the few surviving prehistoric mounds in the region. The mound

SPOTTING STILTSVILLE

Head to the southern shore of **Bill Baggs Cape Florida State Park** and you'll see, in the distance, seven houses standing on pilings in Biscayne Bay. The buildings, known as **Stiltsville** (p71), have been around since the early 1930s, ever since 'Crawfish Eddie Walker' built a shack on the waves. The 'village' was, at times, a gambling den, smuggling haven and bikini club.

At its peak in 1960, there were 27 'homes' here. Predictably, hurricanes and erosion took their toll. No one lives in Stiltsville today, but it's possible to take a boat tour out here with the **Biscayne National Park Institute** (p93) to see the remaining buildings up close.

🍸 **DRINKING IN KEY BISCAYNE: OUR PICKS** — MAP P102

The Cleat: Probably Miami's best spot to raise a sunset glass with toe-in-the-sand vibes, ceviche and Stiltsville views. *hours vary*

Gramps Getaway: Raise a cold one, slurp some oysters and admire the bay views at this Rickenbacker Causeway hangout. *2-11pm Mon-Thu, 11am-midnight Fri & Sat*

The Sandbar: Laid-back local hangout particularly popular at sunset, in the Key Colony community. *hours vary*

Rumbar: Pricy rum drinks served with Old Havana vibes go down too easily at the lobby bar of the The Ritz-Carlton, Key Biscayne. *5pm-midnight*

BEGUILING BOTANICAS

You might notice a few storefronts in Little Haiti with 'botanica' signs. They specialize in the Afro-Caribbean belief system of vodou. Forget stereotypes about pins and dolls. Vodou recognizes supernatural forces in everyday objects. Notice the statues of what look like people; these represent loa (pronounced lwa), spirits that form a pantheon below God.

Whether you're religious or not, botanicas can be a fun place to pick up unique souvenirs like candles, beads, statues, herbs, salts, incense, perfumes, books, oils and the like. An article in the *Miami Herald* posited that Miami might have the most botanicas per square mile of anywhere in the world. Drop a coin into a loa offering bowl before you leave.

Deering Estate at Cutler (p103)

has been repeatedly excavated as far back as the 1860s, although some of the bones removed from the mound have since been reburied. It is thought that the mound is the burial site of 12 to 18 Native Americans. It's accessible via a boardwalk and there is also a fossil site and a midden to see within the property's protected natural areas.

Jewel Box of a Park   MAP p55

Urban green oasis at Arch Creek Park

Just 9 acres, the compact but captivating **Arch Creek Park**, near the Oleta River, is a habitat of tropical hardwood species ensnaring a natural limestone bridge once used by Native American tribes. The park preserve was the hunting grounds for the Seminole until 1830 when the Indian Removal Act forced their removal from their land.

Meandering the area – which includes a butterfly garden and small but well-stocked museum of Native American and pioneer artifacts – with a naturalist on a kid-friendly eco-tour, you might feel the presence of the people who lived here long before you. Its history, greenery and sheer natural beauty makes it a very special place in the middle of Miami.

EATING IN KEY BISCAYNE: BAKERIES & COFFEE SHOPS ———— MAP P102

Piononos: The strawberry pavlova is legendary, but you won't go astray with any of Piononos's pretty pastries. *10am-5pm* $

La Boulangerie Boul'Mich: French baking ethos gets a Latin twist at this sweet spot known for its fresh breads and pastries. *7.30am-6pm Mon-Sat, 8-4pm Sun* $

Flour & Weirdoughs: Maybe it's the fact that they mill their own flour that makes everything here – empanadas, cinnamon rolls etc – so tasty. *8am-2pm Tue-Sun* $

Clasica Victoria: European-style coffee shop with quiches, croissants and more. *7.30am-7pm* $

Places We Love to Stay

$ Budget $$ Midrange $$$ Top End

Miami Beach MAP p53/3, 55

Generator Miami $ Stylish Collins Ave hostel with a vibey pool, dorms and private rooms a block off the beach. Reserve in advance.

Freehand Miami $ Dorms and private rooms, two craft cocktail bars and an outdoor pool, about a mile north of the South Beach nightlife.

Cavalier South Beach $$ The exterior plays with tropical and marine themes. Inside are exposed-brick walls, plus marble bathrooms. Coveted heart-of-South Beach location, just across Ocean Drive from the beach.

Kimpton Surfcomber $$ With a recently renovated pool, happening beach bar and poolside cabanas, this oceanfront property is a short stroll from Soundscape Park.

Faena (p54) **$$$** Sceney, super-luxurious beachfront and art-centric hotel with restaurants, nightlife and entertainment onsite. An Art Basel-crowd favorite.

The Setai $$$ Over-the-top yet understated luxury conjures Asian art deco on the oceanfront, with three infinity pools and an inimitable spa. One of Miami's most luxe properties.

Downtown Miami MAP p65

Dunns Josephine $$ In historic Overtown, themed rooms celebrate the lives of notable Black figures like Ella Fitzgerald and Langston Hughes. Complimentary continental breakfast.

Gale Miami Hotel & Residences $$$ Near the Kaseya Center and Brickell, a 51-story property with a Turkish hammam and rooftop pool.

EAST Miami $$$ Luxury property connected to Brickell City Centre with a tropical rooftop pool and great onsite dining.

Wynwood, the Design District & Allapattah MAP p74/5

Moxy Miami Wynwood $$ Youthful vibes near Wynwood Walls. Small but contemporary rooms and a complimentary cocktail at check-in.

Arlo $$ With gorgeous murals inside and out, this high-rise hotel has beautiful common spaces that draw the neighborhood in.

The Hotel at the Moore $$$ The Design District's lone luxury hotel has just 13 suites and is hidden on the 4th floor of a Historic Landmark building.

Coral Gables & Coconut Grove MAP p88/9

Hotel Arya $$ With a pool, squash court and sweeping Biscayne Views, there's lots to like at this Coconut Grove address.

Mutiny Hotel $$ Rooms with balconies overlook Dinner Key Marina. This all-suite property is a quick stroll from cafes and The Barnacle.

Hotel St Michel $$ Boutique Coral Gables hotel in a Historic Landmark building. Excellent on-site Italian restaurant.

Mr C $$$ Rooms with European glamour wow at this luxe Coconut Grove property. Its rooftop pool gazes out on Biscayne Bay.

Biltmore Hotel $$$ A National Historic Landmark and one of Florida's most storied hotels: championship golf course, 10 lit tennis courts and one of the US's largest hotel pools.

Greater Miami MAP p97, 102

Vagabond Hotel $$ Step back in time to 1950s modernism splashed with 21st-century luxury at this Biscayne Boulevard icon in MiMo. Weekend pool parties are a good time (look for the mermaid on the pool's bottom).

Silver Sands Beach Resort $$ Low-rise, Old Florida-style independent resort just steps from the sand on Key Biscayne. Amenities include a nice pool and rooms with kitchenettes. Crandon Park is nearby.

For places to stay in the Everglades and Biscayne National Park, see p133

ONLYBOUNDARIES/SHUTTERSTOCK

Above: Kayaking, Everglades National Park (p114); Right: Alligator (p114)

The Everglades & Biscayne National Park

MANGROVE MAZES, ISLANDS AND WILDLIFE WONDER

The Everglades is South Florida's massive, quiet oasis, teeming with fauna and flora found nowhere else. Nearby, Biscayne National Park is 95% water, loaded with reefs, islands and shipwrecks.

There's no wilderness in the world quite like the Everglades. Called the 'River of Grass' by Native American inhabitants, it's not just a wetland, lake, river or grassland – it's all of these, twisted into a series of soft horizons, long vistas and sunsets, animated by an ever-changing cast of wild creatures. The park's quiet majesty is evident in the sight of an anhinga opening glistening wings to the sun after a mid-morning feed; in the rhythmic flap of a great blue heron gliding over the mirror-like surface of a saturated prairie; or in the primeval silence of a cypress dome, broken only by a sapsucker's hopeful tapping or the roar of an alligator. Out on Florida Bay, the marsh gives way to an expanse of shallow seabed, with manatees bubbling up to the surface and aquatic birds nesting by the thousands on mangrove-backed mudflats. The third-largest national park in the continental US continues to face threats from encroaching development, invasive species and agriculture. The importance of this ecological treasure, however, is no longer in doubt thanks to tireless preservation efforts by visionary conservationists like Marjory Stoneman Douglas. Beyond recreational bliss, the Everglades is vital, regionally, for water storage and flood control. Nearby and nestled along southeast Florida's shores is Biscayne National Park, best known for its coral reefs and wreck dives, history-themed boat trips and kayaking excursions amid islands fringed with mangroves.

THIERRY EIDENWEIL/SHUTTERSTOCK ©

THE MAIN AREAS

EVERGLADES NATIONAL PARK
Wetlands, hiking, kayaking and flat drives. **p112**

EVERGLADES CITY
Islands gateway, stone crab capital. **p122**

HOMESTEAD
Speedway central, tropical fruits, quaint downtown. **p125**

BISCAYNE NATIONAL PARK
Boating adventures, paddling and bird-watching. **p128**

Everglades City, p122

In the home of the Gulf Coast Visitor Center of Everglades National Park, nosh on stone crabs before embarking on a boating excursion to mangrove islands.

CAR

To maximize an Everglades adventure, a car is essential. The four entrances to Everglades National Park are several miles apart; once inside the park, roads to key attractions can be long – for example, the 38-mile road between the Earnest Coe Visitor Center and Flamingo Marina.

BICYCLE

Generally narrow roads and long distances make this an impractical destination for cyclists. However, if a Shark Valley visit is in store, its pristinely paved loop is primed for a ride. You can also rent bikes on-site.

BOAT & AIRBOAT

Airboats aren't just kitschy tourist vehicles – they are vital in delicately navigating the wet prairies. Within Everglades National Park, there are authorized airboat businesses. For navigating Biscayne National Park, boat tours and rentals are bookable at its main visitor center.

Find Your Way

Everglades National Park spans 1.5 million acres, anchoring the central remote portion of Southern Florida, with Miami within proximity of its northeast corner. To the east of the Everglades, Biscayne National Park protects an island-filled marine reserve.

Biscayne National Park, p128
Before hopping in the waters to snorkel above reefs, stroll along the Convoy Point Jetty Walk, which has a wooden boardwalk and benches on the coast.

Florida's Turnpike (toll)

Fort Lauderdale

ccosukee Indian eservation

Hollywood

North Miami Beach

Hialeah

Miccosukee Village

Shark Valley
Tram Tour

Miami

Key Biscayne

Kendal

ATLANTIC OCEAN

verglades ational Park

Peters

Goulds

Boca Chita Key

Florida Keys National Marine Sanctuary

Coral Castle

Homestead

Biscayne National Park

Dante Fascell Visitor Center

Elliott Key

Florida City

Biscayne Bay

Adams Key

Anhinga Trail

Homestead, p125
Explore a human-made castle made of coral and enjoy a fresh mango (or five) at the Robert Is Here fruit stand and farm.

Card Sound

Barnes Sound

Key Largo

Key Largo National Marine Sanctuary

Florida Bay

Key Largo

Everglades National Park, p112
Take a tram (or opt to cycle or walk) around the Shark Valley loop, pit-stopping midway at its observation tower where gators often sunbathe in the marshes below.

Plan Your Time

You can get a taste of the Everglades within a drive-centric day. Allow bonus days to mix in cycling, overnight camping and night walks. Count on a full day for a proper boating adventure at Biscayne National Park.

Shark Valley Observation Tower (p112)

OLIVIA NOVAK/SHUTTERSTOCK

If You Only Have One Day

● Venturing along the Tamiami Trail, head to **Shark Valley** (p112) and rent a bike for a spin on the 15-mile loop road – you'll see gators, birds, turtles and snakes lounging roadside. Pit-stop at the observation tower midway for lush green vistas in every direction. If you don't feel like biking or hiking, a tram will take you all around.

● Afterwards, learn about Indigenous traditions at nearby **Miccosukee Indian Village** (p115), an open-air museum with gator demonstrations, airboat rides through sawgrass and handcrafted jewelry. Further along Hwy 41 is a scenic drive on a forest-lined **loop road** (p119), with stops for hikes and taking in even more wildlife.

Seasonal Highlights

June through September is muggy and buggy. Winter (November through February) brings noticeably cooler temperatures, and spring is optimal for wildlife viewing.

JANUARY
The heart of **snowbird season** (October to April), when folks from all over the world converge on South Florida to escape the cold temperatures – the Everglades are not excluded.

FEBRUARY
The pleasant, near-perfect weather continues, providing opportunities for seeing raptors and wading birds along the **Tamiami Trail** and from a distance at local boat ramps.

MAY
Wet season begins (lasting through August), which equates to sparse crowds. With full waterways, **kayak** the Sandfly Island Loop and Turner River near Everglades City.

Making a Weekend of It

● After a day of cycling and driving loops, head east to **Biscayne National Park**. Hit the **Dante Fascell Visitor Center** (p128) to learn about nearby shipwrecks and the 600 species of fish looming off the park's coast – you can see some along the **Convoy Point Jetty Walk** (p130). Make sure to book a boat cruise or snorkeling outing.

● Afterwards, you've earned a tropical-fruit concoction from **Robert Is Here** (p127). Head back into the **Everglades** via the **Royal Palm Visitor Center** (p116) entrance. A stone's throw from the visitor center is the **Anhinga Trail** (p115). As you follow the path, you'll have a solid shot at seeing gators, turtles and the trail's namesake, the anhinga – a large water bird with a tail that resembles a turkey.

A Long Weekend & More

● When you reach the **Flamingo Visitor Center** (p114), rent a kayak for a paddle along a mangrove-lined canal or out onto Florida Bay, or else book a boat tour. Keep an eye out for manatees and the rare American crocodile. Book a site at the 275-pitch campground on-site for an extended stay.

● For a different perspective on the region, head to **Everglades City** (p122), gateway to the **Ten Thousand Islands** (p122) and a watery wilderness famed for its dolphins and birdlife. No trip to Everglades City is complete without some seafood at **Diving Pelican** (p124), a chickee-hut-meets-restaurant. Pop in the pink house–resemblant **Museum of the Everglades** (p124) to explore the region's 2000 years of human history.

JULY	SEPTEMBER	OCTOBER	DECEMBER
The summer temperatures swelter, making this a perfect time for dips in the waters of **Biscayne National Park** (p128) and the **Ten Thousand Islands** (p122).	The peak month of **hurricane season** (June through November) in South Florida brings attractive deals on lodgings and excursions.	It's **race month** in Homestead as NASCAR hits the Homestead Speedway. Mango season ends, but fresh mandarins, strawberries and navel oranges become abundant at roadside stands.	The start of the dry season (lasting through April), which means fewer mosquitoes. Local boats can often be seen donning strings of holiday lights.

Everglades National Park

GETTING AROUND

A car is a necessity for accessing and exploring the Everglades' various expanses. Depending on the experiences that you opt to book – kayaking, cycling and boating among them – rental hubs, often sanctioned by or part of the National Park Service, are available throughout.

Stretching serenely across South Florida, Everglades National Park is a wonderland of marshes, sawgrass and mangroves. You can hike, airboat, canoe, kayak or even travel by tram here, with each experience leaving a different impression.

There are four entrances to the park, each providing a gateway to unique outdoor havens. Approximately 40 miles west of Miami, the Shark Valley Visitor Center is home to the famous 15-mile paved Tram Road, great for cycling, walks and (yes) tram rides. The Gulf Coast Visitor Center in Everglades City is a hub for boat excursions and the perfect jumping-off point for exploring the Ten Thousand Islands, a wildlife refuge for water birds. Outside Homestead, Royal Palm Visitor Center provides access to hiking trails (all under a mile), from strolls under canopy trees to walks on boardwalks over the marshland. The Flamingo Visitor Center, about 40 miles south of Royal Palm, is a gateway to the mangrove-draped Florida Bay, canoe trails and the 275-pitch Flamingo Campground.

Primordial Wilderness Vistas

Cycle or tram Shark Valley

A major destination for many visitors to the Everglades, **Shark Valley** *(nps.gov; pedestrian/motorcycle/car $20/30/35)* is named not for its marine life but rather its location at the headwaters of the little-known Shark River, which drains into the Gulf of Mexico. The big draw is the 15-mile paved loop trail that takes you into Shark River Slough. You'll pass small creeks, tropical forest and 'borrow pits' (human-made holes that are now basking spots for gators, turtles and birdlife). Herons stalk their prey along the water and the clouds overhead shimmer like mirror images on the vast expanse of the River of Grass.

Closed to cars, the pancake-flat trail is perfect for bicycles. The halfway point is the spiraling 45ft-high **Shark Valley Observation Tower**, a brutalist concrete structure with dramatic 360-degree views over the landscape. If you don't feel like exerting yourself, the most popular and painless way to

☑ TOP TIP

The culinary landscape is sparse (borderline non-existent) throughout Everglades National Park. Snacks and drinks are available at visitor centers; otherwise, the restaurant attached to the **Flamingo Lodge** (p133) is the sole sit-down option in the entire park. Your best bet is to load up and pack a cooler in nearby Homestead, Florida City, Miami or near the **Miccosukee Casino & Resort** (p115).

EVERGLADES NATIONAL PARK

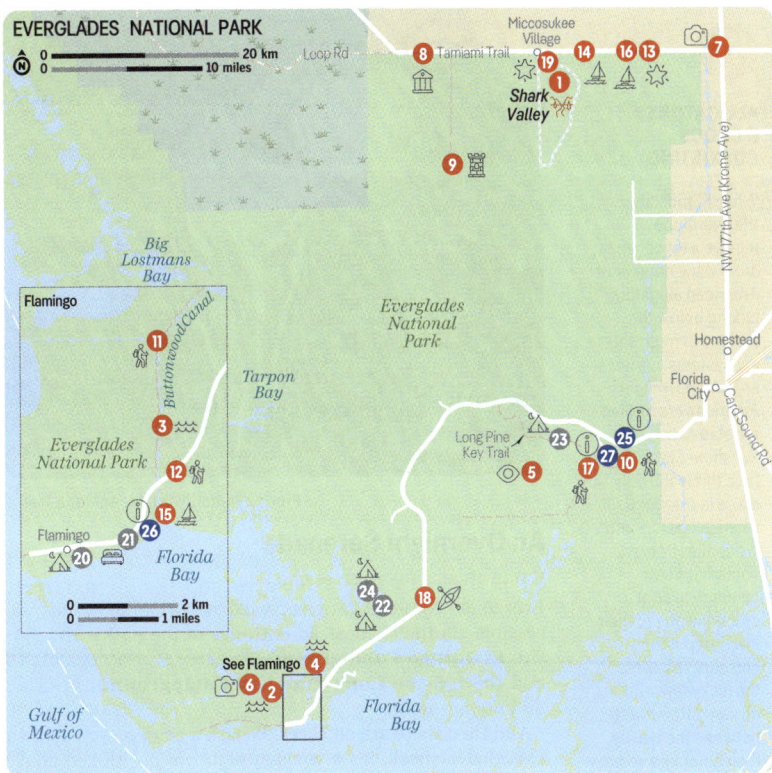

HIGHLIGHTS
1 Shark Valley

SIGHTS
2 Bear Lake
3 Buttonwood Canal
4 Coot Bay
5 HM69 Nike Missile Base
6 Homestead Canal
7 Miccosukee Casino & Resort

8 Miccosukee Indian Village
9 Shark Valley Observation Tower

ACTIVITIES & TOURS
10 Anhinga Trail
11 Bear Lake Trail
12 Christian Point Trail
13 Coopertown Airboats
14 Everglades Safari Park
15 Flamingo Adventures

16 Gator Park
17 Gumbo Limbo Trail
18 Nine Mile Pond Loop
19 Shark Valley Tram Tours

SLEEPING
20 Flamingo Campground
21 Flamingo Lodge
22 Lard Can Campsite

23 Long Pine Key Campground
24 Pearl Bay Chickee

INFORMATION
25 Ernest F Coe Visitor Center
26 Flamingo Visitor Center
27 Royal Palm Visitor Center

immerse yourself in the Everglades is on the two-hour tram tour that runs along the entire loop trail. If you only have time for one Everglades activity, this should be it – the guides are informative and witty, and you may get to see alligators sunning themselves along the road.

You can reserve bikes or tram tours in advance (advisable in the busier winter months) through **Shark Valley Tram Tours** (*sharkvalleytramtours.com; adult/child $33/18*) at the visitor center. Plan to go early in the day, both to beat the heat and the crowds.

FRANCISCO BLANCO/SHUTTERSTOCK

Florida redbelly turtle, Anhinga Trail

ALLIGATORS & CROCS COEXISTING

While Florida and the Everglades receive a lot of hype around the number of American alligators lurking below the surface of freshwater ecosystems, it's not so well known that American crocodiles are also native to the Sunshine State. In fact, this is the only place in the world where alligators and crocodiles coexist. Though it's less common to spot a crocodile due to their lower population and elusive habits, the lucky few who do can differentiate between the two by their color and snout. Alligators tend to be darker with broad snouts and only live in freshwater, while crocodiles are lighter with narrow snouts and can thrive in both fresh- and saltwater environments.

An Overnight Serenade

Camp on an above-water chickee

Everglades National Park has two drive-in campgrounds, accessible via the Homestead entrance of the park – the 274-site **Flamingo Campground** *(nps.gov; $33-60 per night)* and the 108-site **Long Pine Key Campground** *(nps.gov; $33-60 per night)*.

And then there are chickees. What's a chickee, you ask? In Everglades-speak, it's a wooden platform positioned above the water where you can set up a tent; it's like having your own little island with seemingly endless horizon – sunrise and sunsets are unobstructed and, depending on the day, you may see gators coasting by, endless wading birds and frogs crooning you through the night.

Most chickee sites are found near the **Flamingo Visitor Center** *(nps.gov; $20-35 per night)*. You'll need a few things in addition to your camping gear, notably a backcountry camping permit (available from any park visitor center), bug repellant for the inevitable mosquitoes and a canoe (as you can only reach the platforms via water). Canoes and kayaks can be rented from several spots around the park. Off the Hell's Bay Trail are a handful of chickee sites within a 5-mile canoe jaunt, including **Lard Can** and **Pearl Bay Chickee** *(nps.gov; $21 fee plus $2 per person per night)*.

15,000 Years of History

A museum in the middle of it all

Humans have inhabited the Everglades for upward of 15,000 years. Long before European colonization began in the 19th century, tribes like the Seminole and Miccosukee comprised the bulk of the population.

Today, you can learn all about Miccosukee culture, history and legacy at the **Miccosukee Indian Village** *(micco sukee.com; adult/child $28/19)*, less than a half-mile from the park's Shark Valley entrance. The village includes a museum with beadwork and photographs, as well as regular alligator demonstrations, which show the importance of the gators to the tribe. These are strictly ethical presentations, meaning there are no wrestling elements to the show.

Tickets to the museum are available at the front museum desk for a charge; discounted admission is available for children under 12. Notably, the tribe also operates the **Miccosukee Casino & Resort** *(miccosukee.com)*, approximately 20 miles east along the Tamiami Trail.

Beaches, Boardwalks & Prairies

Check off quick hikes aplenty

You'll find fewer than three dozen formal trails in the entirety of this South Florida preserve, many of which are short interpretive trails less than a mile long. Yet the trails you'll find are ones you won't soon forget. Regardless of where your Everglades hiking adventure takes you, you can be sure the route will be flat. Just make sure to pack sun-protective clothing, sunscreen and bug repellant for any Everglades hike to mitigate sun- or mosquito-related headaches.

For a moderate hike with a little history, **Bear Lake Trail**, located 2 miles north of the **Flamingo Visitor Center** (p114) in Homestead, is the top choice. Trickling alongside the trail you'll see the **Homestead Canal**, which was constructed in 1922 to funnel freshwater from the marshland out to sea. The project's (dubious) goal? To create a drier piece of land for future development. The result? Just the opposite, as saltwater entered what had been a freshwater ecosystem, forever creating a hybrid habitat in that portion of the park. The 3.3-mile trail itself features more than 50 different tree species, with hardwood hammocks towering above, culminating in a sweeping vista of **Bear Lake** with dots of mangrove islands. Wear sturdier hiking shoes to navigate the periodic thick grass patches and downed branches.

Christian Point Trail is for the difficult hiking crowd with a multifaceted terrain – slate upwards of three hours for the 3.2-mile experience. You'll find the trailhead 1 mile north of the Flamingo Visitor Center – and once you set out, you'll discover that the trail's difficulty stems from its jagged terrain, including thick mangrove patches and sporadic debris from hurricanes of yesteryear. A stretch of open prairie provides a nice reprieve on dry days. If rain is in the forecast or the area has seen recent downpours, prepare for a muddy experience. Even the flattest prairies are a slushy mud-fest, so bring the right pants and boots.

For families and a gentle saunter, the **Anhinga Trail** is 0.8 miles. This pristinely paved trail – with portions of well-kept and railed wooden boardwalks hovering over the marshland – is perhaps your easiest and best chance to see turtles and a

GUARDIAN OF THE GLADES

One of Florida's most beloved iconoclasts, Marjory Stoneman Douglas (1890–1998) fought tirelessly to save the Everglades decades before conservation was a popular topic. In 1947 (the year Everglades National Park was established), she published her beautifully written classic, *The Everglades: River of Grass*. A commercial success, the book helped shift public perception of the wetlands from 'infernal swamp' to 'national treasure.'

For years afterwards she continued writing and speaking about the threats posed by development and agriculture, and in 1969 (at the age of 79) Douglas formed the Friends of the Everglades, a non-profit that continues to play a pivotal role in garnering political and financial support for the area's restoration.

hearty selection of the Everglades' bird species. To access the Anhinga Trail trailhead, venture to the **Ernest F Coe Visitor Center** *(nps.gov)* in Homestead and head approximately 4 miles south to the **Royal Palm Visitor Center** *(nps.gov).* The trailhead is around 50ft behind the building. If you're itching for a bonus hike, the 0.4-mile **Gumbo Limbo Trail**, draped in massive hammock trees, is a stone's throw from the visitor center.

Everglades Aboard a Buzzing Vessel

Zip through grassy waters by airboat

If the Everglades were to have an official vehicle, it would be the airboat (along the Tamiami Trail, you can't miss all the 'Airboat Tours' signs). These flat-bottomed boats with giant propeller fans on the back are designed to safely navigate the grass- and lily-heavy waters. Most hold a dozen-or-so passengers and are canopied, providing relief from the oft-relentless sun. Aboard, the soundtrack is the propeller fans' endless buzz, light splish-splashes as you glide about, and a tour guide.

While there are oodles of airboat operators beyond the national park's confines, there are only three that operate within the park: **Gator Park** *(gatorpark.com; adult/child $30/20)*, **Everglades Safari Park** *(evergladessafaripark.com; $47-363)* and **Coopertown Airboats** *(coopertownairboats. com; adult/child $30/19).*

As this is a popular family activity, most operators within the national park and beyond offer a children's discount. Coopertown Airboats, for example, has discounts for children ages 6 to 11 and free rides for those under 6. It can be incredibly tempting to reach out to pet wading birds and even seemingly friendly alligators, so if you have a particularly hands-on little one, it's wise to sit toward the middle of the vessel to mitigate temptation.

Immerse Yourself in the Mangrove Islands

Kayak or canoe canopied canals

The **Flamingo Visitor Center** (p114) has an adjacent marina with boat tours of backcountry waters and the Florida Bay. **Flamingo Adventures** *(flamingoeverglades.com; adult/ child $48/24)* runs two different boat tours throughout the day. The 90-minute backcountry excursion takes you through the mangrove-lined **Buttonwood Canal**, along Tarpon Creek and into the mouth of islet-dotted Whitewater Bay. Naturalist guides shed insight into the southern Everglades ecosystems, while pointing out great blue herons, snowy egrets, roseate spoonbills and many other creatures you'll likely see. For less of a jungle-like journey, opt for the Florida Bay tour, which glides out past countless keys in the shallow bay, offering the chance to see ospreys, sea turtles and dolphins. Admission is half price for kids 12 and under. Before or after an excursion, stop a while for some quiet time by the docks. You can sometimes see manatees here, as well as alligators and the rare American crocodile.

GUESS WHO CREATED THE AIRBOAT?

Alexander Graham Bell, best known as the winner of the first US patent for the telephone, was a man of many ideas. He is also credited with creating the first ever airboat in 1905, named Ugly Duckling. The first prototype was heavy and slow, but provided an opportunity to navigate waters without the danger of propellers harming birds and other wildlife. Over the years, the design evolved with the ingenuity of other engineers and even Floridians who took it upon themselves to build versions of their own. The craft became widely popular in the United States in the 1930s and continues to be the preferred method of quick transportation throughout the waters here.

Airboat and alligator, Everglades National Park

At the visitor center, you can also rent kayaks and canoes *($38-55 for 4 hours)* at the marina, meaning you'll receive keys to unlock rentals at nearby ponds and waterways. Among the most popular nearby destinations for kayaking and canoeing is the **Nine Mile Pond** loop, which takes you through mangrove islands and grassy landscapes (though it's actually 3.5 miles to 5 miles depending on your route). Paddle carefully, as wading birds, crocodiles, alligators and other critters roam about in the waters.

Paddling along Buttonwood Canal, you can see a wide range of wildlife, and if you're lucky, manatees in the water and alligators basking along the banks. It's about 3 miles to paddle up to **Coot Bay**. Allow yourself three or more hours to make the return trip, including time to stop and admire the scenery. If a do-it-yourself rental is too much to coordinate, Everglades National Park Institute also has guided tours.

A Cold War Hotspot

Tour a missile base

After the Cuban Missile Crisis of 1962, the US Army Corps of Engineers erected a **Nike Hercules missile defense site**, known as Alpha Battery or HM69, in the Everglades to protect the country from a potential Soviet air attack from nearby Cuba. The site utilized then-great advances in defense technology. Hawk missiles were part of the defense, providing a mobile system of protection against lower-altitude aircraft. HM69 is open to visitors between December and late March; a ranger-guided tour is included with admission to the park. Three missile barns, a missile assembly building, barracks, Nike Hercules missiles and more make this one of the best-preserved Cold War relics you'll find anywhere.

LORE AMID THE LUSHNESS

There's no shortage of lore surrounding the Everglades National Park. Its history and remoteness are the perfect backdrop to stories of mystery and paranormal activity. Al Capone was rumored to make moonshine in the desolate Lost City. Hauntings have been reported on aircraft built with scraps from the Eastern Airlines Flight 401 Everglades crash. Several murders were thought to be committed by Ed Watson, an Everglades farmer, and townsfolk took justice into their own hands by killing him. His farm is said to be haunted. Today, you can backcountry camp at Watson Place, view memorials for plane crashes, and visit the now abandoned, and difficult to locate, Lost City.

Beyond Everglades National Park

Beyond the national park, you'll find a bonus nature reserve, dolphin encounters and swampland surrounds for scenic drives.

Places

Marco Island p118

Big Cypress National Preserve p119

Big Cypress Indian Reservation p121

Just beyond the Everglades National Park are more opportunities to dabble in ever-swampy and island landscapes. On the southwest coast of Florida, approximately 30 miles west of Everglades City, sits Marco Island. A glitzy enclave of higher-end resorts, golf courses and marinas, it has a colorful, boutique-dotted downtown resembling a cozy Caribbean capital. It's also a treasured destination for dolphin sightings.

Also operated by the National Park Service is the 1139-sq-mile Big Cypress National Preserve. Its principal visitor center is approximately 10 miles north of Everglades City, providing a gateway to driving tours, swamp buggy rides and wildlife sightings. If you're lucky, you may even spot an endangered Florida panther along the way. Within it all and worth a hearty detour is one of Florida's most important Native American museums.

Marco Island

TIME FROM EVERGLADES NATIONAL PARK (SHARK VALLEY): **75 MINS** 🚗

Spot and name a dolphin off Marco Island

Some 65 miles west of Shark Valley, Marco Island is the departure point for one of the best boat tours in Florida. Ever since 2006, the **Dolphin Explorer** *(dolphin-study.com; adult/ child $74/59)* has operated a long-term scientific study of the behavior and movements of southwestern Florida's bottlenose dolphins. Using photo ID of dorsal fins, you'll have the opportunity to get involved in spotting, counting and confirming individual sightings – data which is then shared with the Mote Marine Laboratory in Sarasota and other marine-life organizations around the globe.

As the catamaran sets off, visitors can page through a photo album depicting dorsal fins of the 130 or so cetacean residents. The naturalist on board points out bite marks and tears that will help you tell the difference between dolphins Kay Cee, Wyatt, Dolly and Fireball, and fill you in on various dolphins' life stories: which bulls (males) like to hang out together (Capri and Hatchet, for instance), how they some-

GETTING AROUND

Marco Island is very strollable, bike-friendly, and you may even opt to rent a golf cart to cruise around its confines. Otherwise, count on a car to connect the dots between these adventures and your greater Everglades itinerary.

DIARAMA00/SHUTTERSTOCK

Dolphin near Marco Island

times work together in feeding and defense against sharks, and who has recently given birth. Dolphins recognize the boat and may come up and slap the water with their tails, indicating they want to ride in the boat's wake. Sometimes whole pods will gather to pay a visit, even leaping through the wash behind the boat.

If you spot a dolphin not already cataloged (like a newly born offspring), everyone on board gets to name it. The tour ends with a stop for some shelling at remote and beautiful **Keewaydin**, the largest unbridged barrier island in South Florida. Excursions last three hours and depart from **Rose Marina**.

Big Cypress National Preserve

TIME FROM EVERGLADES NATIONAL PARK (SHARK VALLEY): **25 MINS** 🚗

A Cypress swamp drive

Stretching across nearly 1140 sq miles, **Big Cypress National Preserve** *(nps.gov/bicy)* plays a vital role in the health of its better-known neighbor to the south, the Everglades: rains that flood the preserve's prairies and wetlands get slowly filtered down through the Everglades. One of the best ways to get a taste of the primeval scenery of Big Cypress is to take the 24-mile **Loop Road** scenic drive (aka County Rd 94), just off the Tamiami Trail.

🐾

RARE & RAWR

To hockey fans, South Florida is known as Panther Territory thanks to the NHL's Florida Panthers. The 2024 Stanley Cup champions are based in Sunrise. Big Cypress is also considered panther territory because it's one of the only remaining homes to the endangered species. Approximately 200 remain in the wild today. The panther is reclusive, making sightings in the wild rare – but if you are lucky enough, practice caution. There are no reported attacks on humans by this mountain lion subspecies, but they command respect. Fun fact: the Florida panther doesn't roar. It will purr, hiss, growl and yowl to communicate. So keep your ears peeled for the elusive animal, as well.

🍴 **EATING ON MARCO ISLAND: OUR PICKS**

Doreen's Cup of Joe: Locally roasted coffee and fresh breakfast classics like omelets, skillets or breakfast sandwiches; also serving lunch. *7.30am-2pm* **$$**

Marco Island Brewery: Enjoy craft brews and munch on burgers, sandwiches, pizza and more. *11am-midnight Sun-Thu, to 1am Fri & Sat* **$$**

The Boulevard: Italian and seafood dishes using the freshest farm-to-table ingredients amid cozy vibes. *5-9pm Mon-Sat* **$$$**

Oyster Society: Fine dining and a family atmosphere blend to bring a variety of flavors to seafood and raw bar offerings. *4.30-10pm* **$$$**

JMARRO/SHUTTERSTOCK

AMERICA'S FIRST WILDLIFE PRESERVE

Big Cypress National Preserve, established in 1974 and encompassing 1139 sq miles, is America's first national preserve. The efforts to protect Big Cypress swamp came in the aftermath of the unveiled plans to build the world's largest jetport in the Everglades. Local conservationists, environmentalists, athletes, Seminoles, Miccosukees and seemingly everyone in between came together to establish the preserve. National preserves serve a different purpose than national parks. Essentially, preserves protect an area with less restrictions. The traditional uses of the area, such as land use and occupancy of the native tribes, hunting, private land ownership, offroading, oil and gas exploration and cattle grazing are allowed in Big Cypress, but are regulated with sustainability top-of-mind.

Around 4 miles west of the **Oasis Visitor Center**, look for the brown sign that says 'Monroe Station/Loop Road,' off to your left. This marks the beginning of the scenic drive, which will quickly take you into a landscape of sawgrass prairie.

Around Mile 2.2, you'll reach a small picnic area and the **Gator Hook Trailhead**. For immersion in the swampland, there's no better place. The out-and-back trail (5 miles round trip) initially follows an elevated logging tram road, though you'll soon be ankle- or thigh-deep in water, depending on the season (it's driest in the spring) as you trudge past cypress trees with views over the prairie. Use a walking stick to avoid tripping on roots and other invisible hazards.

Back behind the wheel, cypress strands dot the sides of the road, with memorable views around Mile 5, the so-called **Sweetwater Strand**. Out of slightly deeper water, towering cypresses stand covered with ferns, bromeliads and Spanish moss. Look for alligators and fish in the water and songbirds in the trees.

Near Mile 10, you'll pass the blue-blazed **Roberts Trail**, an 8.2-mile (one-way) trail that goes up to the Oasis Visitor Center on the Tamiami Trail. From there, you can keep going along the **Florida National Scenic Trail**, a meandering, 1500-mile route that travels the length of the state. Be prepared to walk through knee-deep water if hiking the Big Cypress section.

Mile 15.6 offers the chance to take another walk. The short, 0.2-mile **Tree Snail Hammock Trail** winds through hardwood hammock, a jungle-like environment of broadleaf trees such as gumbo limbo that grow on higher (and drier) sections of the wetlands. Look for endemic Liguus tree snails clinging tightly to tree trunks.

A few miles east of there, you'll pass through the remains of **Pinecrest**, an abandoned town that had a population of 400 during its peak in the 1930s. Nearby, you can extend your stay in Big Cypress by pitching a tent at **Mitchell Landing**, a primitive campground with sites scattered along a dirt road.

Milky Way over Florida

The last few miles of the road pass through a Miccosukee community, with private homes sheltering among the dense greenery. At journey's end (which is not technically a loop), you'll intersect at a different point along the Tamiami Trail, from where you can continue back to your starting point 20 miles to the west.

Big Cypress Indian Reservation

TIME FROM EVERGLADES NATIONAL PARK (SHARK VALLEY): 1¾ HRS 🚗

Ancestral landscapes and native traditions

It's a long drive north of the Everglades – nearly two hours from Shark Valley – but it's well worth the effort to visit one of Florida's most important Native American museums. Set on the Big Cypress Indian Reservation, **Ah-Tah-Thi-Ki** *(ahtahthiki.com; adult/child $10/7.50)* lives up to its name, which in the Seminole language means 'a place to learn; a place to remember.'

Start off your visit here with the 17-minute film *We Seminoles,* which touches on the tribe's history, myths and traditions, then explore the galleries of the museum with displays of clothing, basketry, jewelry and impressive 30ft dugout canoes that were once poled through the wetlands. Dioramas with life-sized figures depict various scenes out of traditional Seminole life, from the formal meeting of a soon-to-be married couple at the bride's mother's house to the colorfully attired celebrants taking part in the Catfish Dance – a key component of the sacred Green Corn Ceremony held each year.

Nature plays a starring role at Ah-Tah-Thi-Ki: behind the museum is a 1-mile boardwalk trail that loops through a lush cypress dome. Signs along the way point out plant and animal species that are vital not only to the Seminoles (like marsh pennywort, a traditional treatment for asthma and other lung ailments) but for the entire Everglades ecosystem. Other stops along the boardwalk pass beside ceremonial grounds and the dwellings and workshops of a re-created traditional Seminole village.

DEEP IN THE DARKNESS

Big Cypress National Preserve is recognized as an International Dark Sky Place by nonprofit DarkSky International. It is one of the last regions in Florida with a protected night sky, which means there is minimal light pollution and a significant amount of the Milky Way can be viewed by the naked eye. Dark Sky Places also help to protect and view or study nocturnal wildlife. Big Cypress National Preserve offers ranger-led astronomy programs to immerse visitors in its wonders. Once a month, constellation tours and telescope viewings take place. You can learn more about the stars, star clusters, planets, nebulae and galaxies on an evening expedition.

Everglades City

ISLANDS GATEWAY | WATER EXCURSIONS | HISTORICAL GEMS

GETTING AROUND

For a quick offshoot amid the Everglades landscape, a car remains vital. In Everglades City, there are select airboat tour companies to navigate the swampy terrains. A handful of fishing charters are located on the southern end of town for fishing and exploring the islands across Chokoloskee Bay.

The western edge of the Everglades intersects the estuarine mangrove forests of the Ten Thousand Islands, a large wilderness reserve that sets the stage for aquatic adventures both large and small, from multiday canoe-camping trips to short boat rides through the tangled maze of tree-covered islands.

While it's mostly uninhabited, there are a few developed nooks here including Everglades City (population 400). Consider Everglades City about as commercial as this corner of the state gets, with the smallest selection of mom-and-pop restaurants, museums showcasing the historic moments of the broader region and quaint lodge-style accommodations. It's worth a slow stroll and overnight stay if you're looking for a semi-modern reprieve from all the Everglades greenness.

Just south of Everglades City is the small, inhabited island of Chokoloskee (population 350), with its own super-intimate lodging selections – there's a trading post turned museum on its southern shore that is the island's biggest draw.

☑ TOP TIP

Nearby Marco Island has the highest saturation of lodging options, with major beachside resorts, Airbnbs and the in-between. As this is an exclusive enclave, pricing is higher. If you're looking in Everglades City proper, plan accordingly as the options are scarce.

Wilderness Meets Islands

Boat through the island landscape

The **Ten Thousand Islands**, a series of mostly uninhabited islands and mangrove islets, provide scenes like few others. Pods of bottlenose dolphins glide through the waters, with ospreys and bald eagles soaring overhead; loggerhead turtles nest on sandy islands while great blue herons, alligators and even the rare American crocodile stealthily stalk their prey just offshore.

To dive right into these scenes (quite literally in some instances) in Everglades City, the National Park Service (NPS) has its **Gulf Coast Visitor Center** *(nps.gov)* nestled near the southwest edge of town, typically with regular kayak, canoe and water sports programming. Do keep an eye on the NPS

EVERGLADES CITY

website, as the visitor center has been shuttered in recent times due to Gulf Coast hurricane damage.

Non-NPS options include **Everglades Florida Adventures** (*evergladesfloridaadventures.com; from $65*), which runs 90-minute tours aboard a 45ft catamaran, taking you through Chokoloskee Bay, Indian Key Pass and various mangrove islets in the Everglades. You can also rent your own kayaks and canoes, for a few hours or up to 10 days of island-hopping explorations. For guided excursions, book a private tour with **Everglades Adventures Kayak & Eco Tours** (*everglades adventures.com; from $89*), which runs regular itineraries, camping under starry skies at islands along the way. The same outfit also offers shorter (two- and three-hour) paddling tours.

From Skunk Ape to Smallwood
Explore the spectrum of historical spots

For a smaller town, Everglades City has a solid selection of quirkier museum-esque destinations. On Route 41 heading into town, the **Skunk Ape Research Headquarters** (*skunk ape.info; adult/child $10/5*) is worth a quick stop. Appealing to fans of cryptozoology (mythical creatures like Bigfoot, Mothman and the Jersey Devil being within the realm), the

STONE CRAB CAPITAL OF THE WORLD

Though a self-pro-claimed title, 'Stone Crab Capital of the World' is a well-earned one. For some time, stone crabs were thought to be worthless compared with the more popular blue crabs long being harvested in Everglades City. Stone crabs were difficult to cook as a whole, but it turns out they were just misunderstood. Ernest Hamilton, credited with commercializing stone crabbing, discovered that only the claws of the creatures needed to be harvested to provide delicious and lucrative meat. From there, Everglades City stone crabbing boomed to become the 300,000-pound-a-year industry it is today. Everglades City stone crabs can be found at local restaurants and the ever-famous Joe's Stone Crab in Miami.

JILLIAN CAIN PHOTOGRAPHY/SHUTTERSTOCK

Smallwood Store

spot pays homage to its Florida-bred namesake. The skunk ape is said to be resemblant of Bigfoot, large, hairy and lurking throughout Florida's swamps. The 'research headquarters' is mainly a gift shop with T-shirts, keychains and the kitschy in-between, but the staff are full of tales and there's even a reported footprint to get the imagination going.

Perhaps the most comprehensive museum on the Everglades is in the heart of Everglades City. The **Museum of the Everglades** (colliermuseums.com; free) covers over 2000 years of area history, with puzzles, coloring activities and educational crossword puzzles to keep kids entertained.

Nestled just south of Everglades City and on Chokoloskee Island is the **Smallwood Store** (smallwoodstore.com; $5), the island's original market and goods store, dating back to 1906. Since 1990, it has served as a museum and snapshot in time – with soda bottles and candy packages dating decades back, in addition to a gift shop with historic photography, alligator heads and crafts from the Seminole tribe.

EATING IN EVERGLADES CITY: OUR PICKS

Camellia Street Grill: Open-air casual dining on the waterfront serving up seafood and American classics. *hours vary* **$$**

Captain Morgan's Seafood Grill: A Cuban and seafood joint where Latin flavors spice up staples from the sea. *11am-8pm Thu-Sun* **$$$**

City Seafood: Dockside dining offering a mix of seafood and swamp specialties like frog legs and gator bites. *8am-3pm Mon-Fri, to 4pm Sat & Sun* **$**

Diving Pelican: Perfectly fried seafood and themed cocktails with seating available under a chickee hut. *11am-8pm Sun-Thu, to 8.30pm Fri & Sat* **$$$**

Homestead

FRUIT PICKS | LOCAL WINERIES | SUBURBIA REPRIEVE

Homestead and neighboring Florida City make great bases for forays into Everglades National Park. Closer in spirit to Miami (40 miles northwest) than the River of Grass, Homestead is considered part of the ever-expanding South Miami metropolis – it's a bustling suburban corridor that can feel like an endless strip of big-box shopping centers, strip malls and wide-laned boulevards.

Beneath the veneer, there's much more than meets the eye: strange curiosities like a 'castle' built single-handedly by a lovestruck immigrant; a magnificent Buddhist temple that looks like it's been airlifted in from Thailand; a winery showcasing Florida's finest produce (hint: not grapes); and one of the best farm stands in America. For racing fans, Homestead is also home to one of the world's most famous speedways, which especially comes alive with NASCAR races during the fall months.

Coral Like You've Never Seen Before

Admire a one-man-built castle

'You will be seeing unusual accomplishment,' reads the inscription on a rough-hewn quarried wall. That's an understatement. There's no greater temple to one man's obsessive genius than the **Coral Castle** *(coralcastle.com; adult/child $18/8)*, a monumental work of art sitting on the northern edge of Homestead.

The story goes that Edward Leedskalnin, born in Latvia, was jilted by the love of his life one day before his wedding. Heartbroken, he emigrated to the US and eventually found his way to a then-sparsely populated corner of southern Florida,

GETTING AROUND

Rideshare services operate within Homestead, connecting the city with Miami and nearby entrances to national parks (both Everglades and Biscayne). Return trips from the parks may be difficult to book due to limited cell service. Downtown, the Homestead Trolley offers free rides from 6am to 6pm weekdays and from 10am to 2pm on weekends.

☑ TOP TIP

While the area is known as 'Miami's Countryside,' Homestead has an oft-overlooked downtown centered on Krome Ave. Losner Park has outdoor events and neighboring Seminole Theatre has a stately neon sign.

🍴 EATING IN HOMESTEAD: OUR PICKS

Yardie Spice: Small casual mom-and-pop spot with rich Jamaican and Haitian offerings. Vegan-friendly options available. *11.30am-8pm Mon-Sat* **$$**

Shiver's BBQ: Slow-smoked meats and comfort food served up in a cozy atmosphere. The ribs and burnt ends are local faves. *11am-9pm Mon-Thu, to 10pm Fri & Sat* **$$**

White Lion Cafe: English-pub-inspired atmosphere with American fare. Enjoy dining indoors or on the patio. *11am-3pm Tue-Thu & Sat, 5pm-late Fri* **$$**

La Cruzada: Traditional Mexican dishes, a vibrant setting and a margarita selection to match. *9am-10pm* **$**

HOMESTEAD

Everglades National Park

Town Center

0 | 500 m
0 | 0.25 miles

Homestead

See Town Center

Coral Castle

Homestead Miami Speedway

SW 248th St (St Palm Dr)

SW 248th St (Coconut Palm Dr)

SW 147th Ave

Dixie Hwy

SW 268th St (Moody Dr)

Florida City

N | 0 | 2 km
0 | 1 miles

HIGHLIGHTS
1 Coral Castle

SIGHTS
2 Fruit & Spice Park
3 Knaus Berry Farm

4 Schnebly Redland's Winery
5 Wat Buddharangsi

SLEEPING
6 Hoosville Hostel
7 Hotel Redland

8 Tru by Hilton Florida City

EATING
9 City Hall Bistro & Martini Bar
10 Heritage Market

11 La Cruzada
12 Redland Ranch
13 Robert Is Here
14 Shiver's BBQ
15 White Lion Cafe
16 Yardie Spice

where he began his life's work: a massive, castle-like installation dedicated to unrequited love, which he would spend the next 28 years building. This rock-walled compound includes a 'throne room'; a clever sundial that tells both the time and the month; a telescope (of sorts) trained precisely on Polaris; and a revolving, 9-ton boulder gate that was once easily opened with just one finger.

Even more incredibly, all this was built by one diminutive man – Edward was just 5ft tall and weighed 100lb – working alone, without heavy machinery. He accomplished it all using pulleys, hand tools and other improvised devices. Enthusiastic guides point out some of the impressive details hidden within his works, like the Florida-shaped table with its perfectly positioned Lake Okeechobee.

A Slice of Thailand

An unexpected Florida temple

Tucked amid the green fields and palm-fringed lanes northeast of Homestead, the steep golden roofs of **Wat Buddharangsi** (*thaitemplemiamifl.org*) emerge like something out of a fairy tale. Statues adorn the bougainvillea-lined walkways, and two carved lions guard the main entrance. Inside, an elegant, gold-leaf-covered Buddha presides over the peaceful chamber.

Built in 1979, this Buddhist temple was the culmination of two decades of effort by the Thai community to build a suitable gathering place in southeast Florida. Visitors are welcome to Wat Buddharangsi, which is open daily from 7am to 5pm. There are always monks on-site who can guide you.

Floating Through Fresh-Fruit Heaven

An orchard, winery and farm-stand oasis

Farm fields, palm plantations and nurseries are woven into Homestead. You could easily spend the better part of a day taking in some of the exotic wonders flourishing in this verdant corner of southern Florida, starting at the area's most iconic fruit stand: **Robert Is Here** (*robertishere.com*). You'll find loads of Florida-grown fruits you won't get elsewhere in the US – including black sapote, carambola (star fruit) and mamey sapote.

North of Robert's, the **Fruit & Spice Park** (*miamidade.gov; adult/child $15/8*) is a lush, 37-acre garden where you can experience the tropics in all their fecundity. The park makes for a peaceful wander past various species – around 500 different types of fruits, spices and nuts. While you can't pick the fruit, you are permitted to eat anything that falls to the ground.

In winter, from about mid-December to early March, you can pick your own strawberries at **Knaus Berry Farm** (*knausberryfarm.com*), a famed producer that's been around since the 1950s. Knaus also runs a bakery and snack counter – amid fruit-laden cheesecakes and other temptations, its cinnamon buns are famed statewide. The line solely for cinnamon rolls can stretch two hours long; arrive early or on a weekday. The whole place closes down from mid-April through October; it's also closed on Sundays year-round and is cash only.

Schnebly Redland's Winery (*schneblywinery.com; tasting/tour $30/16*) transforms the region's tropical produce into surprisingly good, sweet wines. Wines here are made of mango, passion fruit, lychee, guava, avocado and coconut. Tucked along a quiet farm road west of Homestead, Schnebly is the southernmost winery in America; tastings include five wines.

HOW HOMESTEAD BECAME HOMESTEAD

Homestead's story begins in the late 1890s when the government opened the land for, you guessed it, homesteading. Under the Homestead Act of 1862, people could file to claim government land to settle on. In 1905, when Henry Flagler began to extend the railroad from Miami to Key West, the area quickly became a shipping hub for construction supplies and fruits and vegetables from local farmers. It was dubbed 'Homestead Country' by the engineers who mapped the area since there was no official name established at the time. Homestead Country was eventually shortened to its current form of Homestead and it stuck. The town was officially founded in 1913, becoming the second-oldest municipality in Miami-Dade County.

🍴 EATING IN HOMESTEAD: FARM-FRESH

Heritage Market: Handcrafted dishes like sandwiches and tacos featuring organic ingredients (many grown in the hydroponic garden). *hours vary Thu-Sun* $$

Robert Is Here: Grab fresh fruit including exotic varieties, a smoothie and other snacks on the go at this roadside stand turned iconic market. *9am-6pm* $

Redland Ranch: Farm-to-table spot with open-air seating that feels like a backyard escape, serving American and Latin seasonal favorites. *9am-11pm* $$

City Hall Bistro & Martini Bar: Feast on carefully crafted ceviche, chimichurri lamb chops or Philly cheesesteak egg rolls in a historic hotel. *Hours vary Tue-Sun* $$$

THE GUIDE

BISCAYNE NATIONAL PARK THE EVERGLADES & BISCAYNE NATIONAL PARK

Biscayne National Park

BOATER'S PARADISE | REEF GAZING | BIRD-WATCHING NOOKS

GETTING AROUND

Homestead runs a free bus service to and from the Dante Fascell Visitor Center on weekends between January and early April. Otherwise, given limited service, rideshare options are not reliable once in the park.

Just to the east of the Everglades – and right on Miami's southern doorstep – is Biscayne National Park, 95% of which is made up of the waters of Biscayne Bay and the Atlantic Ocean. A portion of the world's third-largest reef sits here just off the coast, along with mangrove forests and the northernmost Florida Keys. This is some of the best reef viewing and snorkeling you'll find in the USA (outside Hawaii and nearby Key Largo).

The human presence in the park spans more than 10,000 years, from nomadic prehistoric tribes to folly-fueled developers in the 20th century. Mingling aside the reefs are dozens of shipwrecks, some dating back to the 18th century. Although the keys that are part of the national park are today uninhabited, you can learn about the history of former 19th-century homesteaders and Gatsby-esque industrialists here on a visit to the islands.

Gliding Above & Below the Surface

Boating, kayaking and making a splash

Most travelers come for a day's adventure in the national park, which could entail kayaking, snorkeling or island exploring. Biscayne National Park Institute, which operates out of **Dante Fascell Visitor Center** *(nps.gov/bisc)*, runs a variety of excursions, all of which are best reserved before you visit the park. Wherever you go in Biscayne, you're likely to see plenty of seabirds, from cormorants perched on mooring posts and flocks of brown pelicans flying in formation to steely-eyed osprey gliding just above the water. Pods of bottlenose dolphins zip across the horizon, while crabs and lizards scuttle amid the roots of red mangroves along the water's edge.

The **Heritage of Biscayne cruise** *(biscaynenationalpark institute.org; adult/child $83/59)* takes you out across the bay and past **Adams**, **Elliott** and **Boca Chita** keys. Once aboard this half-day tour, guides bring the islands' past to life, relating the stories of some of the people who've lived here over

☑ TOP TIP

The gateway to the park, the Dante Fascell Visitor Center has exhibitions on ecology, marine life and surrounding human settlement. A brief film gives an overview of Biscayne's four ecosystems, while the gallery features nature- and wildlife-themed pieces by artists working in a variety of media.

BISCAYNE NATIONAL PARK

Biscayne Bay

Sands Key

Boca Chita Key

Biscayne National Park

Elliott Key

Hawk Channel

West Arsenicker Key

Arsenicker Keys

Rubicon Keys

Long Arsenicker

Totten Key

Ceasar Rock

Spite Highway Trail

Atlantic Ocean

East Arsenicker

Swan Key

Old Rhodes Key

Card Sound

Gold Key

0   5 km
0   2.5 miles

SIGHTS
1 Adams Key
2 Boca Chita Key
3 Elliott Key
4 Jones Lagoon
5 Mandalay Shipwreck

ACTIVITIES
6 Convoy Point Jetty Walk
7 Elliott Key Loop Trail
8 Spite Highway Trail

SLEEPING
9 Boca Chita Key Campground
10 Elliott Key Campground

INFORMATION
11 Dante Fascell Visitor Center

the years. There was Israel Jones, an African American man who settled on Porgy Key in the 1850s and transformed it into one of South Florida's most prosperous key lime and pineapple farms. His descendants were instrumental in helping to preserve the islands for future generations (instead of taking a hefty payout from developers).

The industrialist Mark Honeywell, on the other hand, left his mark on Boca Chita Key. After founding his eponymous thermostat and home heating company, he bought Boca Chita as a holiday retreat, building an ornamental lighthouse and a chapel and polishing up some old Spanish cannons that would be fired to welcome guests to the lavish parties he loved to host. The cruise typically stops at Boca Chita, where you can admire the views from atop the lighthouse, walk a short nature trail amid the mangroves and enjoy some downtime on the island's tiny beach.

For a closer look at the park's natural beauty, you can sign up for one of several **paddling tours** ($39 per 1½ hours). Hidden between Totten Key and Old Rhodes Key, **Jones Lagoon** has calm, clear waters fringed by mangrove trees. After a 30-minute motorboat ride from the mainland, you'll hop onto a stand-up paddleboard (which allows better perspectives for viewing marine life than a kayak) and look for great blue herons, great egrets and roseate spoonbills as you glide silently along. In the aquamarine waters below, you might spy sea turtles, baby sharks, rays, upside-down jellyfish or sea stars.

Snorkeling trips ($115 per 3½ hours) offer you immersion in Biscayne's most biologically diverse ecosystem. On a half-day trip, you'll visit two different sites, exploring coral reefs, a shipwreck or a bayside setting amid the mangroves, where

Continues on p132

A PARTY ON STILTS

The history of Stiltsville is shrouded in some mystery, but it was once a hotspot for parties and socializing. The collection of wooden shacks on stilts, only accessible by boat, hovers above the water of Biscayne Bay. Stiltsville began when its original core shack was built in the 1930s. Only a handful of the original remain due to the exposed location and havoc-wreaking storms. In 1985, the area became a part of Biscayne National Park. Use of the houses is by permit only, but the structures are preserved to highlight the park's marine resources and remain a reminder of the area's history. You can take a tour to Stiltsville with from Biscayne National Park Institute (p93).

Biscayne to Everglades City

This multi-park trek takes you from Biscayne through the Everglades, highlighting access points to the parks as well as quick stops along the way for snacks and added swampiness. The drive totals 118 miles one way. Expect to spend the greater portion of a day with this itinerary, especially if you'd like a slower pace with your pit stops.

① Dante Fascell Visitor Center

The first stop on this drive takes you to the clear waters of Biscayne National Park. There are plenty of adventures and eco tours that are bookable on-site, if time permits. If a short visit is all there is time for, take the 0.8-mile saunter along the **Convoy Point Jetty Walk**. The path will take you along the mangrove-lined shore out to the jetty, which houses the Colonial Bird Protection Area.

The Drive: Head west toward Florida City. In the tiny suburban town, stop by Everglades Outpost, a nonprofit run by volunteers that rehabilitates injured gators and gives tours.

② Ernest F Coe Visitor Center

This visitor center is a stellar jumping-off point for many popular walking trails nearby. It's also very close to a selfie-worthy Everglades National Park entry sign. Meander around the visitor center to learn more about the park, its critters and the walks around the area. Accessibility ranges from short family-friendly trails such as Gumbo Limbo and a short paved path on the Pinelands Trail to longer, less maintained trails along the Long Pine Key Trails.

The Drive: Make your way north through Redland. Schnebly Redland's Winery is along

Chokoloskee Island and the Ten Thousand Islands

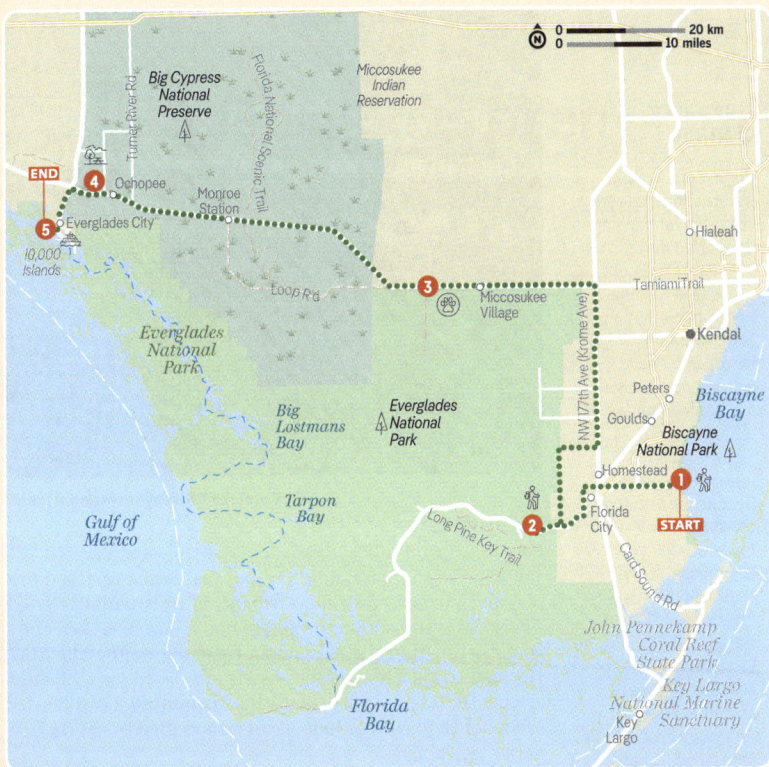

the route, providing a good opportunity to grab some grub or perhaps a fruit-forward libation.

3 Shark Valley Visitor Center

This is the spot for alligator sightings. After you wander through the educational displays and watch the park video, hop on the tram to cruise the 15-mile loop where alligators are likely to be sunning themselves feet away from the path. Halfway through the ride, hop off to climb an observation tower where expansive views of the park and wildlife will delight. Be sure to snag a reservation for the tram in advance.

The Drive: As you venture west into swampland, stop at Clyde Butcher Big Cypress Gallery to view timeless snaps of Everglades landscapes from its iconic namesake photographer and his wife, Niki.

4 Nathaniel P Reed Visitor Center

Peruse the indoor and outdoor exhibits that tell the stories of the natural and cultural history of Big Cypress Swamp. Learn about the swamp, its resources and recreation when you view the preserve film. On occasion there will be art exhibits displayed at the visitor center as well.

The Drive: Continuing along the Tamiami Trail, you'll eventually hang a left to head south towards Everglades City. The food picks are slim until you arrive in stone crab heaven.

5 Gulf Coast Visitor Center

Cruise around Everglades City and peep into the historic buildings like the Bank of the Everglades and the Museum of the Everglades. Everglades City is the launching point for tours of Ten Thousand Islands (p122). A five-minute drive south takes you along a small tree-lined road to Chokoloskee Island, whose top attraction is Smallwood Store (p124), a shop-turned-museum that many say is haunted.

SHIPWRECK CENTRAL

Coral reefs, shallow waters and shoals are notorious for bringing down even the mightiest of vessels – Biscayne National Park is no exception. The geography here, combined with strong currents and unpredictable weather, made this region a hotspot for such tragedies. Despite the eventual construction of the Fowey Rocks Lighthouse, many ships met their dark fate in the shallow waters of the Florida Straits. Six wrecks still visible along its shores include the *Arratoon Apcar, Erl King, Alicia, Lugano, Mandalay,* as well as an unnamed vessel about which very little is known. Underwater plaques at each site tell the full story of each ship and the fate of its passengers and cargo.

Coral reef, Biscayne National Park

Continued from p129

you can see soft coral and sea sponges. Scuba-certified divers can sign on for a six-hour trip including two **dives** *($298)*. There's also the option to explore half a dozen sunken ships contained within the park on an excursion to the Maritime Heritage Trail. Three of the vessels are suited for scuba divers, but the others – particularly the **Mandalay**, a two-masted schooner that sank in 1966 – can be accessed by snorkelers.

A Hike Full of 'Spite'

The national park's longest trail

On Elliott Key, you can hike the longest trail in the national park, a wooded stretch known as the **Spite Highway Trail**. In the 1960s, developers had grand designs on this coastline, envisioning hotels, roads and even a small airport that would be part of the new city of 'Islandia.' Conservationists, however, managed to convince the public that this region was worth preserving. Having lost the public relations battle, developers brought bulldozers to Elliott Key and blazed a six-lane, 7-mile-long swath down the middle of the island in hopes of spoiling the area's preservation. Their wanton destruction failed, however, and President Lyndon B Johnson signed the bill creating Biscayne National Monument in 1968.

Today, the trail is smooth, flat and generally canopied. Particularly during the spring and summer months, make sure to pack mosquito repellant and long clothing as the swarming can be intense. There are no water vistas on the hike – for those, hit the **Elliott Key Loop Trail** that follows the perimeter of the island.

Places We Love to Stay

$ Budget $$ Midrange $$$ Top End

Everglades National Park   MAP p113

Flamingo Campground $
Drive-in campground with heated showers, dump stations, grills, as well as access to fishing and hiking.

Flamingo Lodge $$
Comfortable accommodations deep in the Everglades. Waterfront rooms, on-site dining, rentals, glamping tents and tours available.

Beyond Everglades National Park

The Boat House $$ Spot manatees and dolphins or go fishing off the docks of the property within walking distance of the shops and restaurants in historic Old Marco.

Olde Marco Island Inn & Suites $$$ Old Florida style meets modern design at this lush retreat that's great for families or groups.

JW Marriott Marco Island Beach Resort $$$ Stay at this private luxurious beachfront resort and unwind on the beach, relax at the spa or play 18 holes.

Everglades City   MAP p123

Rod & Gun Club Lodge $$ Quaint rooms with a historic flair. An oasis-like pool, cottages and a screened-in porch overlooking the river add to the charm.

Ivey House Everglades Adventure Hotel $$ Sleep peacefully after a day of Everglades adventures that can be bundled with your stay for extra savings.

River Wilderness Waterfront Villas $$$ Waterfront cabins with amenities like free bicycle and canoe rentals, boat ramp access and a swimming pool.

Homestead & Florida City   MAP p126

Tru By Hilton Florida City $ Budget-friendly stay without compromising comfort and cleanliness.

Hoosville Hostel $ A variety of room options are available at this cozy and conveniently located hostel with amenities like kayak rentals and a fire pit.

Hotel Redland $$ Historic building with recently renovated rooms, where charming common areas meet bright modern accommodations. Conveniently located in the center of town.

Biscayne National Park   MAP p129

Elliott Key Campground $ A hiking trail and fishing on the island. Restrooms and cold showers available. Access by boat only.

Boca Chita Key Campground $ Waterfront views, picnic tables and grills. There are toilets on-site. Access by boat only.

Flamingo Lodge

Florida Keys & Key West

ARCHIPELAGO RETREAT FOR OOOHS AND AAAHS

Imagine 1700 islands with teal-water surrounds, stretches of overwater bridges and endless doings spanning the spectrum of laying low with nature to totally letting loose.

Curling beneath the Miami metropolitan area are the Florida Keys: a 113-mile-long archipelago of sandbar and mangrove islands, aqua waters and memorable sunsets. A journey down the Overseas Highway takes you from the soft bustle of Key Largo to Key West, past arts-loving villages, old-fashioned roadside eateries and stretches of every hue of swamp-esque green. Along the way, cross some 42 bridges (including one that stretches 7 miles across open waters).

Paddling across mirror-like coves and joining the free-spirited party people in Key West is just a sample of the great Florida Keys experience. You can also take in the unusual plant and animal life and explore fascinating history still visible on these shores – from abandoned railroad trestles built in the early 20th century to grand homes and museums filled with treasures (much of which was discovered by the region's once-thriving salvaging industry). 'Salvaging,' by the way, means harvesting shipwrecks, which speaks to a sort of pirate-y roguishness that has long characterized the Keys' identity. Building on this, is a hurricane-surviving resiliency that has particularly shined in recent years.

This is a region that sets its own sunbaked rules, with Key West being the utmost trend bucker. A large society of artists and craftspeople congregated here at the end of the Great Depression, and that community has grown into one of the most renowned and best organized, gay-friendly cities in the country where the pride and party seemingly never stop.

THE MAIN AREAS

KEY LARGO
Coral reefs and cozy abodes.
p140

ISLAMORADA
Best breweries, sportfishing capital, lux resorts. **p145**

MARATHON
Fishing paradise and a bridge like no other. **p150**

BIG PINE KEY
Deer refuge and camping haven.
p157

KEY WEST
Cultural heartbeat, a party for everyone. **p161**

For places to stay in Florida Keys & Key West, see p171

MIA2YOU/SHUTTERSTOCK

Left: Turtle; Above: Overseas Highway (p144)

Find Your Way

Gulf of Mexico

Prepare to island-hop, primarily by car on bridges aplenty above glistening waters. A boat charter or ferry is less about the necessity of getting from A to B, but more about soaking up the Keys' true essence.

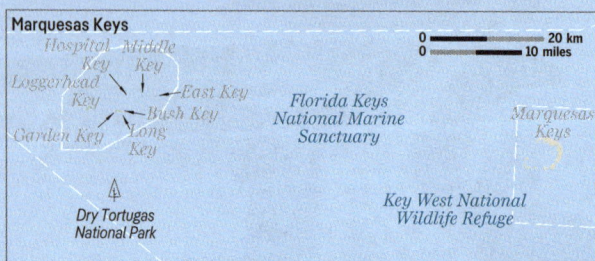

Marquesas Keys

Hospital Key · Middle Key
Loggerhead Key · East Key
Garden Key · Bush Key · Long Key

0 — 20 km
0 — 10 miles

Florida Keys National Marine Sanctuary

Marquesas Keys

Dry Tortugas National Park

Key West National Wildlife Refuge

National K Deer Refu

See Marquesas Keys

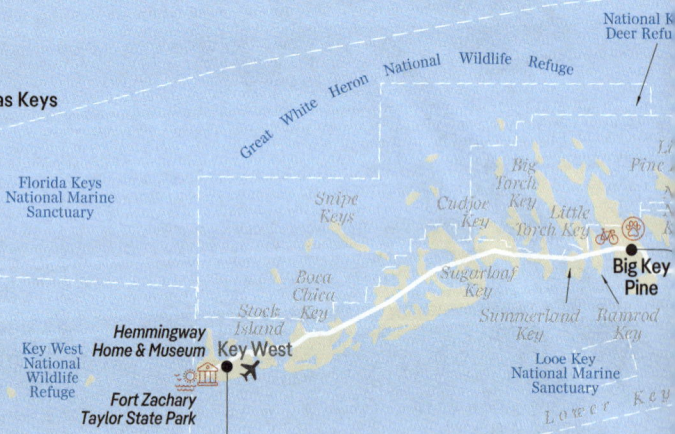

Great White Heron National Wildlife Refuge

Florida Keys National Marine Sanctuary

Marquesas Keys

Snipe Keys

Cudjoe Key

Big Torch Key
Little Torch Key

Li Pine

Big Key Pine

Boca Chica

Stock Island

Sugarloaf Key

Summerland Key · Ramrod Key

Key West National Wildlife Refuge

Hemmingway Home & Museum · Key West

Fort Zachary Taylor State Park

Looe Key National Marine Sanctuary

Lower Key

Key West, p161

Let loose during a Sunset Party at Mallory Square. As the sun dips, fire jugglers, street performers and live music serenade crowds.

Big Pine Key, p157

Venture to Blue Hole in Big Pine Key, a freshwater reprieve amid the key's impenetrable pine forests. Spot endangered Key deer, gators and turtles.

CAR

Driving is the easiest way of getting from key to key. The Overseas Hwy – the vital artery connecting most – assures seamless navigating. Heading to the Keys (southbound) on a Friday and out of town (northbound) on a Sunday, can equate to crawling traffic.

BUS

The Lower Keys Shuttle connects points between Marathon and Key West, stopping primarily along the Overseas Hwy. North of the Keys, Miami-Dade County has buses connecting Florida City and Marathon.

BICYCLE

The Florida Keys Overseas Heritage Trail includes 90-plus miles of paved trails, extending from Key Largo to Key West. The path runs parallel to US-1 and incorporates 23 historic railroad bridges.

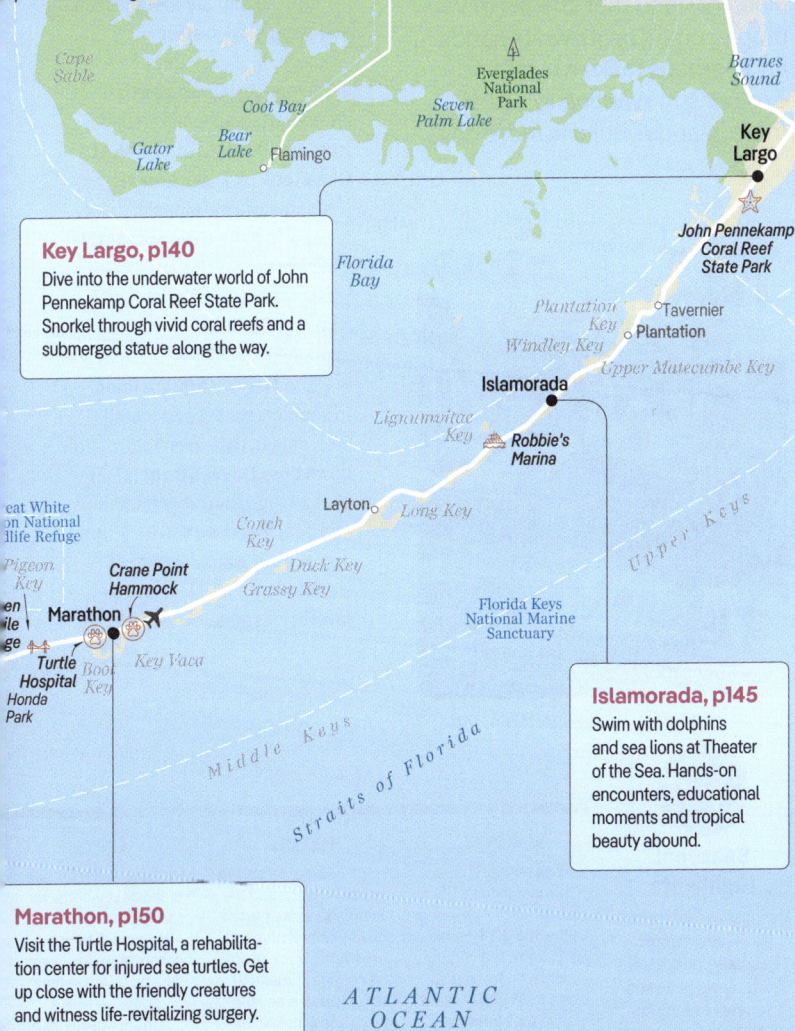

Cape Sable

Coot Bay

Gator Lake

Bear Lake

Flamingo

Everglades National Park

Seven Palm Lake

Barnes Sound

Key Largo

John Pennekamp Coral Reef State Park

Florida Bay

Key Largo, p140

Dive into the underwater world of John Pennekamp Coral Reef State Park. Snorkel through vivid coral reefs and a submerged statue along the way.

Plantation Key

Tavernier

Plantation

Windley Key

Upper Matecumbe Key

Islamorada

Lignumvitae Key

Robbie's Marina

Layton

Long Key

Great White Heron National Wildlife Refuge

Conch Key

Duck Key

Upper Keys

Pigeon Key

Crane Point Hammock

Grassy Key

Seven Mile Bridge

Marathon

Key Vaca

Turtle Hospital

Boot Key

Bahia Honda State Park

Florida Keys National Marine Sanctuary

Islamorada, p145

Swim with dolphins and sea lions at Theater of the Sea. Hands-on encounters, educational moments and tropical beauty abound.

Middle Keys

Straits of Florida

Marathon, p150

Visit the Turtle Hospital, a rehabilitation center for injured sea turtles. Get up close with the friendly creatures and witness life-revitalizing surgery.

ATLANTIC OCEAN

0   20 km
0   10 miles

Plan Your Time

Find an island that speaks to you, plop yourself on its white sands and perhaps make a weekend exploring it. Wanting to build in more islands? Build in more days.

LAZYLLAMA/SHUTTERSTOCK

Robbie's Marina (p145)

If You Only Have Time for One Key

● Land in or venture to **Key West** (p161) at the end of the Overseas Hwy. It's worth the drive for its hybrid of culture, serene landscapes and ever-partying spirit.

● Devote late morning and early afternoon to wandering around town, with pit stops at **Key West Cemetery** (p167) and **Ernest Hemingway's old mansion** (p166) to say hi to some six-toed cats. By choice or not, you'll inevitably lose yourself amid the colorful Caribbean homes of Old Town.

● Go to **Mallory Square** (p166) to soak in a sunset and literally celebrate it, then take a slow stroll down busy **Duval Street** (p167) at night, popping into restaurants and bars that draw you in. **Sloppy Joe's** (p166) was a favorite of Hemingway and will soon be a favorite of yours.

Seasonal Highlights

During snowbird months (November through February), things feel busier in bigger towns. Summer to early fall is for bargain seekers, though tropical weather may affect the area.

JANUARY

With temperatures warmer than its US counterparts – hovering in the mid-60°F to mid-70°F range, day through night – no wonder so many folks ring in a new year in the Florida Keys.

MARCH

South Florida is a **spring break** hotspot, and the Florida Keys are part of the mix March through mid-April. If you're not a college student, **St Patrick's Day** is an all-ages spectacle with festivities archipelago-wide.

APRIL

For fishers, April is one of the best months for snagging a big one. Mahimahi, tarpon, wahoo, blue marlin and yellowtail are in their prime, so plan a **fishing** adventure.

Three Days to Travel Around

● Yes, you can go further west in the Keys than Key West. Book a trip out to **Dry Tortugas National Park** (p169) and have a snorkel around the historic fort there. Back in **Key West** (p161), head to the **Florida Keys Eco-Discovery Center** (p161) to get a grounding in the natural habitat of the islands, which you should begin exploring in earnest.

● Hop in a car and drive north, making sure to stop at **Bahia Honda State Park** (p154) for some super-quiet beach time. Head to **No Name Key** (p155), have a pizza and a beer at the **No Name Pub** (p159), and gawk at some tiny Key deer. Venture back to Key West for a sunset celebration and evening fun.

If You Have More Time

● You'll be driving yet again, this time over the **Seven Mile Bridge** (p152) that connects **Big Pine Key** (p157) to **Marathon** (p150), the center island of the Keys. On Marathon, head into the jungle at **Crane Point Hammock** (p150) to lose yourself amid coastal views and tropical trees.

● Continue on to **Islamorada** (p145). First and foremost, snag a pic with the larger-than-life **Betsy the Lobster** (p149). From there, book a kayaking excursion at **Robbie's Marina** (p145) – after hand-feeding some massive tarpon fish, paddle out to eerie islands like **Indian Key** (p146). Wade into the water at **Anne's Beach** (p147), then head to **John Pennekamp Coral Reef State Park** (p140) at Key Largo to round out the trip with a snorkeling or diving outing.

JUNE

The heat is on and so is hurricane season. June through November, keep an eye on weather systems developing in the Atlantic Ocean and Gulf of Mexico that may affect your trip.

JULY

A darling of dessert menus everywhere, celebrate your love of key lime pie at the **Key Lime Festival** in Key West this month. You'll want that slice of pie extra cool – the weather is scorching all month long.

OCTOBER

Dress up and party for 10 consecutive days at Key West's **Fantasy Fest** (p168). For Halloween traditionalists, there is plenty to do throughout the islands on the big day, and those leading up to it.

DECEMBER

The holidays are celebrated on land and afloat. As colorful as The Florida Keys are year-round, things feel that much cheerier and more vibrant when closing the year with a lighted boat parade.

Key Largo

LAID-BACK LUXURY | PARK PARADISE | GOURMET BITES

GETTING AROUND

Miami-Dade Transit's bus route #301 takes you to Key Largo from Miami's core in 90 minutes. Otherwise, a car is ideal for navigating the town and points beyond. Central portions of the key – notably neighborhoods near the central YMCA – are walkable, but a car or rental bike are necessary for exploring further. Uber and Lyft operate in the area but can be limited late at night and in peak season (December to March). Marinas in town offer boat rentals and charters for off-shore experiences.

☑TOP TIP

Book a snorkeling or diving trip to the Molasses Reef. The water is as clear as it gets, and a historic Spanish ship anchor, bright fish species and boulder coral loom below the surface.

The blanket of mangrove forest that forms the South Florida coastline spreads like a woody morass into Key Largo, the northernmost of the Florida Keys. As you drive onto the island, it resembles a line of low-lying hammock and strip development. The bridges entering Key Largo are painted aqua hues, providing the perfect segue into the watery surrounds that greet you.

The US-1 corridor here can appear tourist trap-esque, with souvenir shops and periodic billboards touting 'the best' key lime pie. But just outside the principal artery, you'll find a blend of elegant resorts and untamed wilderness. Coral reefs await within John Pennekamp Coral Reef State Park, renowned as the Diving Capital of the World.

Historically, Key Largo was a stopover for pirates and traders before evolving into a tranquil retreat for those seeking natural beauty over nightlife. Its rich maritime culture remains reflected in local seafood restaurants, homegrown boutiques and sport-fishing competitions year-round.

Soaking Up Scenery & Sun

Diving into the John Pennekamp Coral Reef State Park

John Pennekamp (*floridastateparks.org; vehicle $8, person 50¢*) has the singular distinction of being the USA's first underwater park. There's 170 acres of dry parkland here and more than 48,000 acres (75 sq miles) of wet: the vast majority of the protected area is the ocean. Before you get out into or onto that water, be sure to take in some of the pleasant beaches and stroll along the nature trails – all part of the park, too.

Three trails are short, flat and more educational than a physical jaunt. The **Mangrove Trail** is a good boardwalk introduction to this ecologically awesome species (the trees, often submerged in water, breathe via long roots that act as snorkels). At a whopping 0.6 miles long, the **Grove Trail** is the longest, and per the name, winds through tropical fruit groves that occasionally attract butterflies. If you're curious

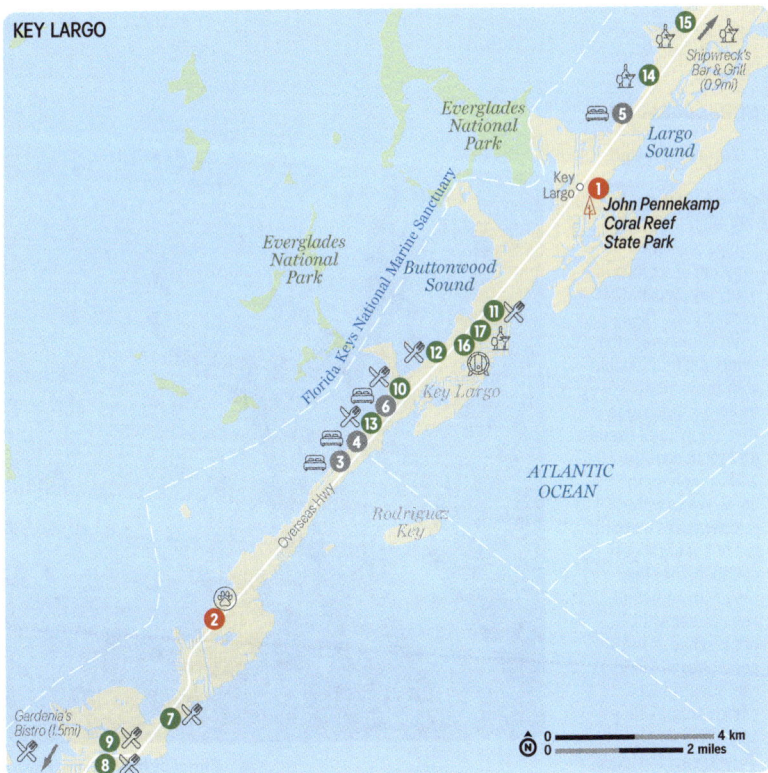

KEY LARGO

HIGHLIGHTS
1 John Pennekamp
Coral Reef State Park

SIGHTS
2 Laura Quinn Wild Bird
Sanctuary

SLEEPING
3 Baker's Cay Resort
Key Largo
4 Playa Largo Resort
& Spa
5 Reefhouse Resort and
Marina
6 Seafarer Resort

EATING
7 Calypso's Sur
8 Casamar Seafood
Market
9 Habanos on the Creek
10 Italian Food Company
11 Key Largo Conch
House

12 Pinecrest Bakery
13 Sol by the Sea

DRINKING & NIGHTLIFE
14 Breezer's Tiki Bar
15 Jimmy Johnson's
Big Chill
16 Shipwreck's Bar & Grill
17 Skippers Dockside

---

about the trees of the Keys, have a saunter around the **Wild Tamarind Trail** where many of the hardwoods are labeled.

Stick around for nightly campfire programs. The **visitor center** is informative and well run, and has a small saltwater aquarium and nature films providing a glimpse of what's

🍽 DRINKING IN KEY LARGO: OUR PICKS

Skippers Dockside:
Rustic charm, waterfront seating, sandy lounge area and live music give this waterfront joint the ultimate Keys vibes. *11am-11pm*

Breezer's Tiki Bar:
Whet your whistle with specialty cocktails and local brews on the beach at Reefhouse Resort & Marina. *4-10pm*

Jimmy Johnson's Big Chill: Sunsets with drink in hand don't disappoint at this famous bar at the Hall of Fame football coach's namesake venue. *11am-9pm Sun-Thu, to 10pm Fri & Sat*

Shipwreck's Bar & Grill:
A low-key spot on a small waterway, with friendly service and live music. *11am-9pm Wed-Sun*

CORAL BLEACHING

Coral reefs develop over thousands of years, with tiny reef-building coral polyps coming together and growing many layers of hard exoskeleton. Their color comes from the symbiotic relationship with zooxanthellae, a microscopic algae that live in coral tissue and produce food and oxygen for the coral. When water temperatures become too hot or coral gets stressed, they lose their zooxanthellae and appear white or bleached. If the coral goes too long without its main energy source, they can starve and die. Coral bleaching leads to larger issues like loss of biodiversity and increased chances of coastal flooding. Widespread restoration efforts in the Keys continue to focus on preventing and repairing one of Florida's important natural resources.

Christ of the Abyss statue

below those waters. To really get beneath the surface, take a 2.5-hour, glass-bottom boat tour. You'll be brought out in a catamaran to **Molasses Reef**, where you'll see filigreed flaps of soft coral, technicolor schools of fish, dangerous-looking barracuda and massive yet graceful sea turtles perhaps.

The park's most famous attraction is the coral-fringed **Christ of the Abyss**, an 8.5ft, 4000-pound bronze sculpture of Jesus – a copy of a similar sculpture off the Portofino Peninsula in northern Italy. On calm days, the park offers snorkeling trips to the statue, 6 miles offshore. You can also arrange diving excursions, which are obviously a big draw, or paddle through several miles of 'blue' trails among the mangroves.

EATING IN KEY LARGO: OUR PICKS

Pinecrest Bakery: Small Cuban bakery open nonstop, serving sandwiches, pastelitos and empanadas. *24hrs* $

Italian Food Company: Indulge in fresh Italian and pizza on a charming outdoor patio. *hours vary Wed-Mon* $$

Key Largo Conch House: Fresh seafood abounds at this waterfront restaurant. For an authentic Keys taste, start with conch fritters. *8am-9pm* $$$

Sol by the Sea: Opt for the Water Table experience where you dine at sunset around a table in the water. *11am-10pm Mon-Fri, from 10am Sat & Sun* $$$

Fine-Feathered Friends to Gawk At

Take a peck at the Laura Quinn Wild Bird Sanctuary

The Florida Keys aren't just popular with tourists. The islands – like much of the outdoors in South Florida – serve as a waypoint for migrating birds; acre for acre, the archipelago is a birding paradise. But many birds sustain injuries over the course of their transit, and that's where **Laura Quinn Wild Bird Sanctuary** *(keepthemflying.org; $10 donation)* – on the southern edge of Key Largo en route to Tavernier – steps up. The seven-acre space serves as a protected refuge for a wide variety of injured birds. A boardwalk leads through various enclosures where you can learn a bit about some of the permanent residents – those unable to be released back in the wild. You can also join guided tours *($20)* that dive into each bird's rescue story and ongoing care. Don't miss the daily pelican feeding sessions, which are a visitor favorite.

Species here include masked boobies, great horned owls, green herons, brown pelicans, double-crested cormorants and others. The same organization also runs a bird hospital just south along the main highway. They're the ones to contact if you see injured birds – or have any other bird emergencies – during your travels.

These Sips Mead Business

Tasting honey wine on island time

Yes, the fabled honey drink of the gods has a producer in Key Largo. For something completely different, stop by for a tasting at **Keys Meads** *(keysmeads.com),* a family-run, artisanal mead producer. Owner Jeff Kesling has an encyclopedic knowledge of all things mead-related and has created many unique varieties of his award-winning libation, all made from locally sourced honey.

During a tasting, you can try 10 meads for $10 or its entire current menu for $24 (small pours, since the alcohol content ranges from 7% to 14%). The lineup changes regularly, but might include lychee, mango, blueberry and habanero-infused varieties. Whichever flavor a tasting entails, you'll learn about the fermentation process and how different honey varieties impact flavor. Mead enthusiasts – perhaps you, after indulging – can purchase bottles to take home, including limited-edition batches not available online. For a bonus treat, and if you have belly room post-tasting, try a mead slushie. While you're in town, keep an eye out for special events which include mead-making classes and pairing affairs.

UNDERSTANDING THE TEQUESTA

The area's earliest known inhabitants were the Tequesta (Tekesta) people who left behind 24 holes, inscribed in bedrock arranged in a perfect circle, in Miami 2000 years ago. The Miami Circle is thought to be the only prehistoric structural footprint of its kind in the Eastern US.

The Tequesta were mostly wiped out by Spanish contact, which brought violence and disease. There is evidence of shell middens left behind by the Tequesta in Key Largo and the Upper Keys. Their lives seem to have been relatively peaceful, even comfortable; the shallow waters of Biscayne Bay provided a ceaseless flow of shellfish, sharks, turtle eggs and other readily available calories.

EATING IN KEY LARGO: NEXT DOOR IN TAVERNIER

Casamar Seafood Market: Select the freshest seafood for home cooking, or dine in at Mar Bar. The fish dip and stone crab are local favorites. *10am-5.30pm* $

Calypso's Sur: The fish tacos are all the rage at this intimate restaurant. Cheese steaks and she-crab soup are other fan favorites. Cash only. *noon-5pm Mon-Fri* $

Gardenia's Bistro: Cute outdoor cafe nestled in a garden center, serving smoothies, bowls, sandwiches and coffee. *hours vary* $$

Habanos on the Creek: Casual Cuban and seafood spot at a marina. Dine on the waterfront and don't skip the Cuban sandwich. 11.30am-9pm $$

HERITAGE TRAIL ROAD TRIP

Cruise the Upper Keys on the Overseas Highway. Pull off the road for biker bars, seafood grills and blissful beaches along the way.

START	END	LENGTH
Dagny Johnson Key Largo Hammock Botanical State Park	Long Key State Park	93 miles; 8 hrs

How many of the 84 protected species of plants and animals – including the elusive American crocodile – can you count at ❶ **Dagny Johnson Key Largo Hammock Botanical State Park**? Drive south next along the Overseas Highway to ❷ **John Pennekamp Coral Reef State Park**. Stroll along the Mangrove Trail, a short loop adjacent to the park's paddling trail. After, whet your whistle at ❸ **The Caribbean Club**, the oldest bar in the Upper Keys, just six minutes' drive down the street from the state park.

As you make your way further south, satisfy your sweet tooth with a slice of authentic key lime pie at ❹ **Blond Giraffe Key Lime Pie Factory**. Down the road in Islamorada, pause to snap a photo with the 30ft-high sculpture of Betsy the lobster at ❺ **Rain Barrell Village** and explore art by local artisans.

Following the highway further south brings you to ❻ **History of Diving Museum** where you can nerd out on the history of underwater exploration. After working up an appetite just learning about diving, fuel up with craft bites and brews at ❼ **Islamorada Brewery**. Keep it classic with a draft of the subtly citrus Sandbar Sunday or taste the Keys with the key lime and coconut-y No Wake Zone. Wrap up your road trip at ❽ **Long Key State Park** with a geocaching session.

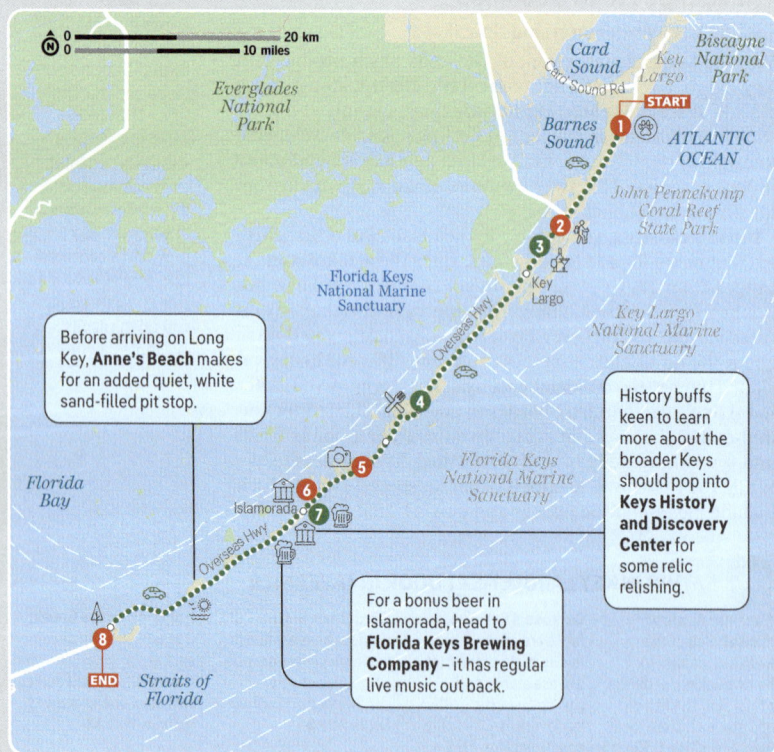

Before arriving on Long Key, **Anne's Beach** makes for an added quiet, white sand-filled pit stop.

History buffs keen to learn more about the broader Keys should pop into **Keys History and Discovery Center** for some relic relishing.

For a bonus beer in Islamorada, head to **Florida Keys Brewing Company** – it has regular live music out back.

Islamorada

SPORTFISHING HAVEN | ARTIST ENCLAVE | GIANT LOBSTER

Though just boasting a population of 7000-plus and a land mass of just over 7 miles, the artistic flair and natural beauty of Islamorada make it feel ten times bigger. Known as the 'Sportfishing Capital of the World,' weekend fishers from South Florida and competitive sportsmen alike flock to Islamorada for trophy catches in its open blue-green waters.

But there's more than just fishing here. Shallow flats and the lushest of mangroves make for total coastal charm. For history buffs, this was the site of a circa 1733 Spanish Treasure Fleet wreck, making for interesting coastal dives. For art lovers, there are quaint galleries and studios, often with beachy work. Plus, you can't miss Betsy, a 40ft-long, 30ft high recreation of a Florida Spiny Lobster looming off US-1. It makes for a stellar Instagram op and is perhaps indicative of just how creative and quirky this key is.

Feed Very, Very Big Fish

Shopping at Robbie's and exploring beyond

Islamorada's scruffy jewel, **Robbie's Marina** *(robbies.com)* covers all bases: it's a local flea market, tacky tourist shop, sea pen for tarpons (massive fish), waterfront restaurant and jumping-off point for fishing expeditions, all wrapped into one driftwood-laced compound. Boat rental and tours are also available.

When you park, you'll first be confronted with the market portion of Robbie's, showcasing crafts and art from around the islands. It's a good spot for picking up a piece of unique memorabilia. If folks aren't perusing paintings, they might be knocking back beers while checking out the waterfront view. If this all feels like it's a bit of sensory overload, you can quickly escape the bustle by hiring a kayak on-site *(kayakthefloridakeys.com; $50-60 per day)* for a peaceful paddle through nearby mangroves, hammocks and lagoons. In fact, this is the major launching point for paddlers looking

GETTING AROUND

Within Islamorada, it's biker-friendly. Multiple rental hubs are tucked along the Overseas Highway, with Backcountry Cowboy Outfitters *(backcountrycowboy. com)* being a popular shop. Twenty miles of the Florida Keys Overseas Heritage Trail runs through the village, making for a flat, paved path through much of town.

While there is no public transit solely dedicated to Islamorada, the Key West Transit Lower Keys Shuttle *(cityofkeywest-fl.gov)* connects the village to other islands, namely Key Largo and Marathon. Rideshares, taxis and charter boats can help you connect the dots. A car is needed for off-island treks.

ISLAMORADA

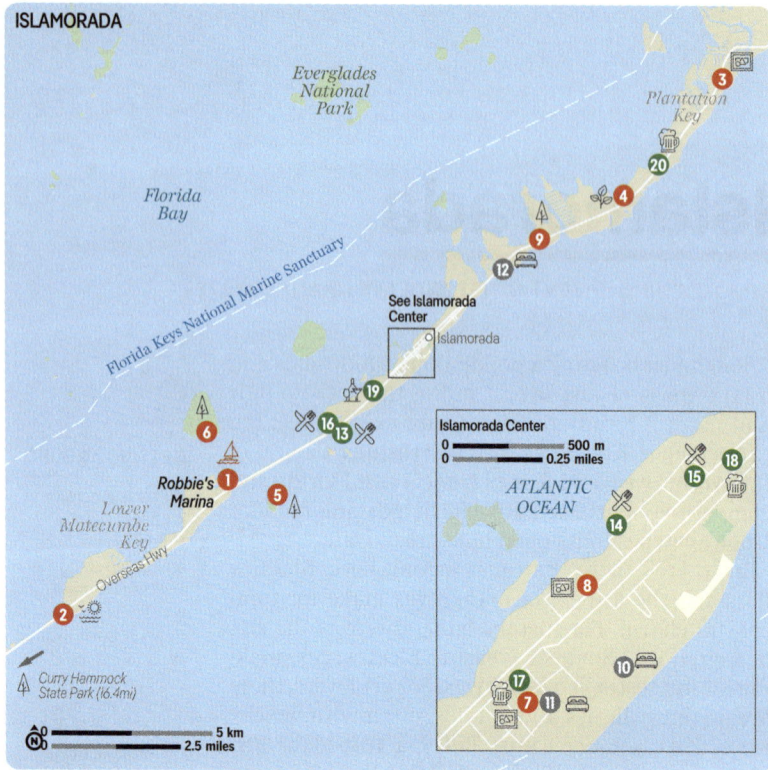

Everglades National Park

Florida Bay

Plantation Key

Florida Keys National Marine Sanctuary

See Islamorada Center

○ Islamorada

Robbie's Marina

Lower Matecumbe Key

Overseas Hwy

↑ Curry Hammock State Park (16.4mi)

0 —— 5 km
0 —— 2.5 miles

Islamorada Center

ATLANTIC OCEAN

0 —— 500 m
0 —— 0.25 miles

HIGHLIGHTS
1. Robbie's Marina

SIGHTS
2. Anne's Beach
3. Coral Shores Performing Arts Center
4. Founders Park
5. Indian Key Historic State Park
6. Lignumvitae Key Botanical State Park
7. MoradaWay Arts & Culture District
8. The Hale Gallery
9. Windley Key Fossil Reef Geological State Site

SLEEPING
10. Cheeca Lodge & Spa
11. The Moorings Village
12. Three Waters Resort

EATING
13. Lazy Days
14. Lorelei
15. Mangrove Mike's Cafe
16. Papa Joe's Waterfront

DRINKING & NIGHTLIFE
17. Florida Keys Brewing Company
18. Islamorada Brewery & Distillery
19. Islamorada Wine Company
20. MEAT Eatery & Taproom

☑TOP TIP

Book a tour to Alligator Reef Light House – don't worry, there are no alligators. Instead, you'll find a decommissioned lighthouse bearing the name of a pirate ship that sank 100 years ago. The waters are crystal-clear and marine life dances below, making it prime for snorkeling.

to get out to Indian Key and **Lignumvitae Key**, two state parks only accessible by boat.

Now lonely and eerie, **Indian Key** was once a thriving town, complete with a warehouse, docks, streets, a hotel and about 40 to 50 permanent residents – it was actually the first seat of Dade County, now dominated by metro Miami, which is just a wee bit larger on the population scale. Lignumvitae Key is a 280-acre island of virgin tropical forest ringed by alluring waters. The official attraction is the 1919 **Matheson House** (*floridastateparks.org; $2.50)*, with a windmill and cistern; the real draw is a nice sense of shipwrecked isolation. Strangler figs, mastic, gumbo-limbo, poisonwood and lignum vitae trees form a dark canopy that feels more South Pacific than South Florida.

Back at Robbie's, you can also book a snorkeling trip and bob amid coral reefs. If you don't want to get out on the water, you can feed the freakishly large tarpon from the dock ($3 per bucket, $2.25 to watch). 'Watch,' in this case, isn't just looking at the fish, but also at the shocked reactions of tourists when a fish the size of a large dog comes snapping out of the water.

A Literal Keys Cross-Section

Soaking up Windley Key and Anne's Beach

To get his railroad built across the islands, Henry Flagler had to quarry out some sizable chunks of the Keys. The best evidence of those efforts can be found at a former quarry-turned-state park **Windley Key Fossil Reef Geological State Park** *(floridastateparks.org; $2.50 per person)*, usually just called Windley Key. The island, now managed by the state, has leftover quarry machinery scattered along an 8ft-high former quarry wall, with fossilized evidence of brain, star and finger coral embedded in the rock. The wall offers a cool (and rare) public peek at the coral that forms the substrate of the Keys – the cake layers of fossilized shells used to be known as Key Largo limestone, or keystone.

There are also various short trails through tropical hardwood hammock that make for a pleasant glimpse into the Keys' wilder side – plenty of birds abound in the tropical hammocks. Borrow a free trail guide from the visitor center to navigate it all.

Creativity Inspired by Tropical Surrounds

Gallery- and arts-hopping

Islamorada's colorful surroundings have attracted a vibrant community of artists who draw inspiration from the striking natural surroundings. Local artist and oil painter Taylor Hale and his wife, Kelly, own **The Hale Gallery** *(thehalegallery. com; free)*, nestled just north of Overseas Highway. The gallery has ever-rotating selections from local artists in addition to in-studio events spanning sound healing, flow yoga and reiki group meditation.

Just south of the gallery is another hub of creativity. The **Morada Way Arts and Cultural District** *(moradaway.org; free)*, a spirited six-block stretch of downtown, is rife with galleries and working studios. Every month, the organization hosts an 'Arts Walk' that brings the area to life with live music, special vendors and plenty of artistry to marvel at.

BEST BEACHES IN THE KEYS

Anne's Beach: Family-friendly Islamorada beach with calm shallow waters, pavilions, a boardwalk and restrooms.

Sombrero Beach: This tranquil beach in Marathon has shaded picnic spots, barbecue pits, a playground, volleyball courts and plenty of space to unwind.

Curry Hammock: Between Duck Key and Marathon, this park sports 1000 lush acres for outdoor adventures.

Higgs Beach: If Fido tagged along for your Keys adventure, this beach has one of Key West's best dog parks.

Fort Zachary Taylor Park: Beyond its historical allure, the park is a stellar spot for a swim in shallow, often serene waters.

DRINKING IN ISLAMORADA: BEER & WINE

Islamorada Brewery: A neon-yellow icon with popular brews like OG Sandbar Sunday and cocktails on tap featuring their own spirits. *11am-9pm*

Florida Keys Brewing Company: A colorful beer garden and tasting room with a large selection of beer, some inspired by local flavors. *11am-10pm Sun-Thu, to 11pm Fri & Sat*

Islamorada Wine Company: Sip wine and snack on specially curated charcuterie in a cozy little wine-bar setting. *hours vary Wed-Thu*

MEAT Eatery and Taproom: Can't-miss burgers and craft beer selection from near and far. *11am-9pm Sun-Thu, to 10pm Fri & Sat*

WHY I LOVE THE FLORIDA KEYS

Jesse Scott, Lonely Planet Writer

I've called Fort Lauderdale home for nearly a decade. We have pristine beaches and stretches of world-class resorts. Honestly, a beach is the last place I want to vacation. But the Keys hit differently. Key West has a bohemian-historic vibe that is seldom found in South Florida and worth the jaunt. Talking to the story-filled locals fuels my soul. As do the ever-orange sunsets – a memorable one being a recent dinner with my wife at the Playa Largo resort. We sat at a 'water table' – literally a table anchored in shallow waters, noshing fresh ceviche and watching kids frolic on floating cabanas nearby. The Keys are a true escape, even if you're a local.

ADORNED PHOTOGRAPHY

MARTIN VALIGURSKY/SHUTTERSTOCK

It's not just the visual arts that flourish in Islamorada. The group **Islamorada Community Entertainment** *(keysice.com),* known locally as ICE, has regular gatherings – primarily concerts and musical events – at the central **Founders Park** *(islamorada.fl.us);* and the **Coral Shores Performing Arts Center** *(keysschools.com)* present an impressive roster of live shows and performances throughout the year. Fans of live music should head to the **Lorelei** (p148) *(loreleicabanabar.com)* for a laid-back vibe and oceanfront views. You may even catch a peek of the Nautilimo, a pink ocean-going Cadillac, in the neighboring marina. The two biggest breweries in town, **Islamorada Brewery** (p147) *(islamoradabrewery anddistillery.com)* and **Florida Keys Brewing Company** (p147) *(floridakeysbrewingco.com),* regularly have live music in their bohemian-esque backyards too.

🍴 EATING IN ISLAMORADA: OUR PICKS

Lorelei: Relax and enjoy drinks, bites and live music on the waterfront. Try the Key lime peppercorn snapper. *7am-10pm* $$

Mangrove Mike's Cafe: This Keys-style diner delights with breakfast classics. It doesn't skimp on the portions either. *6am-2pm* $$

Papa Joe's Waterfront: Opt for more refined dining, inside or with relaxed vibe on the patio. Tailored menus make each environment its own experience. *hours vary* $$$

Lazy Days: Take your pick of award-winning seafood and ocean-view dining environments with tables in the sand, on the patio or indoors. *11am-10pm* $$$

Sombrero Beach (p151), Marathon

The Original Rum Runner

Order a signature cocktail at Tiki Bar

The rum runner is the signature cocktail of the Florida Keys. It's more or less a tropical garden in a glass, made up of pineapple juice, orange juice, banana juice, grenadine and lots of rum. Sometimes it's topped with Bacardi 151. The drink was invented at Islamorada's **Holiday Isle Tiki Bar**, supposedly as a means of getting rid of excess rum before a shipment of liquor arrived. Plan achieved! The Holiday Isle is now the Postcard Inn Resort, but the **Tiki Bar** is still there – a lovely establishment where you can feel the sand squish beneath your toes, which is about as much physical activity as we can recommend after two rum runners.

Meet the World's Largest Lobster

Snap a selfie with Betsy

One of the Keys' most unusual roadside attractions is a 30ft-high and 40ft-long sculpture of a Florida spiny lobster. It's thought that **Betsy** may be the world's largest lobster! She can be found settled into her current home around mile marker 86, just outside the Rain Barrel Village.

Sculpted by Richard Blaze in the early 1980s, Betsy is a commemoration of the significance of the spiny lobster to the Keys' food and commercial fishing scene, and also serves as a symbol of the importance of the broader wildlife found throughout the Keys. Betsy is a great spot to pop to for a photo, wander gardens and peruse one-of-a-kind items from local artisans.

Marathon

KEYS MIDPOINT | FAMILY-FRIENDLY NATURE | TURTLE PATIENTS

GETTING AROUND

Within Marathon, biking is the way to go, with several spots like Marathon Bikeworks *(grit-2-llc. booqableshop.com; from $25 per day)* offering single-speed, tandem, cruiser and electric rentals. The principal parks here – such as Curry Hammock State Park and Crane Point Hammock – have biker-friendly trails in addition to a prospective trek across the Seven Mile Bridge. Otherwise, the Lower Keys Shuttle Bus *(cityofkeywest-fl. gov; ticket $1 to $4)* connects Marathon with neighboring keys. Outfits like Captain Pip's Marina & Hideaway *(captainpips. com; from $199 per half-day)* offer pontoon rentals, fishing charters and the in-between for anchoring at local islands and sandbars.

Geographically the central heart of the Florida Keys, Marathon strikes the balance of laid-back with a bustling US-1 artery sprinkled with big box stores, seafood houses and mom-and-pop water-sports outposts. This is clearly a town local folks flock to for necessities and makes a good home base if you enjoy those comforts. It's also somewhere in between the party-driven electricity of Key West and artsy Islamorada undertones – tiki bars are omnipresent, as are the local bands/duos that jam at them. The island community stretches across 13 islands, with the start of the iconic Seven Mile Bridge looming at its southwestern edge.

Nature lovers can embark on fun, educational, 90-minute tours of the Turtle Hospital, a rehabilitation center for sea turtle neighbors, or splash in the borderline eerily-clear waters of Sombrero Beach. The nearby Crane Point Hammock Museum offers not only an exploration of Marathon's cultural heritage, but trails through native forests and a glimpse into early Keys life.

The Keys' Natural Side in its Prime

Jungle jaunt in Crane Point Hammock

The environment of the Florida Keys is unique and often under threat from overdevelopment; Key West, for example, is almost completely built up. It's hard to find examples of pristine pre-construction ecosystems in the islands, but they exist.

A prime example is Marathon's 63-acre reserve of **Crane Point Hammock** *(cranepoint.net; adult/child $15/10)* encompassing dense tropical hammock (groves), solution holes (karst pits formed when the water table and sea level were lower), a butterfly meadow and a stretch of coastline. A looping 1.5-mile trail, with various boardwalk detours, transports you quickly onto the wild side. Highlights along the way include the restored **Adderley House** (built by Bahamian immigrants in 1903), the jungle-like palm hammock (which only

HIGHLIGHTS
1 Crane Point Hammock
2 Seven Mile Bridge
3 Turtle Hospital

SIGHTS
4 Marathon City Marina
5 Old Seven Mile Bridge

6 Pigeon Key National Historic District
7 Sombrero Beach

ACTIVITIES, COURSES & TOURS
8 Florida Keys Aquarium Encounters

SLEEPING
9 Faro Blanco Resort & Yacht Club
10 Isla Bella

EATING
11 Butterfly Café
12 Castaway Waterfront Restaurant & Sushi Bar

13 Food for Thought
14 Herbie's Bar & Chowder House
15 La Isla Taco Grill
16 Marathon Bagel Co
17 The Stuffed Pig
18 Wooden Spoon

grows between Mile Markers 47 and 60), and a wild bird center (where injured birds are nursed back to health). Begin with a short film that gives an overview of the park, and have a look at the **Natural History Museum** (dugout canoes, pirate exhibitions, a simulated coral reef).

Across the Overseas Highway is **Sombrero Beach** *(ci.marathon.fl.us)*, one of the few white-sand, mangrove-free beaches in the Keys. It's has a small playground and full accessibility for wheelchairs. Turtles (mainly loggerheads) nest here April through October; during these months, human activity is limited where a turtle has laid eggs.

Lessons in Marine Life
Get up close with queen conch and horseshoe crabs

If you passed the Upper Keys without seeing what's beneath the waves, don't worry: **Florida Keys Aquarium** *(floridakeysaquariumencounters.com; adult/child $30/20)* has you covered. Taking in the small, interactive aquarium starts with a free guided tour of local marine ecosystems. But you don't need to relegate yourself to lectured instruction: there are also more immersive experiences such as snorkeling in the coral reef aquarium or lagoon.

☑TOP TIP

Marathon is loaded with tiki huts, many waterside for panoramic sunsets and local entertainment. For fans of Jimmy Buffett, Sunset Grille plays his tunes all day and has vistas of the Seven Mile Bridge – there are few better places in the Keys for catching a sunset.

TURTLE HOSPITAL

There's an odd glut of wildlife-oriented destinations in Marathon. About 4 miles down the road from Florida Keys Aquarium Encounters is Marathon's famous **Turtle Hospital** (turtlehospital.org). Be it a victim of disease, boat-propeller strike or any other danger, an injured sea turtle in the Keys will hopefully end up in this sanctuary. The hospital has 23 individual tanks and a 100,000 gallon saltwater tide pool. The Turtle Hospital houses about a dozen permanent resident turtles here, too injured or traumatized to be returned to the wild. It's sad to see the injured ones, but heartening to see them so well looked after.

Some of the ecosystems you encounter include a mangrove-lined basin full of tarpon, a tidal-pool tank with queen conch and horseshoe crabs, and a 200,000-gallon coral reef tank with moray eels, grouper and several different shark species. You can also observe lion fish, a pig-nosed turtle, juvenile alligators and various fish species from the Everglades, plus snowy egrets and blue herons that may visit.

'Touch tanks' and 'stingray encounters' allow you to handle shallow-water marine species and touch stingrays (the barbs have been trimmed). Note that the stress of human interaction can be detrimental to the well-being of aquatic creatures.

Big Bridge to Little Island

Conquer the Seven Mile Bridge and explore Pigeon Key

Marathon connects to the Lower Keys (specifically, tiny Little Duck Key) via the **Seven Mile Bridge**. If you want to be accurate (or insufferable), feel free to point out that the bridge is actually only 6.765 miles long. Simply crossing the bridge is a cool, only-in-the-Keys endeavor – it's rare to find infrastructure that makes you feel like you've fallen off the face of the Earth.

EATING IN MARATHON: OUR PICKS

Herbie's Bar and Chowder House: Local iconic spot. The service never disappoints and the chowder lives up to its reputation. *11am-9pm Mon-Sat, 9am-2pm Sun* $$

La Isla Taco Grill: Chow down a burrito and drink with the locals at this Mexican food truck stationed next to a tiki bar. *11am-3pm & 4pm-9pm* $$

Castaway Waterfront Restaurant & Sushi Bar: Fresh seafood and sushi plus a large selection of beers on tap. *11am-9pm Mon-Fri, from 10am Sat & Sun* $$$

Butterfly Cafe: Elevated waterfront dining offering seafood as well as Caribbean and American favorites. *6pm-9pm* $$$

Seven Mile Bridge and Old Seven Mile Bridge

While you're crossing, note that there's a parallel bridge. This is the imaginatively named **Old Seven Mile Bridge**, which crosses the little island of Pigeon Key and is only accessible to pedestrians, cyclists and a small tourist train.

For years this speck of land 2 miles west of Marathon housed the rail and maintenance workers who built the infrastructure that connected the Keys. Today you can tour the **Pigeon Key National Historic District** *(pigeonkey.net; $12-25)* or relax on the beach and snorkel. For the historic district, buy tickets from the visitor center at mile 47.5 on the main highway. You can either take a short train ride out to Pigeon Key, or walk or bike via the old bridge. If you go with the latter, note the bridge is only open from 9am to 5pm.

Just before Seven Mile Bridge, on the Gulf side of the highway, is **Marathon City Marina** *(ci.marathon.fl.us),* better known as Boot Key Harbor. This is one of the better-maintained working waterfronts in the Keys, a place where you can watch pelicans fight over the guts left behind by local fishers. Come during Christmas to see a 'parade' of boats decked out with Christmas lights.

SOMBRERO KEY LIGHTHOUSE

One of the gawk-worthy offshore sites in Marathon is the Sombrero Key Lighthouse, standing 142ft tall. Built in 1858, the lighthouse was the tallest iron structure of its kind until the construction of Paris' Eiffel Tower in 1887. It remains the tallest lighthouse in the Keys. Another fun fact: the lighthouse was designed by George G. Meade, better known for his defeat of Robert E. Lee at Gettysburg. Aside from his military career, Meade was a celebrated civil engineer working on government land surveys and designing lighthouses along the East Coast.

The lighthouse can be seen up close with a kayaking adventure out to the reef it defends.

EATING IN MARATHON: WHERE TO BREAKFAST

Food for Thought:
Healthier, lighter breakfast and lunch options. Dine in or grab a smoothie to go with you on your adventure. *8.30am-5.30pm Mon-Sat* $

Marathon Bagel Co:
New York-style bagels baked daily. Order with cream cheese or turn it into a breakfast sandwich. *6.30am-2pm Tue-Sun* $

Wooden Spoon:
Old-school diner with breakfast dishes that will stick to your bones. *6am-1pm* $

Stuffed Pig: This joint comes highly recommended. Eat on the garden patio under the tiki hut. Arrive early to avoid a wait. *7am-1pm Mon & Thu-Fri, to noon Sun* $$

Beyond Marathon

Surrounding the Keys' midpoint and on the homestretch to Key West, find a snorkeling gem, intimate island retreats and a tree named Fred.

Places

Bahia Honda State Park p154

Scout Key p155

No Name Key p155

Looe Key p156

GETTING AROUND

The Lower Keys Shuttle makes several stops between Marathon and Key West, including two stops outside of Bahia Honda State Park. To take in the true beauty of all that is in between – including stops before and after the Seven Mile Bridge – travel by car. Biking is also possible, with vast stretches of flat paths and water vistas along much of the way; be aware of some narrow moments.

For too many, 'beyond Marathon' equates to a nonstop jaunt to Key West. That's a mistake as Bahia Honda State Park and its crisp white sand beaches and clear waters for snorkeling is a major draw on its own. To the south, No Name Key – nestled just east of Big Pine Key – is a comparatively sparsely populated escape and a favorite for those wanting to glimpse the endangered Key deer. Just south of No Name Key is Scout Key, a destination for Boy Scouts to earn various patches for water activities – unbeknownst to most, it's actually open to the public, too, with luxury deluxe tents on-site for family adventuring. In between it all, colorful RV parks and worthy finds – such as Fred the Tree on the Old Seven Mile Bridge – keep your eyes wandering.

Bahia Honda State Park

TIME FROM MARATHON: **20 MINS** 🚗

Bask in bird bliss

A prized stop on the Florida Birding Trail, **Bahia Honda State Park** (*floridastateparks.org; vehicle $8*) is loaded with wildlife and vantage points for taking it all in. On any given day, dozens of species of wood warblers, raptors, snowy egrets, great white herons, sandpipers and more are visible. Come summer, the vulnerable white-crowned pigeon nests in local poisonwood trees.

For the best vantage point, take a stroll on the **Old Bahia Honda Railroad Bridge**. No longer in commission, part of it is still accessible to the public. The bridge eerily juts into the water from the park's most southwestern shore and provides panoramic views of the winged critters within the park's confines. As for the deal with the rail bridge? Down in the Keys, you'll notice everything is named for Henry Flagler, the industrialist who (literally) paved the way for South Florida's mass settlement. This rail bridge was originally part of the Overseas Railway connecting the Keys to the mainland; it was largely destroyed by a hurricane in 1935, and replaced by the Overseas Highway in 1938.

As Keys beaches go, Bahia Honda State Park's often seaweed-strewn white-sand beach (named Sandspur Beach by locals) is probably the best natural stretch of sand in the is-

Bahia Honda State Park

land chain. Heading out on a kayaking adventure is another great way to spend a sun-drenched afternoon. You can also check out nature trails and a science center where helpful park employees help you identify stone crabs, fire worms, horseshoe crabs and comb jellies. Snorkeling is possible near the shore, although you're not likely to see much beyond sand and someone else's feet. The park does offer boat trips out to a reef swimming in sea life to spot.

Scout Key

TIME FROM MARATHON: **22 MINS** 🚗

Earn your badge & some relaxation

A quick stop off the Overseas Highway between Bahia Honda State Park and Big Pine Key's eastern edge, this small, generally inhabited key features the other side of that famous railroad bridge visible from Bahia Honda State Park. On the key's western edge is a Boy Scouting utopia, which hints at the name of the key (actually called West Summerland Key until its name was changed in 2010). Home to **Camp Jackson Sawyer** *(bsaseabase.org),* this is a place where scouts go to earn various water activity-related badges through the year. Non-scouts can get in on the fun, too. October through April, Scout Key hosts a Family Adventure Camp, with bookable sailing, fishing, snorkeling and other outdoor packages. Half the fun is staying on-site in a 'luxury deluxe tent' with cushioned beds and outdoor Adirondack chairs for taking in the views. Scout or not, it's a badge of honor to stay.

No Name Key

TIME FROM MARATHON: **35 MINS** 🚗

Desolate deer watching

Perhaps the best-named island in the archipelago, **No Name Key** gets few visitors – but for a few homes, it's basically a quiet, empty island. It's one of the most reliable spots for watching Key deer, an adorable and endangered subspecies

GEOCACHING IN FLORIDA STATE PARKS

If you loved scavenger hunts as a kid, prepare to fall in love with geocaching – an outdoor activity that uses GPS devices or an app to track down 'geocaches' or little hidden containers. Each geocache has a tiny logbook and occasionally an item to take – in exchange for another item of equal value left in its place for the next discovery. Florida State Parks officially participates in geocaching through a partnership with Geocaching.com. Many state parks in Florida have joined in the exploratory fun, including a few in the Keys like Bahia Honda, Long Key and Fort Zachary Taylor. To, er, "cache" the action, sign up at Geocaching.com.

FRED THE TREE: A SYMBOL OF HOPE

Inspiration comes in many forms and, for the Keys, it's in the lovingly dubbed 'celebri-tree,' Fred. Fred is an Australian pine growing from the Old Seven Mile Bridge. What makes Fred unique? He is rooted in a portion disconnected from land and other spans of the bridge – growing right out of the roadbed without soil! Fred's survival depends on the organic matter in the sand used in construction. Resiliency abounds and locals consider Fred part of the fam. Keep your eyes peeled between mile markers 41 and 42 for the little tree that could. Around the holidays Fred gets dressed up in lights thanks to locals that love him.

of white tail that prances about primarily on No Name Key and Big Pine Key.

Once mainland dwellers, the deer were stranded on the keys during the formation of the islands. Successive generations of the species have grown smaller and had single births instead of large litters, in order to adapt to the archipelago's scarcer food supply. While you won't see thundering herds of these dwarfish deer, you will be rewarded with sightings if you're persistent and practice patience.

From Overseas Highway, take Wilder Road to Watson Boulevard. Cross Bogie Bridge and you'll be on No Name – a small green, square sign welcomes you. Past that novelty, there are some barely signed trails here, including one off to the right about 0.8 miles after crossing Bogie Bridge. It leads through mangrove forest and out to the waterfront, passing an old rock quarry with abandoned machinery along the way. Beyond a quiet stroll on the roadside trails, drive slowly through the key and you may be treated to a small deer sighting – either frolicking in a residential front yard or within a nearby, often fenced-off protected area.

Looe Key

TIME FROM MARATHON: **30 MINS** 🚗

Snorkel a marine sanctuary

Looe (pronounced 'loo') Key (*floridakeys.noaa.gov*), five nautical miles off Big Pine Key, isn't a key at all but a U-shaped reef in the **Florida Keys National Marine Sanctuary**. This is an area of some 2800 sq nautical miles managed by the National Oceanic & Atmospheric Administration. The reef here can only be visited through a specially arranged charter boat trip, best organized through any Keys diving outfit: **Looe Key Dive Center** (*looekeyreefresort.com; from $50),* in a resort of the same name on Ramrod Key, runs half- and full-day trips out to the reef for divers and snorkelers in the mornings and afternoons.

Looe Key itself is named for an English frigate, the HMS *Looe,* that ran aground on the reef in 1744 during the War of Jenkins' Ear, a name that could only have been invented in the 18th century. Apparently unfazed by losing their ship, the crew of the Looe proceeded to board smaller boats and capture a nearby Spanish sloop, before setting fire to their own irreparably damaged vessel.

The remains of the original *Looe* and her cargo form part of the marine sanctuary, but they're not the only sunken ships in this part of the islands. The Looe Key reef contains the 210-foot *Adolphus Busch,* used in the 1957 film *Fire Down Below* and then sunk (110ft deep) in these waters in 1998.

The waters around the reef are generally shallow, making it a good location for snorkelers and beginner divers. A deeper section of the reef with a steep drop (about 100ft at one point) will appeal to advanced divers. All skill levels may spot species like barracuda, jacks and parrotfish, among others.

Big Pine Key

LOCAL CHARM | KEY DEER | DIVE-BAR ROYALTY

If your hope is to find towering pines and a Pacific Northwest-like vibe on this island, temper expectations. This large key – approximately 10 sq miles in total mass – is the last major stop before heading southbound to Key West. It is named for the soaring pines that once dominated its landscape. Its inhabited roots trace back to 1882 and, arguably, its peak of happenings came in the early 1900s, serving as a residential hub for folks working on the Overseas Railway.

Through the years, its tall pine landscape has evolved. Most recently, as a result of powerful Hurricane Irma in 2017, it's estimated that nearly 30% of the island's pines were wiped away. The key is home to a population of just shy of 5,000 people and an estimated 1000 key deer. The tiny and elusive critters can often be seen wandering through streets – learn all about them at the National Key Deer Refuge visitors center on the island.

Shop Quirky Key Finds

Peruse the Big Pine Flea Market

Think of the Florida Keys and beaches, daiquiris and Jimmy Buffett spring to mind. But the daily lived experience really revolves around boats, fishing and the community. And the **Big Pine Flea Market** *(bigpinefleamarket.com)* is very much one of the main markets for said community. It runs from 8am to 3pm on Saturdays and to 2pm Sundays.

A weekend bazaar rivaling local churches for attendance, the market offers an extravaganza of locally made crafts, antiques, vintage clothes, handbags, sunglasses, souvenir T-shirts and beach towels, wood carvings, wind chimes and hand tools plus all the secondhand gear you might need for a fishing trip. For kids, there are inflatable bounce houses and giant critters (yes, a mammoth gator) and local legend Don Young hosts a fish fry on-site from time-to-time. Food vendors abound, so stock up if you're planning a picnic or embarking on a weekend road trip north back to the mainland.

GETTING AROUND

One of the bigger keys to explore, Big Pine Key is primed for biking. **Big Pine Key Bicycle Center** *(bigpinebikes.com; from $25 per day)* has rentals spanning the e-bike, 7-speed and cruiser spectrum for taking in the flat streets. Flixbus, Greyhound and the Lower Keys Shuttle make stops on the island. A well-paved trail runs along US-1 for bikers, particularly if you're wanting to explore the nearby quaint and cute isles to the west such as Little Torch Key, Ramrod Key and Summerland Key.

☑TOP TIP

Beyond booze aplenty, nosh on a slice of homemade, ultra-tangy key lime pie at the **No Name Pub** (p159) dive. Sitting at a yellow-and-blue picnic table outside, you'll agree with the sign donning its front proclaiming 'YOU FOUND IT'.

BIG PINE KEY

National Key Deer Refuge
Big Torch Key
Toptree Hammock Key
Knockemdown Key
Middle Torch Key
Dom Rd
Florida Keys National Marine Sanctuary
Big Pine Key
Great White Heron National Wildlife Refuge
No Name Key
Key Silverside Habitat 2010
Watson Blvd
South St
Little Knockemdown Key
Key Who
Howell Key
Niles Rd
State Rd 4A
Middle Torch Rd
Av D
Wilder Rd
Big Pine
Av A
Cudjoe Key
Summerland Key
Northside Dr
Overseas Hwy
W Shore Dr
O'Quinn Dr
Mariposa Rd
Old State Rd 4A
West Indies Dr
Little Torch Key
Straits of Florida
Ramrod Key
Venture Key
Melody Key
Out Key
Crab Key

0 — 2 km
0 — 1 miles

SIGHTS
1 Grimal Grove

SLEEPING
2 Little Palm Island Resort & Spa
3 Old Wooden Bridge Resort & Marina

4 Parmer's Resort

EATING
5 Good Food Conspiracy
6 No Name Pub
7 Square Grouper Bar & Grill

8 Tindahan Little Asian Store

DRINKING & NIGHTLIFE
9 7 Mile Cafe & Kava Bar
10 Boardwalk Bar & Grill
11 Boondocks Grille and

Drafthouse
12 Kiki's Sandbar

SHOPPING
13 Big Pine Flea Market

Pick Mangoes & Guava

Tour America's first breadfruit farm

For a glimpse into the botanical wonders and agricultural history of the broader Florida Keys, **Grimal Grove** (*grimal grove.com; adult/child $38/20*) on Big Pine Key has quite the story. Known as the very first breadfruit farm in the continental US, Grimal Grove was originally developed in the 1950s by an unconventional inventor, Adolf Grimal, who envisioned a tropical fruit paradise on a very small plot of land. After years of neglect, the grove was revived in the late 2010s, making it a fun stop for plant enthusiasts and curious travelers. By now, if you're wondering what a breadfruit is, it's a large, starchy fruit native to the Pacific Islands – it's used in everything from savory dishes to desserts.

DRINKING IN BIG PINE KEY: OUR PICKS

Kiki's Sandbar: Arrive by land or sea and put your yard-game skills to the test after grabbing a Kikitail at this beachfront tiki bar. *11am-11pm*

7 Mile Cafe & Kava Bar: Take a break from the heat and booze at this cozy cafe serving smoothies, kava and coffee. *7am-3pm Mon-Sat*

Boardwalk Bar & Grill: Cold beer and TVs galore so no one misses cheering on their favorite teams. *hours vary*

Boondocks Grille and Drafthouse: This family-friendly site is a blend of food, drink and activities. A cold brew has never tasted better after 18 holes of mini-golf on-site. *11am-10pm*

Tours here not only spotlight the breadfruit, but also exotic counterparts like sapodilla, canistel and jackfruit. Visitors can learn about sustainable farming techniques and taste some of the fruits in season. Post-tour, there's a market area that regularly sells morsels, including mango, guava, dragonfruit and other fresh finds. Tours typically last 75 to 90 minutes and depart at 10:30 am, 1pm and 3:30pm. Keep an eye on seasonal schedules; organizers typically take Monday and/or Tuesday off from tours.

Underwater Music Festival

Divers put on a concert at Looe Key

As if the subaquatic world surrounding the Florida Keys wasn't already exhilarating enough, the Lower Keys Chamber of Commerce has truly upped the ante with a unique event. Annually, in July, an underwater concert is hosted at the **Looe Key reef** (p156), blending Keys pizzazz and education by taking reef restoration awareness to new depths.

Divers and snorkelers are treated to music piped beneath the surface, creating an immersive experience unlike any other. Expect whimsical playlists featuring ocean-inspired classics that may include everything from The Beatles' *Yellow Submarine* to Jimmy Buffett's extensive catalogue of island-evoking tunes. Participants can explore the vibrant aquatic ecosystems of the reef while supporting local preservation efforts – proceeds from boat charters and donations can go toward coral conservation initiatives, but the primary goal of the event is simply to raise awareness of such a special ecosystem.

Underwater concert attendees may even encounter 'mermaids' and underwater jam sessions where divers pretend to play instruments. In Big Pine Key, **Captain Hook's Dive Center** *(captainhooks.com)* offers trips to the festival, with snorkel and dive packages starting at around $75 per person.

THE BLUE HOLE

Located on Big Pine Key, along Key Deer Blvd off mile marker 30.5, the Blue Hole is a little pond that is now the largest freshwater body in the Keys. That's not saying much, but the hole is a pretty dollop of blue (well, algal green) surrounded by a small path and information signs. The water is home to turtles, fish, wading birds and the odd alligator – don't feed them, as it makes the animals way too comfortable around humans. You can't swim here, nor would you want to (again, alligators). A quarter-mile further along the same road is Watson's Nature Trail and Watson's Hammock, a small Keys forest habitat.

EATING IN BIG PINE KEY: OUR PICKS

Tindahan Little Asian Store: Small Filipino market, good for grabbing snacks and drinks like boba tea to go. *7am-6pm* $

Good Food Conspiracy: This market of many talents acts as an organic health food market, restaurant, juice bar and deli. *10am-6pm Mon-Sat* $

No Name Pub: This legendary pub off the beaten path has a fish dip that can't be missed. *11am-10pm* $$

Square Grouper Bar & Grill: Fresh local seafood worth the quick 10-minute drive to Cudjoe Key. *11am-2.30pm & 5-10pm Tue-Sat* $$$

🚲 PEDAL PART OF THE GREAT FLORIDA BIRDING TRAIL

Get up close and personal with the endangered Key deer and more.

START	END	LENGTH
Big Pine Bicycle Center	Big Pine Bicycle Center	10 miles; 3 hrs

Rent a cruiser or e-bike at ❶ **Big Pine Bicycle Center** then head one-third of a mile along the Overseas Highway to ❷ **National Key Deer Refuge Nature Center**. Pop in to get an overview of the wildlife you may spot along your ride.

Continue along the Overseas Highway and hang a right on Key Deer Boulevard. Keep your eyes peeled along this 3-mile stretch for Key deer roaming. Arrive at ❸ **Blue Hole Observation Platform**. Walk the short, shaded path and scan the old limestone quarry for alligators and birds like green herons and ospreys. From here, a quick trek beyond lies ❹ **Manillo Wildlife and Watson Nature Trails**. These short trails provide views of the wetlands where marsh rabbits, alligators, blue land crabs and birds can be spotted.

Double back to Watson which leads you to ❺ **No Name Pub**. Take a break here and refuel with some pizza and read about the quirky history of this establishment. Once rested, head towards the ❻ **Bridge to No Name Key**. Pause in the middle of the bridge for sweeping views of the ocean. After snapping a couple pictures, begin your ride back to return your wheels, this time taking the road through the neighborhood along Avenue B and Wilder Road.

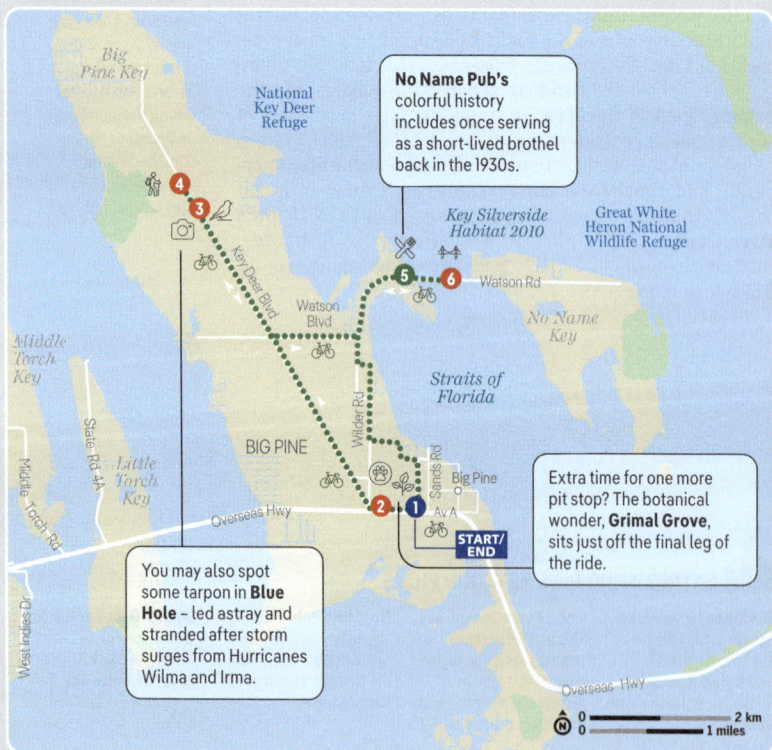

No Name Pub's colorful history includes once serving as a short-lived brothel back in the 1930s.

You may also spot some tarpon in **Blue Hole** – led astray and stranded after storm surges from Hurricanes Wilma and Irma.

Extra time for one more pit stop? The botanical wonder, **Grimal Grove**, sits just off the final leg of the ride.

Key West

CELEBRATED SUNSETS | BOHEMIAN SPIRIT | PARTY-HARDY

Key West is the far frontier: edgier and more eccentric than the other Keys, and also buzzing with nonstop life. At its heart, this 7-sq-mile island feels like a beautiful tropical oasis where moonflowers bloom at night and classical Caribbean homes are so romantic to stroll by, it's hard not to sigh at them.

While Key West has obvious allure, it's not without its contradictions. On one side of the road, there are literary festivals, Caribbean villas, tropical dining rooms and expensive art galleries. On the other, you may see an S&M fetishist parade, frat boys passing out on the sidewalk on a given weekend and grizzly dive bars filled with bearded burnouts.

With all that in mind, it's easy to find your groove in this setting, no matter where your interests lie. As in other parts of the Keys, nature plays a starring role here, with some breathtaking sunsets – cause for nightly celebration down on Mallory Square.

Key to the Natural Keys

Environmental immersion at the Florida Keys Eco-Discovery Center

This much beloved **nature center and science museum** *(floridakeys.noaa.gov; free),* open 9am to 4pm Wednesday to Saturday, is traditionally one of the best places in the Keys to learn about the extraordinary marine environments of South Florida. It makes sense, given this is the flagship museum for the Florida Keys National Marine Sanctuary. After a significant renovation and upgrade in recent years, the museum is now an even better all-round destination for learning about local ecosystems, with an emphasis on interactive and virtual experiences. Visitors can 'dive' into simulated reefs, 'paddle' through created mangrove coasts and undertake similar activities.

GETTING AROUND

Beyond its natural walkability, rideshares and taxis alike zip folks around the clock in Key West. The Duval Loop bus – operated by the city – is free and makes 18 stops throughout the tourist corridor. It operates daily from 8am to 10pm. The Key West Express ferry *(keywestexpress. net; adult/child return $185/135)* connects the island with Marco Island and Fort Myers to the north. As an alternative to flying in and out of Miami, Key West has an international airport *(eyw.com),* too.

☑TOP TIP

The history of Ernest Hemingway and Key West go hand-and-hand – the writer called the island home for more than a decade. Mega fan or not, stop in the Hemingway House and Museum and marvel at the space that inspired him and also some famed six-toed cats.

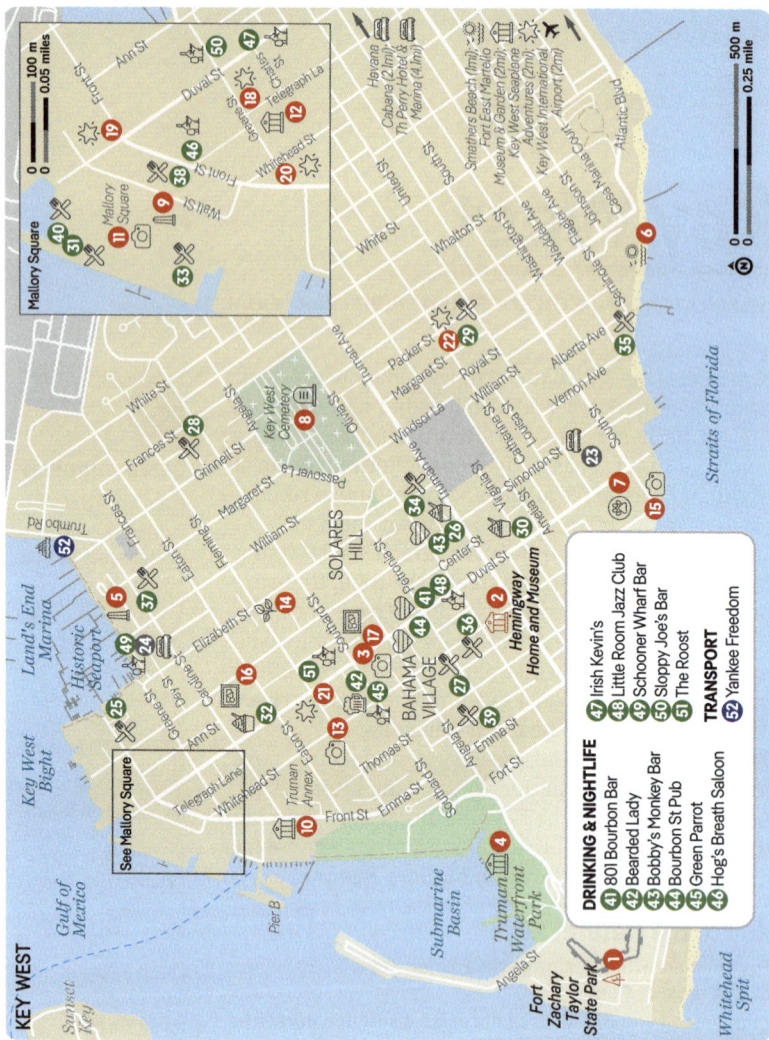

KEY WEST

Mallory Square

See Mallory Square

Sunset Key

Gulf of Mexico

Key West Bight

Land's End Marina

Historic Seaport

Trumbo Rd

Key West Cemetery

SOLARES HILL

BAHAMA VILLAGE

Hemingway Home and Museum

Fort Zachary Taylor State Park

Submarine Basin

Truman Waterfront Park

Pier B

Whitehead Spit

Straits of Florida

Havana (Cuba; 21mi)
Fort East Martello Museum & Garden (2mi)
Smathers Beach (3mi)
Dry Tortugas National Park & Fort Jefferson (70mi)
Key West Seaplane Adventures (2mi)
Key West International Airport (2mi)

Atlantic Blvd

0 — 100 m
0 — 0.05 miles

0 — 500 m
0 — 0.25 mile

HIGHLIGHTS
1 Fort Zachary Taylor State Park
2 Hemingway Home and Museum

SIGHTS
3 Duval Street
4 Florida Keys Eco-Discovery Center
5 Greetings from Key West Postcard Mural
6 Higgs Beach
7 Key West Butterfly & Nature Conservatory
8 Key West Cemetery
9 Key West Historic Memorial Sculpture Garden
10 Little White House
11 Mallory Square
12 Mel Fisher Maritime Museum
13 Mile 0
14 Nancy Forrester's Secret Garden
15 Southernmost Point
16 Studios of Key West
17 Wyland Gallery of the Florida Keys

ACTIVITIES
18 Bone Island Haunted Pub Crawl
19 Ghosts and Gravestones Walking Tour
20 Highlights and Stories of Key West
21 Jimmy Buffett Walking Tours
22 Southernmost Food Tasting & Cultural Tour

SLEEPING
23 Southernmost Beach Resort
24 The Marker Key West

EATING
25 Bel Mare
26 Better Than Sex
27 Blue Heaven
28 Café Solé
29 El Siboney
30 Flamingo Crossing
31 Hot Tin Roof
32 Kermit's Key Lime Shoppe
33 Key West Original Conch Fritters
34 Little Pearl
35 Louie's Backyard
36 Moondog Cafe
37 Pepe's Cafe
38 Salty Frog's Bar & Grill
39 Santiago's Bodega
40 Sunset Pier

DRINKING & NIGHTLIFE
41 801 Bourbon Bar
42 Bearded Lady
43 Bobby's Monkey Bar
44 Bourbon St Pub
45 Green Parrot
46 Hog's Breath Saloon
47 Irish Kevin's
48 Little Room Jazz Club
49 Schooner Wharf Bar
50 Sloppy Joe's Bar
51 The Roost

TRANSPORT
52 Yankee Freedom

Meet Robert the Doll

Museum hop, discover haunts and history

Fort East Martello Museum & Gardens *(kwahs.org; adult/ child $15.50/7.50)* was built to resemble an old Italian Martello-style coastal watchtower, a design that quickly became obsolete with the advent of the explosive shell. Now the fort serves a new purpose: preserving the past.

Historical memorabilia explores Key West's role in the Civil War, its wrecking and cigar industry heyday, plus the folk art of Mario Sanchez (self-taught son of a cigar roller) and 'junk' sculptor Stanley Papio (a Canadian-turned-Conch who turned scrap metal into things of chaotic, anarchic beauty). Perhaps the most haunted thing in Key West is kept here: 'Robert the Doll,' a child's toy from the 19th century who reportedly causes much misfortune to those who question his powers. Children as early as the 1940s claimed to see Robert act in an un-doll-like manner. Reports of him moving, laughing, throwing things and the illusion of breathing have come in over the years from people of all ages (you can get more accounts and the full backstory on robertthedoll.org). Indeed, the doll looks like it's about to step out of a Stephen King novel and devour your soul, so that's fun. Admission to the museum or booking a nighttime ghost tour are the way to go to see if you'll be spooked by the dude, too.

For a less creepy, fascinating glimpse into Key West's complicated history through the lens of the waves, visit the **Mel Fisher Maritime Museum** *(melfisher.org; adult/child $17.50/8.50)* near the waterfront. It's best known for its collection of gold coins, rare jewels and other treasures scavenged from Spanish galleons by Mel Fisher and crew. That said, the more thought-provoking material is the exhibition devoted to the slave trade. Artifacts from the wreck of *Henrietta Marie,* a merchant slave ship that sank in 1700, throws light on how central chattel slavery was in an often-romanticized Old Florida. Find the museum at home in a turn-of-the-20th-century neoclassical building that once served as a local storehouse for the US Navy.

Truman's Retreat Lives On

Tour a southern White House

This sprawling 1890s mansion (a former naval officer's residence) is where President Harry S Truman vacationed when he wasn't molding post-WWII geopolitics. In fact, the first time the president came down here was in 1946, when a doctor told him that he needed a warm weather break. Truman arrived in Key West in November and after one visit vowed to return every year.

Plenty of visiting dignitaries and big wigs visited the **Little White House** *(trumanlittlewhitehouse.org; adult/child $23/10)* where Truman would treat them to (what else?) fishing trips on the water. In March 1948, the president convened the Joint Chiefs of Staff (the heads of the American military) at the Little White House, where they drafted the Key West

THE CONCH REPUBLIC: ONE HUMAN FAMILY

A Conch (pronounced 'conk') is someone born and raised in the Keys. You will see the flag of the Conch Republic everywhere in the islands. In 1982, US customs agents erected a roadblock at Key Largo to catch drug smugglers. As traffic jams mounted, tourists disappeared. Subsequently, a bunch of Conchs formed the Conch Republic and made three declarations: secede from the USA; declare war on the USA and surrender; and request $1 million in foreign aid. Today the Conch Republic is largely a marketing gimmick, but that doesn't detract from its official motto: 'One Human Family.' An emphasis on tolerance and mutual respect has accelerated acceptance of peoples of all backgrounds, sexual orientations and religions.

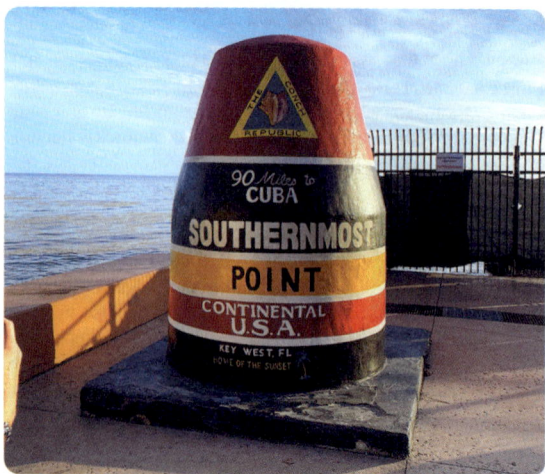

Southernmost Point Buoy

BEST WALKING TOURS

Highlights and Stories of Key West: Tours (2.5hrs) through historic Old Town feature the culture, legends, secrets and sights of Key West.

Jimmy Buffett Tour: A 1½-hr exploration of spots important to the life and career of the island-vibed musician.

Southernmost Food Tasting & Cultural Tour: Three hours to sample five can't-miss dishes, while learning about Cuban and Caribbean influences on the island.

Ghosts and Gravestones: This 1hr part-trolley, part-walking tour uncovers the dark and mysterious side of Key West.

Bone Island Haunted Pub Crawl: Bar-hop for two hours through the island's most haunted and chilling locations.

Agreement, a policy paper that had a huge bearing on the organization and function of the armed forces.

The Little White House is a beautifully preserved space, open daily, and one of the finest slices of architecture on the island. It is only open for guided tours, although you are welcome to visit one small gallery for free, with photographs and historical displays (and a short video) on the ground floor. Plenty of Truman's possessions are scattered about, but the real draw is the tour guides – each intensely knowledgeable, quirky and helpful.

Winging It in Local Gardens

Spot birds and butterflies

The **Key West Butterfly & Nature Conservatory** (*keywest-butterfly.com; adult/child $15.50/$12.50*) is a domed escape where folks can stroll through a lush, enchanting garden of flowering plants, tiny waterfalls and colorful birds (including flamingos). There are also up to 1800 fluttering butterflies, comprising some 50 species – all live imports from around the globe. Shimmery blue morpho butterflies winging past are particularly captivating. Don't miss the small viewing area where butterflies emerge from their chrysalises, most frequently in the morning. There are butterfly-friendly birds here too that won't make a meal of the other conservatory res-

EATING IN KEY WEST: FINE DINING

Louie's Backyard: Feast on fresh seafood in a Victorian home-turned-restaurant with sweeping ocean views. *11.30am-2-30pm & 6-9pm* **$$$**

Little Pearl: An elevated dining experience centered around a custom four-course tasting menu. Three daily seatings. Reservations required. *5-9pm Mon-Sat* **$$$**

Bel Mare: Cozy up on the waterfront for homemade pasta and coastal Italian flavors paired with wine. *5-10pm* **$$$**

Café Solé: Savor classic French cuisine in a romantic, intimate atmosphere. Choose your pairing from an extensive wine list. *hours vary* **$$$**

idents and represent a palette of feathers as rainbow-bright as the butterflies.

As for a well-kept 'secret' for seeing our winged friends? **Nancy Forrester's Secret Garden** (*nancyforrester.com; adult/child $10/5*) is the brainchild of an environmental artist and fixture of the Keys community. She welcomes visitors into her backyard oasis where a veritable flock of chatty rescued parrots and macaws await. She gives an overview of these marvelously intelligent, rare birds ('Parrot 101' as she calls it) daily. This secret garden is a great place for kids, who often leave inspired by the hands-on interactions; family-friendly activities down here can feel same-samey, but this experience is utterly unique. Musicians are welcome to bring their instruments to play in the yard. The birds love it – particularly flutes!

From Ernest Hemingway to US President Harry Truman to Florida railroad builder Henry Flagler, so many folks have left a lasting mark on Key West. All of the aforementioned are part of the 36 men and women honored at the **Key West Historic Memorial Sculpture Garden** (*keywestsculpturegarden.org*). The garden is tucked between Mallory Square and a string of shops. It's small, shaded and provides a quiet reprieve from the nearby hustle and bustle.

Southernmost Snaps

Take a selfie at Mile 0

US Route 1 runs through 14 states and the District of Columbia, stretching nearly 2400 miles. It is the longest north-to-south road in the US. As for its starting point? **Mile 0** is in Key West. Mile 0 markers are not common whatsoever, so the one here makes for a unique photo opportunity. Find it at the corner of Whitehead and Fleming Streets.

The distinction of most Instagrammed spot on the island goes to **Southernmost Point Buoy**. Technically it's not even the southernmost point, but alas, no trip to Key West is complete without a picture here. Located at the corner of Whitehead and South Streets, you may have to wait a few minutes in line to snag a pic, but it's worth it.

If that's not enough southernmost charm for you, over at 284 Margaret Street is a retro **postcard-esque mural** with waves, palm trees and 'Greetings from Key West, Florida – The Southernmost City in the USA' tagline. If you and yours need a sunny, colorful backdrop for that next holiday card, consider it a strong candidate.

HEMINGWAY'S OLD HAUNTS

Touring his house is not the only way to nerd out over the renowned author. Just about anywhere you wander on the island holds Hemingway memories. The most famous? Sloppy Joe's. He 'pissed away' so much money there that he stole a urinal (turned fountain, still on display at the museum). Today, **Sloppy Joe's** (p166) is not in its original location, bringing us to **Captain Tony's** which is housed in the original Sloppy Joe's building (there's some controversy over who gets the claim to fame). Dine at **Blue Heaven** and you might catch the faint aroma of the boxing matches Hemingway officiated every weekend. Our guy also frequented **Dry Tortugas National Park** (p169) to patrol for German U-boats during WWII.

🍴 EATING IN KEY WEST: RELAXED ATMOSPHERE

Blue Heaven: Customers (and free-ranging fowl) flock to dine on Caribbean fare in a ramshackle tropical garden. *8am-2.30pm & 5-10pm* $$	**Santiago's Bodega:** A brunch to remember, with unlimited tapas and your choice of sangria, mimosas or wine. Reservations recommended. *11am-10pm* $$$	**Pepe's Cafe:** Stop by this classic steakhouse, established in 1909 and Key West's oldest eatery. *7.30am-9.30pm* $$$	**El Siboney:** Super casual, family-friendly restaurant in Old Town, with authentic Cuban offerings. *11am-9.30pm* $$

The Write Place
Spot the cats at Hemingway Home

Key West's most famous resident, Ernest Hemingway, lived in a gorgeous French Colonial house in Key West from 1931 to 1940. He moved here with his second wife, Pauline Pfeiffer, Vogue fashion editor and (former) friend of his first wife (she left the house when he ran off with his third wife). *The Short Happy Life of Francis Macomber* and *The Green Hills of Africa* were produced here, as well as many cats – maybe? The cats could have been owned by a neighbor, but either way, their descendants run the grounds today. About half of them are polydactyl (six-toed) and regularly purr about – in total, some 60 cats frequent the grounds. Can you spot 'em all? If not, there's an app (Hemingway Cats) to track and learn about them.

The home would be worth a visit even if one of the iconic novelists of the 20th century hadn't lived here. It was built in 1851 by famed salvager Asa Tift and looks like a tropical wedding cake. Note the pool, which apparently cost twice the purchasing price of the house itself. Pfeiffer had it built while Hemingway was reporting. He threw a penny down and told her to take his last cent; she later had the coin embedded in the concrete adjacent to the pool (after Hemingway started enjoying it, along with a habit of swimming in the buff – hence, the high brick walls). Admission to the **Hemingway Home and Museum** *(hemingwayhome.com; adult/child $18/7)* includes a guided tour. You're also free to poke around the house and grounds on your own.

Rays the Roof
Sunset celebrations at Mallory Square

A sunset in Key West is a visual spectacle in itself. At **Mallory Square** *(mallorysquare.com)* – Key West's epicenter, loaded with restaurants, museums and shopping options – nightly sunset celebrations kick off two hours before sunset.

Celebrations are never the same two nights in a row. In a nutshell, take all the energies, subcultures and oddities of Keys' life and focus them in one torchlit, family-friendly (but playfully edgy), sunset-enriched street party. The result of all these raucous forces is cinematic and a bit tourist-clogged. The waterfront location is magnificent, and food vendors often congregate here. Among the oft-kitschy activities, you can watch a dog walk a tightrope, a man swallow fire, and British

🍸 DRINKING IN KEY WEST: ICONIC SPOTS

Sloppy Joe's: A bar with as much character as it has history, often patronized by Hemingway. Try a Sloppy Rita for a good time. *9-4am Mon-Sat, from 10am Sun*	**Green Parrot:** A good place to let loose with good people, strong drinks and live music. *10-2am, to 4am Fri & Sat*	**Irish Kevin's:** This memorable Irish bar has music all day, classic pub food, cold drinks and a lively atmosphere to boot. *11-3.30am*	**Hog's Breath Saloon:** Throw back strong libations in this rustic and tropical, laid-back watering hole. *10-2am*

Hemingway Home and Museum

acrobats tumble and sass each other. The showmanship and camaraderie of the performers is matched by the energies of the crowds and the dying fires of the day.

Then – lucky you – you'll find yourself positioned right at the top of **Duval Street**, ready for the **Duval Crawl**. Duval Street is the main drag in Old Town Key West, a conglomeration of neon and historic buildings. Its upper reaches in particular are packed with bars and restaurants, while the southern end has more galleries and gift shops – although it certainly doesn't lack for bars and restaurants either. From Mallory Square, you'll want to pace yourself as two of Duval Street's biggest dive bar draws, **Hog's Breath Saloon** (p166) *(hogsbreath.com)* and **Sloppy Joe's Bar** (p166) *(sloppyjoes. com)*, are right there.

Dead Center of Town

Get lively at Key West Cemetery

A cemetery, really? A darkly alluring Gothic labyrinth beckons at the center of this pastel town. Built in 1847, the **Key West Cemetery** crowns Solares Hill, the highest point on the island (with a vertigo-inducing elevation of approximately 16ft). Some of the oldest families in the Keys rest in peace – and close proximity – here. With space at a premium, mausoleums stand practically shoulder to shoulder.

🍸 **DRINKING IN KEY WEST: LGBTQIA+ FAVORITES**

Bobby's Monkey Bar: Classic dive bar with an everybody-knows-your-name feel. Come for reasonable prices, stay for nightly karaoke. noon-4am	**22&Co:** The cocktails are fresh, the bartenders are fun and the tutus (and flamingos and unicorns) are everywhere. *2pm-2am*	**Bourbon St. Pub:** Speedo-wearing dancers, a garden bar, a clothing-optional pool area and entertainment of all sorts. *10-4am*	**801 Bourbon Bar:** Chill atmosphere downstairs and nightly drag shows upstairs. This lovely bar has something for everyone. *10am-4am*

BAHAMAS VILLAGE

Bahamas Village was the old Bahamian district of the island, and in days past had a colorful Caribbean feel about it. Today, many areas have been swallowed into a pseudo-Duval Street periphery. If you want a taste of the old rhythms of Bahamian Village life, visit during **Goombay Festival** *(facebook.com/ keywestgoombay2018).* It occurs around the time of **Fantasy Fest** *(fantasyfest. com),* an adults-only, costume-filled extravaganza, typically the third weekend of October. Goombay is a more family-friendly party, although the music still gets loud. Conch fritters are a treat, best washed down with a Switcha (a tangy, carbonated limeade and the national drink of the Bahamas) or a Goombay Smash (a cocktail that does what the name promises).

Wyland Gallery of the Florida Keys

What makes Key West Cemetery a top free thing to do is spotting the wildly quirky things written on the gravestones. Among the classics are the tombstone of BP 'Pearl' Roberts that reads 'I told you I was sick', and Edwina Lariz' stone that reads 'Devoted Fan of Singer Julio Iglesias'. For history buffs, a large monument honors the 260 US soldiers that were killed aboard the *USS Maine* in Havana Harbor in 1898.

Works of Heart

Snag some sunny art to take home

Key West is an artsy haven. Fortunately for visitors and locals alike, much of that art is on full display. Among a number of free art galleries, the **Wyland Gallery of the Florida Keys** *(wylandgalleriesofthefloridakeys.com)* has an incredible pulse on the Key West scene and hosts regular shows. Revel in its selection of local and handcrafted pieces – often spanning sunsets and marine life. With a visit, you may easily decide to purchase and take home a little piece of Key West with you.

Also worthy of a peruse, **Studios of Key West** *(tskw.org)* is a nonprofit showcasing about a dozen artists' studios in a three-story space. It hosts some of the best art openings in Key West, as well as open-studio showcases, on a regular basis. Besides its public visual arts displays, it also hosts readings, literary and visual workshops, art auctions, painting

⚘ EATING IN KEY WEST: MALLORY SQUARE

Key West Original Conch Fritters: Skip the sit-down meal and snag a classic Key West snack from this stand at the heart of the square. *10.30am-6pm* $

Salty Frog's Bar & Grill: Relax over tranquil vibes at this laid-back beach bar. Taste a bit of Tennessee with a Nashville hot chicken sandwich. *11am-10pm* $$

Hot Tin Roof: Local ingredients and seasonal produce are featured in Cuban and Caribbean cuisine. Lovely hand-painted ceilings and ocean views. *hours vary* $$$

Sunset Pier: Top-tier views from this spot, poised for best sunset dining, are undeniable. *11.30am-8.30pm* $$$

boot camps, concerts, lectures and community discussion groups. The Studios also have a popular residency program, which helps explain the constantly rotating presence of creative talent on the island. Don't miss **Hugh's Views**, the Studio's rooftop deck, open to the public on Tuesday evenings from 6pm to 8pm, and offering a fine perspective over town.

Southernmost Parks

Dabble in history and white sands at free beaches

Fort Zachary Taylor Historic State Park *(florida stateparks.org; vehicle $6)*, dubbed 'America's Southernmost State Park,' is home to an impressive fort, built in the mid-1800s that played roles in the American Civil War and in the Spanish-American War. You can actually see these roles come to life, too – local re-enactors conduct demonstrations the third weekend of each month. The beach here is the best one Key West has to offer. It has white sand to lounge on (but is rocky in parts), water deep enough to swim in, and tropical fish under the waves. You can learn more about the fort on free guided tours offered at 11am.

The beach is also a great spot to watch the sunset – a fine alternative to the mass-induced mayhem of Mallory Square. But you won't be able to stick around and watch the colors light up the sky: all visitors are ushered out right after the sun sinks below the sea. If coming by foot, it's about a half-mile walk (10 minutes) from the entrance to the beach.

For a free dose of white-sand goodness, the half-mile stretch at **Smathers Beach** *(cityofkeywest-fl.gov)* is the largest public beach in town. Come spring break season in the Keys, it's beyond packed with college bros and gals. **Higgs Beach** (p147) *(cityofkeywest-fl.gov)* is another free option, with a long wooden pier to gawk at the surrounding turquoise water from.

Fortress with the Mostest

Catch a ride to Dry Tortugas National Park

Key West may have 'west' in its name, but it's actually not the most western attraction in the Keys. Situated in the heart of the Gulf of Mexico, that honor goes to **Dry Tortugas National Park** *(nps.gov/drto; adult/child $15/free)*. It comprises seven islands and is perhaps the most isolated destination within the entire US national park system. Getting there requires a two-plus hour ferry ride aboard the **Yankee Freedom III** *(drytortugas.com; from $220)* or a private boat charter. **Key**

LOGGERHEAD NESTING SEASON

Walk along the beaches, May to October, and you may notice the occasional brightly colored, roped-off area and low-intensity lighting on buildings. These elements are there for a reason: protecting vulnerable turtle nests. Female turtles return to their birth beach to lay eggs and bury them in the sand to incubate. Local volunteers and organizations set up stakes and signs to designate nest locations to warn beachgoers to steer clear. The warm lighting, usually orange or yellow, prevents confusion for the hatching turtles – turtles use the light of the moon to find their way into the water and any bright cool-toned lights could draw them in the wrong direction. So, don't mess the turtle nests, y'all.

EATING IN KEY WEST: DESSERTS

Flamingo Crossing: This playful ice cream shop serves up creamy, dreamy, homemade scoops. Check out the rotating seasonal flavors. *11am-11pm* $

Kermit's Key Lime Shoppe: A popular place to relish all things key lime flavored. The frozen, chocolate-dipped key lime pie bar is a hit. *10am-9.30pm* $

Better Than Sex: A dimly-lit, romantic, dessert-dedicated restaurant with indulgent sweet treats that bear punny names. *6-11pm Tue-Thu & Sun, to midnight Fri & Sat* $$

Moondog Cafe: Cakes, pies and pastries to be enjoyed in an eclectic environment. *7.30am-10pm* $$

VARINA C/SHUTTERSTOCK

Dry Tortugas National Park (p169)

KEY WEST SONGWRITERS FESTIVAL

For nearly three decades, Key West has proudly hosted its renowned Songwriters Festival, an event that has become a beloved tradition. Typically held the first week of May, this festival lives up to its billing, attracting an ever-changing line up of budding talents and well-established creatives from across the music scene. The gigs happen all over the island at a variety of venues, with sessions going down at hotel pools, bars, theaters, the beach, music halls and seemingly every cozy haunt in between. Many of these gigs are intimate affairs, providing a unique opportunity to chit-chat with the artists and perhaps even throw back a brewski with 'em.

West Seaplane Adventures *(keywestseaplanecharters.com; from $466 per person)* takes up to 10 passengers on half-day tours to the island; flight time one way is 40 minutes and you spend 2½ hours on the island. Reserve well in advance.

Once there, vivid coral reefs, a massive Civil War-era fortress (Fort Jefferson) and secluded beaches like no other await. On paper, the Dry Tortugas covers an extensive area – over 70 sq miles. In reality, only 1% of the park (about 143 acres) consists of dry land, so much of the park's allure lies under the water. The marine life is quite rich here, with the opportunity to see tarpon, sizable groupers, lots of colorful coral and smaller tropical fish, plus the odd sea turtle gliding through the sea.

Some history: explorer Ponce de León named this seven-island chain Las Tortugas (The Turtles) for the sea turtles spotted in its waters. Thirsty mariners who passed through and found no water later affixed 'dry' to the name. In subsequent years, the US Navy set an outpost here as a strategic position into the Gulf of Mexico. But by the American Civil War, Fort Jefferson – the main structure on the islands – had become a prison for Union deserters and at least four other people, among them Dr Samuel Mudd, who had been arrested for complicity in the assassination of Abraham Lincoln. Hence a new nickname: Devil's Island.

The name was prophetic: in 1867 a yellow fever outbreak killed 38 people, and after an 1873 hurricane the fort was abandoned. It reopened in 1886 as a quarantine station for smallpox and cholera victims, was declared a national monument in 1935 by President Franklin D Roosevelt, and was upped to national park status in 1992 by George Bush Sr.

🍸 DRINKING IN KEY WEST: LOW KEY VIBES

Bearded Lady: Escape the hustle and bustle of the town's busiest areas to imbibe in a variety of craft beers. *11am-midnight*

Little Room Jazz Club: Sip cocktails while listening to live jazz five nights a week in this small music lounge. *5pm-midnight Tue-Sat*

Schooner Wharf Bar: Local charm oozes from every corner. Open-air seating is set against the backdrop of yachts docked at the Historic Seaport. *8am-2pm*

The Roost: A casual lounge-like setting makes for a non-pretentious version of a fancy cocktail bar. *noon-11pm*

Places We Love to Stay

$ Budget $$ Midrange $$$ Top End

Key Largo
MAP p141

John Pennekamp Coral Reef State Park $ The park has campsites that can accommodate both tents and RVs. Restrooms, hot showers and coin laundry on-site.

Seafarer Resort $$ Cute cottage motel situated on the water. Simple accommodation, complimentary breakfast, free kayaks and that old Keys feel.

Playa Largo $$$ This oceanfront resort is the classic combination of luxury and secluded. Check out their 'chimenea with s'mores' experience on the water.

Reefhouse Resort & Marina $$$ Island-inspired vibes and modern amenities. On- and off-property adventures are easily bookable for guests.

Baker's Cay Resort Key Largo $$$ Waterfront resort on a historic pineapple plantation with a secluded feeling and sustainability at the forefront.

Islamorada
MAP p146

Bud N' Mary's Marina $$ A true, quirky Keys lodging experience with everything from motel rooms to house boats. Located near Papa Joe's Waterfront Private boat docking available.

Three Waters Resort $$$ Upscale resort on 15 acres of oceanfront property, with chic guest rooms and nine unique dining experiences.

Cheeca Lodge & Spa $$$ Luxury resort with private beach access, a fishing pier and boat slips for water arrivals.

The Moorings Village $$$ Private, one-bedroom cottages or three-bedroom houses beautifully meshing with tropical surroundings.

Marathon
MAP p151

Curry Hammock State Park $ Beautiful sunrises and beach access are standard at this campground. Some campsites offer ocean view.

Isla Bella $$$ Comfortable oasis where every room overlooks the water. Relax with waterfront amenities or dabble in watersports at the marina.

Hawk's Cay Resort $$$ Laid-back tropical vibes and a plethora of on-site adventures like dolphin encounters and scuba diving.

Faro Blanco Resort & Yacht Club $$$ Recently renovated resort with sweeping ocean views. On-site programming includes fishing and yoga.

Big Pine Key
MAP p158

Bahia Honda State Park $ Gravel campsites with water, electric and picnic tables. Waterfront sites are available. Restrooms and hot showers are on-site.

Parmer's Resort $$$ A range of island accommodation, from basic hotel rooms to suites, cottages and studios sprinkled in its grounds.

Old Wooden Bridge Resort & Marina $$$ Modest but comfortable cottages and aqualodge (houseboat) accommodation.

Little Palm Island Resort & Spa $$$ Splurge on a private West Indies-style bungalow or suite that gives the illusion of being on a totally secluded island.

Key West
MAP p162

Seashell Motel & Key West Hostel $ Basic dorm-style housing conveniently located near Old Town Key West.

NYAH Key West $$ Adult-only, elevated, dorm-esque lodging, plus a continental breakfast. Private rooms available.

Havana Cabana $$$ Adults-only hotel with vibrant influences of the art and culture of Cuba, plus Key West's largest pool.

Southernmost Beach Resort $$$ Modern romantic resort rooms or contemporary coastal guesthouses in the heart of Historic Old Town, within walking distance of Duval Street.

The Marker Key West Harbor Resort $$$ Lux accommodation tucked in a quiet corner near Key West Harbor.

The Perry Hotel & Marina $$$ A sleek and refined modern hotel with touches of the nautical, situated right on the water's edge.

TOOLKIT

The chapters in this section cover the most important topics you'll need to know about in Miami & the Keys. They're full of nuts-and-bolts information and valuable insights to help you understand and navigate Miami & the Keys and get the most out of your trip.

Arriving
p174

Getting Around
p175

Money
p176

Accommodations
p177

Family Travel
p178

Health & Safe Travel
p179

Food, Drink & Nightlife
p180

Responsible Travel
p182

LGBTIQ+ Travelers
p184

Accessible Travel
p185

Street Talk
p186

Nuts & Bolts
p187

✈ Arriving

Most travelers arrive at Miami International Airport (MIA), a major international hub. Fort Lauderdale–Hollywood International Airport (FLL), about 45 minutes north, also serves the area, especially for budget airlines. From Miami, you can take the Overseas Highway (US-1) to venture through the Keys or use shuttle services, rental cars or regional flights to Key West International Airport (EYW).

Customs

International travelers entering via MIA or FLL will encounter a customs queue upon arrival. The **Mobile Passport Control app** (*cbp.gov*) helps expedite the process and lines, as does Global Entry for US citizens.

Rideshare

Rideshare pickups are available at arrival and departure points in airports. Double-check and communicate with your driver directly to ensure you are on the same level – a typical point of local confusion.

Train

At MIA, the MIA Mover is an airport train moving between the terminals. Go to the Central Station/Car Rental stop, where you can connect to trains serving the broader Miami area or Miami/Keys bus routes.

Wi-Fi

South Florida's airports and train stations offer free wi-fi, often with different networks in different terminals. Connect to the networks to navigate or arrange onward transportation, including rideshare services.

Travel from Airports to City Center

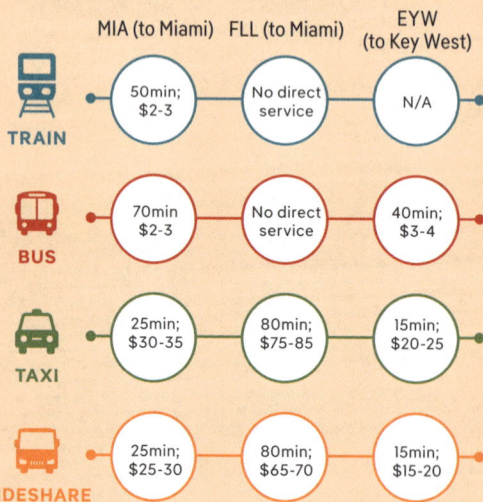

	MIA (to Miami)	FLL (to Miami)	EYW (to Key West)
TRAIN	50min; $2-3	No direct service	N/A
BUS	70min $2-3	No direct service	40min; $3-4
TAXI	25min; $30-35	80min; $75-85	15min; $20-25
RIDESHARE	25min; $25-30	80min; $65-70	15min; $15-20

FLORIDA ENVIRONMENTAL PROTECTION

Spanning Florida, and inclusive of Miami and the Keys, are strict agricultural and environmental protections. When landing at an airport, travelers may encounter questions about bringing fruits, plants or other organic materials to the state. Florida has stringent regulations to prevent invasive species and agricultural pests. Additionally, in the Keys, there are unique conservation rules due to the fragile coral reef ecosystem. Items like live coral and certain shells are strictly regulated. The year-round tropical climate also means customs may screen for health-related concerns related to mosquito-borne illnesses, particularly during surges in instances.

Getting Around

Getting around is easiest by car, though traffic can be intense during weekday rush hour and on weekends to/from the Keys. Public transit and rideshare present flexibility; bike rentals and scooters are great for shorter distances.

TRAVEL COSTS

Car rental
From $40/day

Gasoline
Approx. $3.10/ gallon

EV charging
35¢/kWh

Bicycle rental
Approx $35/ day; free with select hotels

Honk, Honk

Driving in South Florida can be lively. Locals aren't shy about honking, as a friendly reminder or, often, to signal total impatience. Traffic can be intense, especially during rush hours. Stay alert, use GPS for navigation and you'll savor the slower, scenic drive on the Overseas Highway when heading to the Keys.

The Grid

Miami's roads generally follow a grid system, with streets, lanes and drives running east–west and avenues running north–south. Flagler St and Miami Ave are the central dividing lines in the City of Miami – you'll see addresses including directional indicators (NW, NE, SW, SE) to guide navigation.

TIP

Miami-Dade Transit (*miamidade.gov*) has a GO Connect app for planning trips in Miami-Dade County and connecting points beyond. It optimizes a trip for shortest distance and smallest cost.

HIGHWAY TOLLS

Toll roads in South Florida are mostly cashless, using license plate recognition to send bills by mail. You can save approximately 25% on tolls with a SunPass transponder, available at many retailers; installation and activation is required. Car rental agencies often offer SunPass for a fee, so plan your routes in advance to decide if it's worth any upfront costs.

DRIVING ESSENTIALS

Drive on the right.

.08
The blood alcohol limit is 0.08%.

25
Some interstate stretches allow speeds up to 70mph, otherwise it's typically 55mph on highways and 25mph to 35mph in municipal areas.

Renting a Car

A rental car gives you flexibility for visiting beaches, towns and attractions in between. Major rental companies operate at MIA, FLL and along the Keys. Double-check your credit card benefits before opting in to select insurance packages, as a minimum liability insurance is required.

Transportation Passes

The EASY Card and EASY Ticket offer reloadable access to Miami-Dade Transit, including buses, Metrorail and routes that connect with the Keys. Options include daily, weekly and monthly passes. The Brightline rail, connecting to Orlando, offers modern amenities, speedy service and passes for day trips.

Bicycle

You can borrow a bicycle from scores of kiosks around Miami and Miami Beach through **Citi Bike** (*citibikemiami.com*). Miami is flat, but traffic can be abundant and fast-moving, and there isn't much of a cycling culture. Citi Bike has a handy app that shows you where the nearest stations are.

175

Money

CURRENCY: US DOLLAR ($)

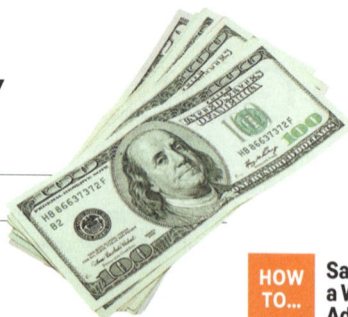

Credit Cards

Credit cards are widely accepted throughout Miami and the Florida Keys. However, if it's not a US card, check whether foreign transaction fees apply. Many creditors charge 2.5% or higher.

Sales Tax

Florida sales tax sits at 6%, applied to most goods and services. Locally, this includes restaurants, shopping and attractions, so keep this in mind when budgeting your trip.

ATMs

ATMs are easy to find across the region, but fees can add up. Local banks may charge $3 to $5 per withdrawal, in addition to fees charged by a cardholder's bank.

Tipping

Tipping is standard in Miami and the Keys. For dining, leaving 20% of the bill – as a starting point – is common. Bartenders typically receive $1 to $2 per drink or higher. Hotel staff and tour guides may encourage tipping for their services.

HOW MUCH FOR...

Parking at the beach
$25-50/day

State park entrance fee
$6

Valet parking tip
$3-5 upon pickup

Beach chair rental
$30-50/day

HOW TO... **Save on a Water Adventure**

If 'being on the water' is the goal, you can skip pricey private boat tours and opt for public ferries or group charters for activities like snorkeling and island hopping. For example, the Island Queen Cruises from Miami is a scenic, affordable alternative to luxury options. For water sports, consider booking directly with local operators instead of through resorts to avoid markup fees.

SENIOR DISCOUNTS

Many retailers offer perks, often in the 5% to 30% range to those who've earned the privilege – minimum qualifying ages range from 50 to 65. If signage isn't visible, ask a retailer if you qualify.

SAVING MONEY ON CURRENCY EXCHANGE

Credit card transactions often provide better exchange rates than local banks or currency exchange kiosks, especially at South Florida airports or hotels. Withdrawals from ATMs also tend to offer competitive rates, though it's best to limit transactions to avoid fees multiple times. For significant amounts – for example, real estate transactions or extended stays – consider using a professional currency exchange service such as Firma, which can save money on large transfers. Local exchange shops may charge higher fees, so plan ahead to maximize your budget.

Accommodations

Houseboats

Experience the ocean and Intracoastal Waterway in Miami or the laid-back vibes of the Florida Keys by staying on a houseboat. From cozy floating cottages to high-end yachts, options abound. Rates start around $150 per night for smaller boats to thousands of dollars per night for the most mega of yachts. Docked near trendy Miami marinas or serene keys, rentals often come with wi-fi and kayaks.

Vacation Rentals

In Miami, Airbnb ranges from trendy high-rise condos in Brickell to colorful bungalows in Little Havana. In the Keys, options include oceanfront villas or quirky cottages on stilts. These rentals are perfect for groups or extended stays, with kitchens to save on dining out. Book early for prime spots, especially during high season or festivals. Check out Vrbo, Booking.com and other homestay sites, too.

Chickees

On the ultra-basic front, you can immerse yourself in Seminole culture with an overnight stay in a chickee, which is a thatched-roof, open-air hut. Sprinkled through the Everglades, these rustic accommodations are for true nature lovers seeking a unique experience. Pack essentials like bug spray and a flashlight. Check Miccosukee-run sites as well as the National Park Service for booking and availability.

Hotels

Miami and surrounding hotels cater to every vibe, from chic boutique stays in South Beach's Art Deco district to the luxe beach resorts like the Fontainebleau Miami Beach. In the Keys, waterfront properties with private beach access abound. Watch for resort fees when booking and try last-minute booking apps like HotelTonight for deals, especially in shoulder seasons for the best rates.

HOW MUCH FOR A NIGHT IN...

a hotel room
$200-300

a glamping tent
$150-225

a houseboat
$150-225

Glamping

You can trade basic tents for glamour throughout Florida, certainly including its southern locales. Glamping sites offer canvas tents with plush bedding, air conditioning and sometimes outdoor soaking tubs or fire pits. Some eco-resorts combine sustainability with luxury. These are perfect for a romantic getaway or family adventure – setups often offer the beauty of the outdoors without sacrificing comfort.

BOOKING INLAND

That ocean view often comes with a premium, and booking hotels further inland can significantly cut costs. Staying a bit removed from the beachfront buzz can still give you easy access to attractions. Properties further inland may also offer lower parking fees and smaller immediate crowds to navigate. Balance your budget by exploring inland neighborhoods then driving to the beach for the day to soak up the sun. If you're in an oceanfront or waterfront hotel, booking rooms with city, courtyard or non-ocean views can potentially save hundreds of dollars per night, too.

Family Travel

Consider this a paradise for families, with something for all ages. Kids can enjoy hands-on learning at museums at every corner, with a handful of children's museums, too. Animal encounters bring smiles to all ages, whether out in the wild in the Everglades or at Zoo Miami. Beaches, parks, snorkeling and boat tours only add to the family appeal here.

Saving Money

Despite its oft-pricier allure, traveling with kids in Miami and the Keys can be affordable. Free or low-cost activities include visiting beaches, exploring parks or walking popular beachside promenades. Consider a lodging option with a kitchen to save on meals. Some spots, including major museums, have free-entry days or discounted group rates.

Children's Discounts

Kids often enjoy free or reduced fares on public transport, and many attractions provide group rates. Passes like the Go City Miami Pass offer discounts on visiting multiple attractions in one day, or an unlimited number of attractions within a specified timeframe.

Facilities for Babies & Kids

Many hotels provide cribs, highchairs and even babysitting services, while restaurants often feature kids' items, whether listed on the menu or not. Attractions offer stroller-friendly pathways and rest areas. Public beaches frequently have playgrounds, shaded areas and family restrooms, making outings with little ones less stressful and more enjoyable.

Animal Encounters

Animal encounters are common, be it snorkeling excursions or seeing alligators sunbathing by a lake. During organized programs supervised by trained staff, children should obey all guidelines. Out in the wild, all wildlife should be left alone, and children should steer clear.

KID-FRIENDLY PICKS

Miami Children's Museum (p70)
Interactive exhibits including a miniature cruise ship and construction zone, for hours of hands-on fun.

Everglades Airboat Tours (p116)
Kids can safely observe alligators aboard a giant, fanned craft, gliding through mangroves and marshes.

Biscayne National Park Snorkeling (p129)
Explore underwater wonders with family-friendly snorkeling tours over coral reefs.

Robbie's Marina (p145)
In Islamorada, families can paddle through lagoons or feed huge tarpon from the dock.

AIRBOAT RIDES WITH KIDS

Exploring the Everglades on an airboat is a thrilling family adventure. To ensure everyone has a safe and fun experience, keep the following in mind:

- Spotting alligators and birds is exciting, but kids should stay seated and keep hands inside the boat. Always follow guides' instructions for a safe journey.

- Many operators provide ear protection as the fans on the boats are loud, but bring child-sized earplugs or noise-canceling headphones for extra-sensitive ears.

- Pack sunscreen, hats and bug spray to stay comfortable amid the Everglades' elements. Choose family-friendly tours with experienced guides who cater to younger adventurers.

Health & Safe Travel

INSURANCE

The state of Florida and local jurisdictions don't require foreign travelers to carry insurance, but with the high cost of healthcare in the US, purchasing coverage is a smart choice. It's wise to pay a bit extra for insurance that includes protection against lost luggage, costs related to trip cancellation or interruption, and adventure activities like diving and boating.

Hurricanes

South Florida has been prone to hurricanes in recent years, especially during hurricane season (June to November), often peaking in August and September. They bring heavy rain, strong winds and storm surges that can cause significant damage and pose serious risks to safety. Residents and visitors alike must stay informed and follow all official directives during storm emergencies.

Jellyfish & Sea Urchins

These saltwater creatures are often found near the shores, especially after storms. Encounters can be painful but rarely dangerous. If stung by a jellyfish or stepping on a sea urchin, carefully remove any tentacles or spines with tweezers and immerse the affected area in hot water. Seek medical attention for severe pain, allergic reactions or difficulty removing spines.

TAP WATER

Tap water here is considered safe to drink; it meets all federal guidelines for quality. You may notice a distinct taste due to the high mineral content.

FLORIDA BEACH WARNING SIGNS

Green flag
Low hazard. Calm conditions, exercise caution

Yellow flag
Medium hazard. Moderate surf and/ or currents

Red flag
High hazard. High surf and/or strong currents

Red flag + Red no swimming flag
Water CLOSED to the public

Purple flag
Stinging marine life present

Cannabis Laws

Although cannabis products are widely used, recreational use remains illegal in Florida. Only individuals with a valid medical marijuana authorization may legally buy and consume these products. Possession of up to 20 grams is classified as a misdemeanor, punishable by up to one year in jail and a fine of up to $1000. Enforcement varies, but penalties are significant.

PERSONAL SAFETY PRECAUTIONS

In Miami, neighborhoods can shift dramatically within a few blocks, so stay aware of your surroundings. Exercise caution near bus depots and transit hubs. Aggressive driving is common in South Florida, with frequent speeding and signal-less turns. Pedestrians should be extra vigilant, particularly when crossing busy streets, even though they have the right-of-way. The Keys are generally more relaxed but always stay aware.

Food, Drink & Nightlife

Where to Eat & Drink

Restaurants offer varied cuisines, from Cuban to seafood-centric dishes. Vibrant decor, lively energy and tropical flavors are the regional norm.

Bars often mix tropical cocktails, wine tastes, craft beers and live music. Rooftop views, tiki vibes and good old casual fun dominate the scene.

Cafes serve cafecitos, pastelitos and strong Cuban espresso. A relaxed ambiance, perfect for people-watching, light conversations or remote work.

Clubstraunts are a fusion of dining and nightlife – trendy spaces serving gourmet bites with cocktails. Expect DJs and dancing, too.

MENU DECODER

Conch fritters Chopped conch (a type of sea snail) is the noticeabl chewy ingredient in these deep-fried dough balls, also with a hint of chef's-choice spices.

Mamey sapote A tropical fruit with a somewhat ooey-gooey, orange-like texture. This is a common smoothie ingredient.

Pastelitos Typically flaky pastries that come in a variety of fillings spanning meat to sugary. The guava-and-cream-cheese combo is prevalent region-wide.

Ropa vieja A traditional Cuban dish (meaning 'old clothes'). There are no clothes in this stew, but instead shredded beef, vegetables (often tomatoes, onions and peppers) and spices.

Cafecito A small but mighty Cuban espresso concoction, mixed with sugar while brewing. It's often served in tiny cups, but don't be fooled – it carries a caffeinated punch.

HOW TO... Eat a Stone Crab Claw

Stone crabs are iconic menu staples around these parts and a must-try delicacy that's as synonymous with the region as sunshine and turquoise waters. They grace menus from culinary icons, like Joe's Stone Crab in Miami, to intimate, no-frills establishments along the Everglades' edges and throughout the Keys. The succulent claws dominate menus during stone crab season (October to May), when they're harvested sustainably. This means crabs are returned to the ocean after claw removal.

As for when your plate arrives, pre-cracked claws are the norm, and you can often simply dig in. First, snap away any remaining shell pieces to expose the tender meat. You'll want to dip generously into the oft-mustardy sauce accompaniment, which is typically zesty and creamy with a hint of spice. Use the small fork provided to extract every morsel of meat from the crevices and, yes, savor away.

HOW MUCH FOR A...

Dinner for two at a Michelin-star restaurant
$700-800

A pound of stone crabs
$70-90

Cuban sandwich
$10-12

Slice of key lime pie
$7-10

Cafecito
$1-3

Specialty coffee
$6-8

Bottle of beer
$7-9

Glass of wine
$10-12

HOW TO...

Pinpoint the Perfect Cuban Sandwich

The Cuban sandwich is a culinary icon in Miami, an edible embodiment of the city's Cuban heritage. Its roots trace back to the late 1800s, when Cuban workers in Tampa's (yes, that other Florida city) cigar factories enjoyed this on-the-go concoction. Over time, Miami adopted the sandwich, omitting Tampa's addition of salami to create the purist version known today. Now, the Cuban sandwich is a cornerstone of Miami's food culture, found on menus ranging from casual cafeterias to upscale Cuban gems. It makes appearances south, in the Keys, too.

So, how do you pinpoint the perfect Cuban sandwich? Authenticity is everything. A true Cuban sandwich consists of roasted pork marinated in mojo, glazed ham, Swiss cheese, tangy pickles and yellow mustard, layered inside fresh Cuban bread. Crucially, there are no extraneous ingredients like mayonnaise, lettuce or tomato – purists know these additions stray from tradition.

The bread is the unsung hero of the sandwich. True Cuban bread, with its distinctive crispy, flaky crust and airy interior, is essential. The sandwich must be pressed on a *plancha* (flat grill) until the bread is golden and crunchy and the cheese melts into the layers of meat. Each bite should balance warm, savory flavors with the tang of pickles and mustard, creating a harmonious dish. Don't be afraid to grill your server on the essentials before your sandwich is grilled.

A Culinary Melting Pot

While Tampa and Miami battle on the Cuban sandwich's origins, it has cultural roots well beyond Florida. Having evolved from Cuban, Spanish and Italian influences, it symbolizes the melting pot of immigrant communities in Florida since the 19th century.

WAHOO! (THE FISH)

Welcome to wahoo country – you'll want to exclaim the name of this fish when you try it. Wahoo is a fast-swimming oceanic fish prized for its firm, flaky texture and slightly sweet flavor. Often dubbed the 'steak of the sea,' wahoo is a staple of the region's seafood scene. It's caught year-round in the warm waters off Miami and the Keys, among other locales – it's a favorite among anglers and chefs for its versatility.

Throughout South Florida, wahoo can be the star of any seafood-centric meal. You'll often find it simply cooked to highlight its flavor, though its clean, rich taste can equally shine in ceviche or thinly sliced as sashimi. Local chefs often pair wahoo with tropical ingredients like mango, lime and coconut, paying that much more of a homage to South Florida culinary magic.

For visitors, eating wahoo is a culinary experience that transcends the plate. Several fishing charters offer a catch-and-cook option, allowing you to reel in your own wahoo and have it expertly prepared at a nearby dockside restaurant – it's a truly immersive way to taste the freshest possible fish aside from what you'll find on local menus. Wahoo is most abundant during the fall and winter months. Whether it's your first bite or your tenth, it's a flavor-packed reminder of the local fishing culture – and, remember, it's only one fish in the sea.

Responsible Travel

Climate Change & Travel

It's impossible to ignore the impact we have when travelling; Lonely Planet urges all travellers to engage with their travel carbon footprint, which will mainly come from air travel. While there often isn't an alternative, travellers can look to minimize the number of flights they take, opt for newer aircrafts and use cleaner ground transport, such as trains. One proposed solution — purchasing carbon offsets — unfortunately does not cancel out the impact of individual flights. While most destinations will depend on air travel for the foreseeable future, for now, pursuing ground-based travel where possible is the best course of action.

The **UN Carbon Offset Calculator** shows how flying impacts a household's emissions

The **ICAO's carbon emissions calculator** allows visitors to analyse the CO2 generated by point-to-point journeys

Volunteering

Reef Environmental Education Foundation (reef.org) Based in Key Largo, REEF focuses on marine conservation. Volunteers can participate in 'citizen science projects' like fish surveys or assist with coral restoration efforts.

Miami Waterkeeper (miamiwaterkeeper.org) Champions clean water and a healthy marine ecosystem in Miami and beyond. Volunteers help with beach cleanups and mangrove plantings to keep local waterways pollution-free.

The Turtle Hospital (turtlehospital.org) Located in Marathon, this facility rescues, rehabilitates and releases injured sea turtles. Volunteers can assist with daily operations or public outreach to help spread awareness.

Airboats

Airboats are widespread and an integral part of life in South Florida, as well as an important way for people of all abilities to experience these unique wetlands. However, there are concerns about their use: they are noisy and create a significant disturbance to local wildlife. There is also a worry that their speed, in spite of their flat-bottomed design, affects the sediment below the surface, to the detriment of the animals that live there. We recommend researching airboat tours before booking and considering alternatives like paddle boat tours or on-land bicycle or walking tours.

Camp at one of South Florida's state or national parks, state forests or one of the myriad private camping and RV parks across the region.

Where possible, opt for eco-tours like kayaking or paddleboarding (rather than gas-powered boats) to explore the region's natural beauty.

SUPPORT LOCAL ARTISTS

Rather than buying imported goods, visit local markets – like those ever-present in Miami's Wynwood or in Key West – to purchase handmade goods and support local creators.

EXPLORE INDIGENOUS COMMUNITIES

Venture to the Miccosukee Indian Village or Big Cypress Reservation for authentic cultural experiences that honor Native American history. Any funds or proceeds benefit the tribe directly.

Spend Time in Nature

Visit botanical gardens and arboretums to learn more about sustainable resources and eco-friendly gardening. Visit nature centers and wildlife refuges to learn more about conservation efforts and how you can help. Donations are encouraged, when possible.

Respect the Sea Turtles

Sea turtles nest on the beach from May to October. Getting too close, shining lights or using flash photography can scare or disorient them – and it's illegal. Note coastal hotels and businesses that have orange-hued lighting to not disturb the natural nesting environment.

Leave a Positive Footprint

Use eco-friendly transportation whenever possible. Consider cycling (rentals are abundant) when traveling short distances. Most areas in Miami and the Keys are bike-friendly. Canoes and kayaks are widely available for rent and have little effect upon the environment.

Clean Beaches

Baskets can be found at select beach access points for visitors to thoughtfully dispose of trash. If none are present, consider bringing a bag and gloves of your own to the beach to help clean up.

Snorkel or Dive Responsibly

Book a Blue Star–recognized dive or snorkel operator, meaning the company promotes and adheres to sustainable practices designed to mitigate harm to coral reefs.

Support local farmers markets and buy locally produced organic food products. Find one at *farmersmarket toolkit.org*.

Choose accommodations certified for sustainability like eco-friendly hotels to reduce your carbon footprint.

Coral Reef

The Florida Keys are home to the world's third-largest coral reef, with sustainability-focused eco-tours and conservation programs aplenty. These typically support reef restoration and protect marine biodiversity for future generations.

RESOURCES

floridaconservationcoalition. org
Focused on protecting natural resources through conservation.

eco-usa.net/orgs/fl.html
Alphabetical list of Florida's environmental organizations.

evergladescoalition.org
Nonprofit focused on protecting and restoring the Everglades.

LGBTIQ+ Travelers

Despite the state government's well-publicized 'Don't Say Gay' agenda, this region remains one of the world's most popular LGBTIQ+ destinations. Many inclusive municipalities continue to roll out the rainbow carpet, offering millions of those within the LGBTIQ+ community a warm and welcome embrace each and every year.

The Best 'Gayborhoods'

Miami Beach
South Beach, particularly around the main drags of Ocean Dr and Collins Ave, is a hub for LGBTIQ+ nightlife, drag brunches and chic, queer-friendly hotels. Expect a vibrant energy mixed with classic Art Deco district vibes.

Key West
Head to Duval St to hit up the district's famous bars, clubs and endless stores. Check out 801 Bourbon Bar for entertaining drag shows.

Downtown Miami
Brickell and Wynwood are growing LGBTIQ+ havens, with trendy bars, inclusive art galleries and queer-focused events tied to Miami's cultural scene.

FABULOUS RAINBOW FESTIVALS

Key West Pride in June features a week of sunset cruises, drag shows and a lively street fair. October's Fantasy Fest brings colorful costumes, a spirited parade and inclusivity island-wide. Miami Beach Pride in April offers a week of parties, art and one of the country's most iconic Pride parades. The Winter Party Festival in March (also in Miami) celebrates the community with beach parties and live tunes.

Same-Sex Marriage Tourism

After same-sex marriage was legalized in 2015, Florida saw a boom in gay-wedding tourism. Couples from across the country flocked to Florida's beaches to marry even when their unions weren't recognized in their home states. For a list of LGBTIQ+ friendly wedding vendors serving the region, visit *engaygedweddings.com/florida-gay-wedding.html*.

TAKE A LGBTIQ+ STROLL

Join Miami's 90-minute Gay & Lesbian Walking Tour to explore the community's significant historical contributions and visit contemporary hot spots. Tours start at the Art Deco Welcome Center (1001 Ocean Dr) at 11am on the second Saturday of each month.

Resources
Key West LGBTIQ+ info: *gaykeywestfl.com*

Miami's Gay Scene: *miamiandbeaches.com/travel-interests/lgbtq-miami*

LGBT Visitor Center Miami Beach: *gogaymiami.com*

Florida Gay Nightlife: *hotspotsmagazine.com*

GLORIOUS LGBTIQ+ FRIENDLY BEACHES

Miami Beach: The 12th Street Beach is Miami's best-known, and sometimes rowdy, LGBTIQ+ beach.
Key West: Fort Zachary Taylor Historic State Park is nicknamed Liz Taylor Beach by the local LGBTIQ+ community.
Key West: Higgs Beach, on the southern edge of town, is a popular gathering spot for everyone of all backgrounds.

Accessible Travel

Visit Florida's 2021 campaign, 'Limitless Florida,' highlighted efforts to position the state as the world's leading accessible destination. Wheelchair-accessible beaches like South Beach's Beachwalk and adaptive water-sports hubs in the Keys showcase the commitment to inclusivity.

ADA-Friendly Beaches

Many popular beaches are wheelchair-accessible, with ramp access to boardwalks. Several offer Mobi-mats (interlocking pads that create a solid path over the sand). Miami's Crandon Park has accessible paths and manual beach wheelchairs. In the Keys, John Pennekamp Coral Reef State Park offers beach wheelchairs and accessible trails.

Airport

South Florida airports provide barrier-free paths and accessible services throughout their terminals, including guided mobility assistance at designated locations. If a wheelchair is required upon arrival, request it in advance through your airline.

Accommodation

Compliance with the Americans with Disabilities Act (ADA) may be less consistent in smaller lodgings; verify their status in advance. Higher-end hotels and resorts offer fully ADA-accessible facilities. State parks and many campgrounds provide fully accessible services.

RESOURCES

Visit Florida (*visitflorida.com/things-to-do/accessible-travel*) provides an extensive list of accessible sights and attractions in the region, along with resources for wheelchair and scooter rentals, childcare services, oxygen supplies and other relevant topics.

Bright Feats (*brightfeats.com*) helps families and loved ones of children with special needs find resources to plan successful vacations across the region and broader state.

HIGHLY ACCESSIBLE ATTRACTIONS

Vizcaya Museum & Gardens
This Miami landmark has wheelchair-accessible pathways and elevators for exploring the historic estate and surrounding gardens.

Miami Seaquarium
Wheelchair rentals and accessible exhibits available year-round at the marine park.

Everglades National Park
Select accessible trails, boardwalks and boat tours, ensuring all visitors can enjoy the wildlife surroundings.

Florida Keys Eco-Discovery Center
A free, wheelchair-accessible center with interactive exhibits about the region's ecosystems and conservation efforts.

Vision-Impaired Visitors

Braille guides and signs are increasingly common at tourist attractions. State law mandates that all public facilities allow trained service dogs, a requirement widely embraced by Florida's many pet-friendly business owners.

Mobile on the High Seas

Mobility challenges needn't restrict fun on the water. Accessible catamarans and adaptive sailing and boating experiences are widely available in Florida, with providers like **Shake-A-Leg** (*shakealegmiami.org*) in Miami making excursions easy and enjoyable.

Many attractions strive to provide sign language services; advance bookings of up to two weeks may be required. Printed guides are often available for museum/gallery tours. Some locations offer Assistive Listening Systems (ALDs) to enhance sound clarity for hearing aids and cochlear implants.

Street Talk

English is the predominant language throughout South Florida, though Spanish speakers, stemming from dozens of different nations, are ever-present. A unique blend of 'Spanglish' has emerged throughout the region in recent years, where conversations can intertwine English and Spanish for strings at a time. Learning a little Spanish before you come can help in certain situations where a speaker's native language may not be English.

Dale (*dah-leh*) Meaning 'let's go,' 'do it' or 'come on.' Popularized by Miami's own Pitbull.

Bro (*broh*) Miami's universal way of addressing anyone, regardless of gender or relationship.

Qué bola (*keh bo-lah*) Cuban slang for 'What's up?' or 'How's it going?'

Fresco (*fres-koh*) Used to mean 'cool' or 'fresh.' A compliment.

Chancletero/a (*chan-kleh-teh-ro/rah*) Someone who dons flip-flops everywhere, in a funny way.

Pata sucia (*pah-tah soo-syah*) Means 'dirty feet,' but used to poke fun at someone who walks barefoot in public places, which is common here.

Asere (*ah-seh-reh*) Cuban slang for 'buddy,' often heard in Little Havana.

Tremendo/a (*treh-men-doh/dah*) Means 'awesome' but can also emphasize drama.

Mango (*mahn-go*) Slang for a hottie.

Ventanita (*ven-tah-nee-tah*) A small coffee window to snag a cafecito at or hang out and chat.

Nuts & Bolts

OPENING HOURS

Banks 9am to 5pm Monday to Friday. Some branches open Saturday mornings.

Shops 10am to 8pm Monday to Saturday. Areas like Lincoln Rd and Duval St often stay open later and some shops operate on Sundays.

Museums 10am to 5pm, though some have extended evening hours on specific days, especially in Miami. Many are closed on Mondays.

Restaurants Lunch noon to 3pm, dinner 5pm to 10pm. Casual spots may stay open much later, especially in Miami Beach and Key West.

Bars/clubs Many stay open until 2am, and some clubs operate until 5am or later. Key West bars, especially along Duval St, often stay open past midnight.

Smoking & Vaping

In Florida, smoking is prohibited in most businesses, including restaurants, bars and their outdoor patios. It's also prohibited inside workplaces. Locally, counties and municipalities have extended restrictions to include beaches and parks. Vaping often falls under the same rules as smoking in businesses.

Weights & Measures

The US uses inches, feet, miles, gallons and pounds. Temperatures are given in degrees Fahrenheit.

Wi-Fi

Free wi-fi is widely available at restaurants, cafes, bus stations, airports and train stations.

GOOD TO KNOW

Time zone
EST

Country code
+1

Emergency number
911

Population
2.78 million

Electricity
120V/60Hz

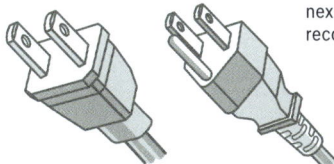

Type A
120V/60Hz

Type B
120V/60Hz

PUBLIC HOLIDAYS

Eight public holidays are recognized throughout the year in Florida. On these dates, government offices and most businesses (except essential services) are closed.

New Year's Day
January 1

Martin Luther King Jr Day Third Monday of January

Memorial Day Final Monday of May

Independence Day
July 4

Labor Day First Monday of September

Veterans Day
November 11

Thanksgiving Fourth Thursday of November

Christmas December 25 (if Christmas falls on a Sunday, the next day is also a recognized holiday.)

THE MIAMI & THE KEYS

STORYBOOK

Our writers delve deep into different aspects of Miami & the Keys life

A History of Miami & the Keys in 15 Places

Culture through the ages

Terry Ward

p190

Meet the South Floridians

The people of Miami & the Keys

Terry Ward

p194

Miami English

Listen and learn

Terry Ward

p196

Florida's Other Famed Pink Bird

The roseate spoonbill

Jesse Scott

p199

At Nature's Mercy

A delicate tropical masterpiece

Jesse Scott

p202

Everglades National Park (p112)

JUSTIN FOULKES FOR LONELY PLANET

189

A HISTORY OF MIAMI & THE KEYS IN
15 PLACES

Miami and South Florida were built on a cycle of boom and bust, by dreamers who took advantage of nice weather and opportunists who took advantage of natural disasters. Every chapter of the region's saga has been closed by a hurricane, building boom or riot – in between are fascinating stories of human resilience, survival and innovation. By Terry Ward

THE HISTORY OF Miami and the Florida Keys is one of discovery and development, set to a subtropical backdrop where nature is always trying to get a word in, edgewise.

It begins with the Tequesta Indians, who settled near Biscayne Bay and were largely wiped out by the effects of Spanish colonization. The Caloosahatchee culture flourished in the region until 1750. Present-day Florida changed hands between Spain, Britain and back to Spain before being purchased by the US in 1821. Tensions with the Seminole tribes led to the Seminole Wars, waged by the US government. It's often said that the Seminoles remain 'unconquered' since they never signed a peace treaty.

In the late 19th century, Henry Morrison Flagler extended his railroad to Miami after a freeze devastated Florida's citrus crops. Miami was officially incorporated as a city in 1896 and grew rapidly with Flagler's railroad and land sales. The Florida Keys flourished through wrecking and sponge industries and Key West became Florida's wealthiest city. The US Navy kept it in the Union during the Civil War, despite strong Confederate sympathies among residents.

Miami boomed again after WWII, spurred by Cuban immigration following Fidel Castro's 1959 revolution. In 1980, the Mariel Boatlift brought 125,000 Cubans to the city, reshaping its demographics with both middle-class exiles and prisoners. Hurricane Andrew caused massive destruction in 1992; Miami recovered through revitalization efforts, including the development of skyscrapers that reshaped its skyline.

Today, as one of the fastest-growing US cities, Miami faces rising sea levels, frequent hurricanes and extreme weather events fueled by climate change – all while maintaining its role as a global hub for Latin American culture.

1. Miami Circle National Historic Landmark
ANCIENT HISTORY REVEALED

It's otherworldly to stand – surrounded by shiny skyscrapers and multi million-dollar condos – at this ancient archaeological site where the Miami River meets Biscayne Bay. At the Miami Circle, holes and basins are carved into the shallow limestone where humans are thought to have lived as far back as 4000 years. Black earth midden deposits were found here during construction-related excavations in 1998, as well as other artifacts from the native Tequesta culture that suggest the area was part of a far-reaching trade network. Miami Circle was named a National Historic Landmark in 2009.

For more, see p72, 143.

2. Indian Key Historic State Park
FORMER SALVAGING SPOT

Just south of Islamorada in the Florida Keys and accessible only by boat, Indian Key is an offshore island thought to have been inhabited by Native Americans as far back as 800 CE. The island was bought in 1831 by native New Yorker Jacon Houseman, who made it a base for his empire wrecking and salvaging cargo from shipwrecks. Native Americans attacked the island in 1840 during the Indian Key Massacre, with all but one building destroyed (Houseman was lucky to escape with his life). Today it's a peaceful place to paddle a kayak or go bonefishing in the grassy flats.

For more, see p146.

3. Key West Historic Seaport
ONE PARTICULAR HARBOR

Sea captains first started using the safe anchorage of Key West, which they called Cayo Hueso, in the 1700s. By the 1800s, Key West operated as a hub for maritime activities ranging from sea turtle processing and canning and diving for sponges to the commercial fishing and shrimping industries, the latter of which boomed in the mid-20th century and declined in the late 1980s due to overfishing. Today, visitors descend on the Key West Historic Seaport's original location at the northern tip of Margaret St to listen to live music and dine on fresh seafood at waterfront restaurants and bars.

For more, see p162.

Cape Florida Lighthouse

4. Fort East Martello
CIVIL WAR BASTION

This fortress on the US National Register of Historic Places was constructed by the US Army in 1862 during the Civil War on Key West's southeastern coast to defend it against a possible Confederate sea assault. The city remained under Union control during the war, however, and Key West was never attacked. Built from bricks and with an 8ft-thick granite and brick wall surrounding it, the fort's design models a Genoese defense system from Corsica that dates to the 16th century. Come to see Civil War relics and to ogle the infamous Robert the Doll, the most legendary haunted object in all of the Keys.

For more, see p143.

5. Cape Florida Lighthouse
A BEACON FOR MARINERS

On Key Biscayne, Miami-Dade County's oldest structure is like a time capsule of Florida history. Built in 1825, the lighthouse at Bill Baggs Cape Florida State Park was originally built as a lookout to protect the area from pirates and to guide sailors around the treacherous Florida reefs. Native Seminoles attacked the lighthouse during the Second Seminole War, when the assistant lightkeeper threw a keg of gunpowder into the belly of the tower but survived the attack (with bad burns). Today, you can climb 109 steps to the top of the lighthouse for sprawling ocean and bay views.

For more, see p103.

6. Barnacle Historic State Park
A RESIDENCE WITH HISTORY

In Miami's Coconut Grove neighborhood, you'll find Miami-Dade County's oldest still-standing house at the 5-acre Barnacle Historic State Park. Built in 1891 and still in its original location, the Barnacle was the home of American yacht designer Ralph Middleton Munroe, who was one of the original founders of Coconut Grove. Families enjoy strolling the tree-lined paths within the park and relaxing in rocking chairs on the home's front porch while gazing out on Biscayne Bay. Live theater performances and concerts are often staged on the park's grounds, too, with the historical house as a backdrop.

For more, see p95.

7. Overseas Railway

TOURISM ARTERY FOR THE AGES

When you drive across the Seven Mile Bridge in the Florida Keys, connecting the Middle Keys to the Lower Keys, consider the eccentric railway tycoon, Henry Morrison Flagler, who was the first with the idea (and means – it cost him more than $50 million) to create an overseas railway system to bring tourism to the region. The Overseas Railway was built between 1905 and 1912, when it was dubbed the 'eighth wonder of the world,' and met its demise in 1935 during the Labor Day hurricane. You can still see parts of the Old Seven Mile Bridge here.

For more, see p154.

8. Black Archives – Historic Lyric Theater

STAGE FOR GREATS

Miami was segregated until the 1950s and '60s. And in the Jim Crow era of the decades before, the downtown Miami neighborhood of Overtown was the city's only central location that wasn't designated for 'whites only.' Once known as Miami Black Wall Street and the Harlem of the South, the neighborhood boomed as a cultural hub in the 1930s. At its heart, the historic Lyric Theater, built in 1913, hosted such stars as Ella Fitzgerald, Louis Armstrong and Billie Holiday. You can still see jazz performances and other shows at the 400-seat theater, added to the US National Register of Historic Places in 1989.

For more, see p70.

9. Ocean Drive

NEON AND DECO DREAMS

Miami Beach was first incorporated in 1915 and truly developed as a resort town in the 1920s. Then, as now, Ocean Drive was its beating heart and main thoroughfare. Most of the art deco structures for which the street is still known today were built between 1923 and 1943. During WWII, many of the buildings lining the street were used as barracks to house military personnel (soldiers took swimming lessons at the Roney Plaza Hotel, one of Ocean Drive's first major resorts that was demolished in 1968). Today, the neon-lit facades lined with swaying palms make the ultimate photo backdrop while restaurants, bars and nightclubs lure the masses to be entertained.

For more, see p61.

10. Venetian Causeway

BRIDGE TO THE BEACH

Added to the US National Register of Historic Places in 1989, this structure linking downtown Miami to Miami Beach across Biscayne Bay was built in 1925 and remains one of the city's most critical infrastructure links. The arched Venetian Causeway replaced a wooden causeway called the Collins Bridge, at the time the longest wooden bridge in the world, which was built in 1913 as a link from the mainland to Miami Beach. The causeway is 2.5 miles long and has 12 bridges, and is a popular place to run, bike or walk.

For more, see p67.

11. Freedom Tower

ELLIS ISLAND OF THE SOUTH

Amidst the gleaming condos and office buildings along Biscayne Boulevard in downtown Miami, the 289ft-high, Spanish Renaissance–style Freedom Tower stands apart. Modeled after the Giralda bell tower of the Seville cathedral in Spain, it has distinct Moorish embellishments and was famed as the 'Ellis Island of the South,' thanks to its role as the Cuban Assistance Center in the 1960s and '70s. It was a beacon of relief (healthcare, housing, education and more) for Cuban refugees who had come to Miami seeking political asylum from Fidel Castro. The tower turns 100 years old in 2025, when it's scheduled to reopen following extensive renovations.

For more, see p70.

12. Dry Tortugas National Park

STRATEGIC OFFSHORE FORT

Ponce de León first discovered these remote islands about 70 miles west of Key West in 1513, and the Dry Tortugas were named for the thriving population of sea turtles swimming in their waters. The islands soon became an important navigational marker and strategic location for Spanish explorers, and the ocean passageway here was heavily trafficked by treasure fleets. Today, Dry Tortugas National Park, established in 1935, is mainly known for Fort Jefferson, built from some 16

Old Bahia Honda Railroad Bridge (p154), Overseas Railway

million bricks during the mid- to late 19th century to protect the strategic deepwater anchorage here.

For more, see p169.

13. Everglades National Park

A RIVER OF GRASS

Rampant development and ever-burgeoning skylines of condos and skyscrapers plague large swaths of the Sunshine State. But in its southernmost reaches in Everglades National Park, established in 1947, Florida will remain home to the country's largest stretch of subtropical wilderness into perpetuity. The park's establishment was the successful culmination of a 19-year effort led by Ernest Coe and author Marjory Stoneman Douglas to protect the Everglades from the harm done by dredging and draining. Some 1.5 million acres of primarily wetland habitat – home to alligators, black bears and the Florida panther – are protected here within the unique place the author famously called the 'River of Grass.'

For more, see p112.

14. John Pennekamp Coral Reef State Park

REEF-RIDDLED WONDERLAND

The snorkel- and scuba-tank-toting crowds who make their way through the Florida Keys largely have this state park to thank for the thriving reefs and underwater wonders found throughout the island chain. John Pennekamp Coral Reef State Park was established in 1963 as the first undersea park in the US. Together with the adjacent Florida Keys National Marine Sanctuary, it helps preserve some 178 nautical square miles of fish-laden coral reefs, seagrass beds that serve as important habitat for manatees and vital mangrove swamps.

For more, see p140.

15. Little Havana

WHERE THE DIASPORA DESCENDS

There's no talking about Miami without talking about the neighborhood of Little Havana and its main drag, Calle Ocho. The area grew into ground zero for the Cuban diaspora in the 1960s as Cuban dissidents fled Fidel Castro's regime for a new life in Miami. Today the city's Cuban-American population spreads all over town (not to mention Florida and far beyond). But Little Havana remains the heart of the Cuban-American community, drawing those newly arrived from the island and people who've been here since the '60s from far and wide whenever there's something to protest or celebrate (or just to grab a cafecito at Versailles).

For more, see p81.

MEET THE SOUTH FLORIDIANS

The people of South Florida come from as many diverse backgrounds, cultures and walks of life as there are sunny days in the year. TERRY WARD introduces them.

SOUTH FLORIDA, AND its people in particular, are so much more than most people think. On Florida's sunniest stage, in Miami and the Florida Keys, they welcome the world – and they are the world, too.

Over 25% of Florida's more than 22 million people are Latino, with more than 20% of Floridians born in a foreign country. And when you zoom in on South Florida, those percentages skew even higher. More than half of the population in Miami-Dade County was born outside the US. Spanish is far and away the most spoken language in Miami, where it's estimated some 70% of the population speaks it. But South Floridians represent cultures from all over the globe – and within them, every walk of life.

South Floridians are Cubans in guayaberas who arrived on rafts decades ago and still meet at Máximo Gómez Park to play dominoes. They're an entirely younger generation, too, who just arrived at the US border last year after a long and treacherous journey north (nothing will make you more grateful for this state than chatting with any of them and hearing why). They are Venezuelans who escaped Nicolás Maduro, and Haitians and Jamaicans in search of a better go, too. They are Uruguayans and Argentineans who ventured so far north on the continent perhaps to play polo or follow a love. Ecuadoreans, Peruvians, Dominicans, Brazilians and others...they are the entire rainbow of Latin American and Caribbean colors.

Floridians are Brits and Scandinavians who swapped gray skies for something entirely sunnier. They're Floridians, born here, who left to make it big elsewhere and swore they'd never come back – then missed never having to force boots over their toddler's feet in winter snow.

They're New Yorkers who found a real estate deal they couldn't resist and bagels they could accept, and Canadians who just want to warm the heck up. They're Michiganers who fell in love on spring break, found jobs in a dive shop and never left. They're Wisconsinites who wouldn't miss a Green Bay Packers game at the marina bar by the sailboat where they live.

They're scuba divers and marine biologists, famous writers and treasure wreck divers and commercial fishers. They're airplane pilots and pilot boat captains who all found this state the perfect place to follow their dreams, making a living doing what they love.

They're born-and-raised-under-the-Florida-sun types, too, who know all the state's faults but still wouldn't live anywhere else for that promise that's never undelivered of a perfectly mild winter and nonstop sunshine the rest of the country craves.

They're also just people who never want to shovel snow another day of their lives and pointed the moving truck as far south as the road would go.

Who & How Many

According to 2023 data, Miami-Dade County and the Florida Keys are home to more than 2.7 million people. Some 54% of the population in Miami-Dade was born outside the United States.

Pictured clockwise from top left: Domino players, Little Havana (p84); a 'snowbird' (p33); local guide, Evergaldes National Park (p112); stallholder, Legion Park farmers' market (p101)

SOUTH FLORIDA THROUGH A FRIENDS & FAMILY LENS

My relationship to Miami and the Florida Keys has changed throughout my life. As a college student at the University of Florida, my friends and I lived for long weekends when we could drive through the night all the way from Gainesville, in North Florida, to where the road ended in Key West – suddenly transported to the tropics with coral reefs to explore. Many a South Beach bachelorette party ensued in the decade that followed. And when I married a Cuban many years later, Miami took on new interest and meaning when we'd visit from our home in Tampa and I got the chance to see the city differently through my husband's new-to-the-US eyes. Today, I bring my own young kids to learn to snorkel and kayak in South Florida's unique natural spaces. One day soon, I hope to be back in these waters with them as newly certified scuba divers. The adventures here just go on and on.

195

MIAMI ENGLISH
LISTEN & LEARN

A Miami professor of linguistics shares a theory: a new dialect distinct to Miami has emerged. By Terry Ward

THE NEXT TIME you find yourself in an English conversation with someone who was born and raised in Miami, listen not only to what they're saying but also how, exactly, they're saying it.

Linguistic researchers at Miami's Florida International University made national headlines in 2023 after releasing a research paper determining that Miamians speak English with their own unique dialect. The findings went viral and were plunged into the spotlight far beyond the 305.

And if you think we're referring to Spanglish, you're wrong. In fact, some of the people speaking this unique-to-Miami dialect may not even speak Spanish at all.

'Objectively speaking, the fact is that everyone who speaks a language speaks a dialect of that language. And all dialects come from somewhere – just like all languages come from somewhere,' explains Phillip M Carter, a professor of linguistics at FIU, who co-authored the research paper about Miami's distinct dialect with FIU master's student Kristen D'Alessandro Merii.

When it comes to the dialect of English widely spoken in Miami by people born in South Florida into Latinx communities (the parlance Carter and Merii call 'Miami English'), it has been formed by both the Spanish language influencing English and the other way around. The first thing Carter wants people to know about it is that it's not Spanglish.

'When I talk about Miami English, I'm not talking about Spanish words, and I'm not talking about Spanglish,' Carter states. 'I'm talking about, specifically, the dialect that mostly Cuban Americans – but Latinos in general, who were born in South Florida, in Miami-Dade County – learn to speak when they grow up here.'

According to Carter, the Miami English dialect is characterized by several things, among them grammatical elements, pronunciation and word-choice differences that may be almost imperceptible to those who aren't linguists studying it.

Its evolution can be traced back to the arrival of Cubans in Miami in the 1950s, following the Cuban Revolution.

FIU's linguistic research posited that years of the local population being exposed to Spanish (widely spoken in Miami now by roughly 65% of the population) has led to the adoption of certain phrases unique to the people from here that are commonly recognized and understood – both by native Spanish speakers, native English speakers with no proficiency in Spanish and everyone in between.

To understand what's happening, you have to understand what linguists call the bilingual continuum, says Carter. 'You have people on one end who are monolingual English speakers, who only speak English, and on the other end those who are monolingual Spanish speakers,' he explains.

In the middle, you have every degree of speaker of both languages – from people who are proficient English speakers but don't have literacy, to really proficient Spanish speakers who don't have literacy.

'There's this massive mix of things going on in the middle, and many people engage in code-switching behavior, alternating between the two languages,' Carter adds. This kind of language usage is a natural phenomenon all over the world and one of the things humans evolve to do.

'So it is true that the presence of Spanish in South Florida – in the speech community and in the minds and mouths of bilingual people – affected the way that folks spoke English,' he says. Fascinatingly enough, that applies whether the people speaking the Miami English dialect even speak Spanish at all.

If that sounds confusing, perhaps some examples of calques – 'loan translations,' meaning a word or phrase borrowed from another language and translated directly – will help understand what to listen for when you're listening to Miami English.

'Get down from the car' is a phrase commonly used by speakers of Miami English. It's easy enough for those of us who might speak another English dialect to understand that anyone saying this phrase means 'get out of,' or exit, the car. But if you've never been exposed to spoken Spanish, the phrase's origins might be less clear. 'Get down from the car' is in fact a direct translation of the Spanish expression *bajar del carro*.

THERE'S THIS MASSIVE MIX OF THINGS GOING ON IN THE MIDDLE, AND MANY PEOPLE ALTERNATE BETWEEN THE TWO LANGUAGES

Viernes Culturales (p84), Little Havana

ALEKSANDR DYSKIN/SHUTTERSTOCK

Another example of a calque typical of the Miami English dialect is the expression 'make the line' instead of 'get in line' or 'join the line.' Again, this comes from a direct translation of the Spanish phrase *hacer la fila*.

What might be most interesting is that phrases like these are used not only by native Spanish speakers who are speaking English, but also by native English speakers in the Miami area.

In the Spanish language, Carter explains, the word *carne* can refer to meat in general or specifically to beef, and its usage also ties into Miami English. 'When it comes to a lot of folks in Miami, you're never going to hear them say the word beef,' he says. 'They'll refer to a chicken empanada, a pork empanada, a spinach empanada and a meat empanada.'

Beyond the calques in Miami English, distinct vowel pronunciations used by the people from here also sound a little bit more like Spanish than English in some cases, according to Carter. 'It can be very subtle, and people may not even notice it, but we found significant differences in the way that people pronounce things,' he says.

While only a visitor with a very keen ear may pick up on these subtle pronunciation differences, Carter notes that his students from Miami at FIU often make an interesting observation when they head just north. When they leave Miami-Dade County for Broward County, they say people sometimes ask them what country they're from.

For all the fast-paced action in Miami, take time to slow down, listen and learn – real-life lessons in linguistics are all around.

FLORIDA'S OTHER FAMED PINK BIRD

Spotting a treasured roseate spoonbill in the wild at Biscayne National Park, amid other avian characters and the efforts to preserve them. By Jesse Scott

WHEN MOST PEOPLE think of 'Florida's pink birds,' it's easy for the flamingo to steal the limelight. Its near-neon feathers and tall stature make it a worldwide symbol of tropical bliss, Florida certainly included. While once common, wild flamingos in Florida have faced rapid decline due to hunting during the 1800s as well as the gradual drainage of the Everglades, which, combined, has nearly wiped them out completely in recent decades. The flamingo population is making a small comeback – a group of volunteers with Audubon Florida counted a total of 101 birds in the state in February 2024, marking a slight uptick from prior years.

But the Sunshine State has another pink and comparatively under-the-radar avian friend: the roseate spoonbill. Often overshadowed by its taller, slender relative, the flamingo, the roseate spoonbill is a South Florida gem, especially when you lay your eyes on one within Biscayne National Park. Its distinct bubblegum-pink feathers, unique spoon-shaped bill, and graceful flight make it an exciting sight, whether you're a bird enthusiast or not. There are approximately 2400 roseate spoonbills in the park – here's the scoop on catching a glimpse of one.

Biscayne National Park's Most Colorful Resident

Biscayne National Park, located south of Miami, is known for its watery expanse, with 95% of the park lying below the surface. Visitors to the park quickly realize that getting out on the water is essential in order to explore the hidden wonders above and below the waves. For birders, the park's venture-worthy and desolate keys, sprawling mangroves and shallow bay waters make it one of the best spots to observe the roseate spoonbill in its natural wonder.

The spoonbill has found a haven within Biscayne National Park's shallow waters, which typically teem with small fish and crustaceans, perfect for the bird's seemingly nonstop diet. Its unusual bill is not just for looks – it plays a vital role in the spoonbill's feeding regimen. The bird sweeps its bill from side to side in the water, using its delicate sensitivity to detect small prey such as fish, shrimp and aquatic insects. When spoonbills soar, their broad wings bubble with pink and white, creating a spectacle against skies of any hue.

Spotting one within the park requires adventure, patience and, sure, a bit of luck. To appreciate its habitat as well as Biscayne National Park's broader birdlife, you'll need

to explore the more remote locations. Start your birding journey at the Dante Fascell Visitor Center, where you can catch glimpses of wood storks and mangrove cuckoos, but the real spoonbill excitement lies well beyond. Hop on a boat to explore Biscayne Bay or venture to Boca Chita Key and Elliott Key, approximately 7 miles offshore. These areas are known for their abundance of wading birds, and you might just spot a roseate spoonbill gliding low over the water or standing in the shallows, its pink feathers reflecting the sun's rays on a crisp Florida day.

The prime feeding grounds for spoonbills are the park's vast mangrove forests and seagrass beds – the Biscayne Bay Coastal Wetlands Project has played a significant role in protecting these vital habitats. Among the organization's efforts in recent years, the project has constructed pump stations and re-established vital wetlands, helping reduce harmful freshwater discharge into the bay. This effort directly helps the roseate spoonbill and other aquatic bird species by improving feeding and nesting grounds.

THERE ARE MORE THAN 170 SPECIES OF BIRDS IN BISCAYNE NATIONAL PARK, MAKING IT ONE OF THE DENSEST AVIAN HABITATS IN THE SUNSHINE STATE

More Avian Treasures of Biscayne National Park

While the roseate spoonbill is a prized sight, the park offers much more for bird lovers. There are more than 170 species of birds in Biscayne National Park, making it one of the densest avian habitats in the Sunshine State.

Among the most common winged residents are brown pelicans, typically perched on channel markers or diving in the water for a fish snack. The white ibis, with a curved bill and noble white feathers, often feeds in groups along the shore. Blue herons can be seen comparatively motionless in the mangroves, waiting to snatch a snack of their own, while the green heron cleverly uses tools like twigs to lure fish.

Other wading birds frequently spotted include snowy egrets, recognizable by their popping yellow feet and contrasting black bills, and tricolored herons, known for their blend of blue-gray, white and red-

dish bodies. Biscayne's mudflats are also home to the endangered wood stork, another rare treat for bird gawkers.

Biscayne National Park's location along the migratory bird route regularly attracts rare Caribbean visitors. A couple of examples are the Bahama mockingbird, known for its melodic song, and the Antillean nighthawk, with white-striped wings. Additionally, during migration seasons, one may encounter colorful warblers like the yellow-throated or the ever-vivid American redstart, adding even more flashes of color to the mangrove landscapes.

Preservation Initiatives: A True Community Effort

The National Park Service and compassionate local nonprofits alike have stepped up big-time amid the elements, spanning climate-change-induced disasters to natural population evolution. Among those organizations, Audubon Florida, in 2022, launched a habitat restoration initiative targeting mangrove forests, which are key for migratory birds and waders like the roseate spoonbill. Their educational programs have reached thousands of locals and visitors, raising awareness about bird protection and conservation.

Friends of Biscayne Bay also focuses on preserving the park's delicate ecosystems via meaningful community action. Recent projects have included large-scale cleanup events. Their 2023 Biscayne Bay cleanup alone equated to the removal of more than 10,000lb of debris from bird habitats. Additionally, they regularly collaborate with South Florida and global researchers to monitor bird populations and the health of Biscayne's waters, which, like so many other bodies of water, hit record temperatures with each new year.

With so many colorful and resilient critters, this region is certainly a visual masterpiece worth cherishing – and protecting for generations to come.

Roseate spoonbill
MICHAL DOBES COM/SHUTTERSTOCK

AT NATURE'S MERCY

The Florida Keys remain a delicate tropical masterpiece. Here's a look at its geographic challenges, how it is preparing for the future, and the people preserving it. By Jesse Scott

THE FLORIDA KEYS, a stretch of coral islands nearly 120 miles long, dangle off South Florida like a glistening diamond necklace. Beachgoers, fishing anglers, divers and outdoor enthusiasts all flock to its waters, vibrant reefs and palms. But paradise – whether visiting or living in it – is coming with a growing anxiety. This idyllic landscape, which attracts upwards of 5 million visitors annually, is vulnerable like few others to nature's fury.

In recent years, rising seas, intense hurricanes and other climate-related issues have been reshaping the Keys' approach. As weather roulette plays out – literally leaving the entire state at hurricanes' mercy – local conservationists and climate warriors are racing to protect this delicate region from ultimately diminishing.

The Heat is On

The Keys are uniquely at risk – a hair above sea level and sandwiched between the Atlantic Ocean and the Gulf of Mexico. While this geographic scenario equates to stunning beauty, it also exposes the islands to climate-change stress and avenues aplenty for tropical systems. The water has risen around the Keys by nearly 9in since 1913, and some scientists are projecting a rise of another 2ft to 4ft by 2100, which would submerge much of the Keys.

Pictured clockwise from top left: Flooded Everglade grassland; flooded residential area; Florida Keys National Marine Sanctuary; coral nursery

Related to rising temperatures is coastal erosion. As the ocean heats and rises, the Keys' shores are degrading into the sea. Low-lying areas like Sugarloaf Key and Big Pine Key experience regular tidal flooding, accentuated by king tides, which are visibly higher-than-normal tides that occur during new and full moons. During king tides, it's not uncommon throughout the Keys and much of South Florida to get knee-deep in water in order to stroll down a street or access your car.

It's not just the land that's being impacted. Coral reefs, which are the backbone of the Keys' coastal ecosystem, are sensitive to temperature changes. Rising water temperatures have spearheaded vast coral bleaching, eradicating up to 40% of coral cover in the Florida Reef Tract, the third-largest barrier reef in the world. Without the reefs to serve as organic storm barriers, the islands face more exposure to storm surge, which has reached 10ft-plus with recent major storms.

Nature's Wrath Unleashed

Hurricanes, tropical storms and major rain events have long tested the Florida Keys, but climate change is visibly intensifying such storms. Recent storms offer sobering examples of the damage Mother Nature can inflict.

In 2017, Hurricane Irma, a Category 4 storm with winds peaking at 130mph, ravaged the Keys, with a storm surge that submerged stretches of land. The director of the Federal Emergency Management Agency at the time said that more than 25% of homes in the Keys were destroyed and 65% of them experienced significant damage. Irma also reshaped the coastline, eroded beaches and left behind debris, some of which took years to clean up.

In 2022, Hurricane Ian struck, bringing sustained winds of over 150mph and torrential rain. It made landfall in Punta Gorda in Southwest Florida, due north of the Keys. Though it spared the Keys a direct hit, Ian intensified damage from Irma – notably damage to the Overseas Highway and the delicate coral bedrock system below that upholds the road.

Beyond geographic tolls, these storms cripple the local economy, especially businesses – from large resorts to quaint tiki huts – that rely on tourism. The rebuilding process is becoming an unfortunate cycle in this region, where so many folks have uprooted their lives to relax and enjoy paradise.

Standing Up for the Future

Residents and organizations alike aren't just sitting back and doing nothing amid these happenings and what may be ahead. Their efforts are vital, not just to preserve the islands' charm but also to mitigate future storm harm.

A leading initiative is the Keys Restoration Project, spearheaded by the Nature Conservancy and other local stakeholders. It focuses on restoring the protective coral reefs damaged by bleaching and storms. Among the project's actions, scientists are creating heat-resistant strains of coral that can better stand up to warming waters. This new coral is being transplanted into damaged reefs, with a goal of rebuilding the habitat.

Local governments are also boosting green infrastructure to combat flooding and erosion. In Key West, for example, city officials have raised roads, improved stormwater drainage systems and constructed 'living shorelines,' which are natural walls that incorporate mangroves, seagrass and wetlands to soak in stormwater.

The Florida Keys National Marine Sanctuary is another big player. The sanctuary and its team is working to limit damage from boat anchors, coral poaching and overfishing in the region. They do so by enforcing 'no-take zones,' meaning spots where fish populations can recover, equating long-term marine health.

On the subject of land, nonprofits like the Florida Keys Land Trust are working to protect vital habitats. Its efforts focus on purchasing and preserving parcels of land at risk of development and habitat loss. This land protection often also creates added buffers that help absorb the impact of storms.

Remaining Resilient

The Florida Keys are truly a paradise on the frontlines of climate change. In a conversation with any Keys local, you'll pick up on a laid-back vibe felt nowhere else in the United States. But don't mistake that chillness for nonchalance when it comes to protecting their home and its future. Anyone who resides in the Keys – many of them welcoming visitors with open arms to their nook of the globe – has either lived through horrors and/or is actively preparing for whatever may be next. It's a landscape and place worth fighting for. **203**

INDEX

Map Pages **000**

Heading to the beach? Miami has many to enjoy (p62)

The world's largest collection of 1920s and 1930s art deco buildings (p61)

Mapping data sources:
© Lonely Planet
© OpenStreetMap http://openstreetmap.org/copyright

THIS BOOK

Destination Editor
Caroline Trefler

Production Editor
Jeremy Toynbee

Book Designer
Dominic Allen

Cartographer
Val Kremenchutskaya

Assisting Editors
Natalie Howard, Brana Vladisavljevic, Nicola Williams

Cover Researcher
Kat Marsh

Thanks Sophie Andersen, James Appleton, Fergal Condon, Gwen Cotter Melanie Dankel, Darren O'Connell

MIX
Paper | Supporting responsible forestry
FSC
www.fsc.org   FSC™ C021741

Paper in this book is certified against the Forest Stewardship Council™ standards. FSC™ promotes environmentally responsible, socially beneficial and economically viable management of the world's forests.

Published by Lonely Planet Global Limited
CRN 554153
10th edition – Aug 2025
ISBN 978 1 83869 409 8
© Lonely Planet 2025 Photographs © as indicated 2025
10 9 8 7 6 5 4 3 2 1
Printed in Malaysia